Marco Eimermann and Anders Trumberg (eds)

Place and Identity

A New Landscape of Social and Political Change in Sweden

Santérus
Academic Press
Sweden

www.santerus.se

© 2015 The authors and Santérus Academic Press Sweden
ISBN 978-91-7335-044-0
Cover art: Landscape with house at Ceret by Juan Gris from 1913 (trimmed)
Cover profile: Sven Bylander
Santérus Academic Press is an imprint of
Santérus Förlag, Stockholm, Sweden
academicpress@santerus.se
Printed by BOD, Germany 2015

Contents

HÅKAN FORSELL & MARCO EIMERMANN

Introduction; themes and trajectories of urban
and regional development in Swedish society   7

CHRISTINA HJORT ARONSSON

1. Ageing, identity and place – senses of belonging   15

MARCO EIMERMANN

2. "I felt confined" – Narratives of ambivalence among
   Dutch lifestyle migrants in rural Sweden   31

CHARLOTTE FRIDOLFSSON

3. Multiplying the unique – the place-identity of a
   rural Swedish landscape   57

EVA GUSTAVSSON AND INGEMAR ELANDER

4. Greenest of them all? Climate change mitigation
   and place branding in three Swedish towns   76

ANDREAS K.G. THÖRN

5. Group identity and church buildings – the Philadelphia
   church in Stockholm 1930   97

CHARLOTTE FRIDOLFSSON AND INGEMAR ELANDER

6. Place and religion: Swedish Muslim identity formation   118

SUSANNA NORDSTRÖM

7. The place of music – the place of becoming. Heavy
   metal identity formation in Gothenburg city   141

ANDERS TRUMBERG

8. You and 'the other' – the school as a meeting place   159

MONIKA PERSSON

9. Place and unsafety – does place affect feelings
   of unsafety?   180

MAJA LILJA AND PETER SUNDSTRÖM

10. The construction of people and place in Swedish
    residential projects   205

Contributors   226

Introduction

Themes and Trajectories of Urban and Regional Development in Swedish Society

Håkan Forsell & Marco Eimermann

The point of departure for this volume is the history of Swedish modernisation. This modernisation follows the Swedish industrial golden age (1930–1975), which rested on strong features of socialization into employment, interest expressions organized in political parties and trade unions, the consumption of public services and leisure activities clearly separated from work. It was a homogeneous society with strong equality ideals and commitment to the formal democratic decision-making processes. Above all, the smaller industrial towns gained most from the welfare-building process.

The 'horizon of expectation' (Koselleck 1992 [1979]) created by the industrial society during these decades was not compatible with the social and political landscape that took shape and direction after the industrial crises of the mid-1970s. The developments were increasingly characterized by labour-market flexibility, deregulation, consumer lifestyle, individualization and privatization of public welfare services. At the time, Henri Lefebvre (1979: 290) noted an 'explosion of spaces', in which industrial geography, patterns of urbanization, every-day life and the regulating power of the nation state were instable and distorted. This tendency has increased through globalization, neo-liberalism and the urbanized labour market.

Generally, the traditional social democratic welfare model that made Sweden world-famous during the post-war period has been dismantled and deprived of many of its economic and political instruments. The initial distributive allocation model has been transformed into a market-oriented hierarchy of activities, regions and cities. The global economy has undergone similar changes. Since the late 1970s, national, regional and local policies no longer aim at redistribution of resources in order to counteract uneven geographical developments. Rather, the policies result in the emergence of areas as winners or losers in sub-national competition for resource-allocation (Andersson *et al.* 2008). In most cases, this development favours knowledge-intensive and financially governing urban regions, with international connectivity.

In detail however, this transformation has proceeded in different ways depending on historical, geographical and institutional circumstances. This anthology is written in light of these structural changes in economy, politics and society. The localities and identities that the Swedish welfare model created were strongly related to a distributive national system of cities and production locations. But metropolitan areas and university cities have in recent decades taken on a decisive leading position in economic and demographic development. An ever-widening gap has emerged between small towns and rural areas on the one hand and major cities on the other hand. In recent decades, reasons for population growth in large Swedish cities are less connected to domestic rural-urban migration, but more to high urban nativity and international migration. Countless small towns in the countryside experience an alarmingly aging population and schools with a decreasing number of school-children. This is a result of a redistribution principle and choice of investment locations that stand in stark contrast to the economic and political landscape which once formed the basis for the Swedish welfare society.

Against this background, the aim of this anthology is to present research on place distinctiveness, identity formation and social change in Sweden, aided by international theories and concepts. At the time of writing, the authors were PhD candidates and senior researchers at the research school Urban Studies (FUS) within the Centre for Urban and Regional Studies (CURES) at Örebro University, Sweden. The studies collected in this volume relate to various interpretations of the concepts of place and identity.

Therefore, this introduction now turns to a short discussion of these concepts. Before a more critical stance is offered towards the end of this chapter, the concepts are first approached broadly here. In lay discourse, the word 'place' is used in many ways in different contexts. Someone or something can be put 'in place' or become 'out of place'. The word can also be used as a verb, when scholars are 'placing a phenomenon in time and space'. Similarly, identity can be formed by age, gender, ethnicity, religion and so forth. As such, identity is used in many ways to describe senses of belonging to or alienation from groups or places.

As an academic concept, 'place' has been discussed by sociologists (*e.g.* Urry 2007), human geographers (Massey 1991, Relph 1976, 1996, Tuan 1977, 2005) and other social scientists. As Massey (1995) argues, places are unique in that they are different, while simultaneously having aspects in common in an interrelated world. According to Castree (2006: 170), place can have different, often overlapping meanings. These are place as location (distinct points on the earth's surface), sense of place ('how different individuals and groups [...] both interpret and develop meaningful attachments to those specific areas where they live out their lives') and place as locale (the scale at which people's daily life is typically lived). It is neither possible nor desirable to reach consensus on what constitutes place, which is why it is so exciting to study social phenomena in relation to 'place'!

Place has been characterised both as fixed and as fluid. As such, the concept has been associated with settlement and stasis as well as with mobilities and dynamics of everyday life. Urry (2007: 269) suggests that 'places are economically, politically and culturally produced through the multiple mobilities of people, [...] capital, objects and information'. As the chapters and various empirical materials in this volume witness, place is never completed (Thrift 1999: 317).

Yet, in relation to the concept of identity, place can be studied from a particular angle. The concepts of identity and place can be combined so as to ascribe identity to a certain locale (place identity) or for human beings to derive their identity partly from a place with which they identify (Gren & Hallin 2003: 143–145). As such, place identity can be derived from historical human activities in or around that place. It can also be created by contrasting places with each other or focusing on similarities between places. Moreover, through music, people may relate their identity to places by expressing emotions of joy, sadness, hatred or rebellion felt in connection to those places.

This volume discusses on-going multi-disciplinary explorations of geographical and cultural change within the social sciences on the one side, and recently intensified transformations of Swedish society on the other. The chapters represent various reflections on these transformations and how they are connected to people's relationship to particular places. They contribute to an adjusted perspective on the history of Swedish modernisation by looking at its different consequences during the post-war period.

The rapidly growing research on the situation of the elderly population has spread widely across demographic analyses. Christina Hjort Aronsson's contribution examines the conditions for the elderly in depopulated municipalities after the turnaround from a publicly funded nursing care to a cost-effective and competitive market in line with New Public Management. How did this policy transition affect the elderly care especially when it comes to sensitive issues like dignity, belonging and social interaction? Do elderly people today live less or more in congruence with contemporary society than previous generations? Hence, this first chapter focuses on a rural society.

Current issues in contemporary rural society are also highlighted in Marco Eimermann's study on Dutch migrants in Hällefors, a municipality in rural Sweden. This chapter relates place-identity to the field of lifestyle migration (*e.g.* Torkington 2012). Eimermann discusses post-migration challenges faced by lifestyle migrants, as an illustrative contrast to *e.g.* refugees' post-migration everyday lives that seem challenging for more obvious reasons. In many cases, a mismatch occurs between pre-migration aspirations – partly raised by visiting migrant fairs where Swedish depopulated municipalities attempt to attract new residents from Holland, Belgium and Germany – and post-migration experiences in the rural Swedish destinations. Although the natural beauty, space, low property prices and a general sense of freedom motivates many lifestyle migrants to move, the (lack of) social relationships established after migration determine much of the migrants' quality of life.

Particular characteristics of the rural landscape are studied in the third chapter. Taking a story that relates contemporary rural Swedish landscape to historical events as its point of departure, the chapter by Fridolfsson connects place and identity to issues of uniqueness in an era of globalisation. The author relates a particular place in the rural Swedish Bergslagen area to nostalgic sentiments referring to the heydays of this area before and during the Swedish industrial golden age (see also Isacson *et al.* 2009). She investigates these developments within the context of emerging ecotourism in rural Sweden.

After these chapters with a rural focus, the collection turns to a rather urban focus. The chapter by Eva Gustavsson and Ingemar Elander on local climate policy in three Swedish towns corresponds to the 'selling' perspective on urban and regional development. As municipalities increasingly compete when attracting jobs, investment and international interest, environmental strategies have become an integral part of the 'branding' of the location – but the outcomes differ in terms of success, as Gustavsson & Elander also discuss in the chapter.

Besides the social fabric of a place, physical surroundings are also important. Places can also be designed, built and constructed for different purposes. Both Andreas Thörn's study of the Pentecostal Church in Stockholm during the earlier twentieth century and the chapter by Charlotte Fridolfsson and Ingemar Elander on contemporary mosques in Swedish cities deal with sites created for specific groups' needs of both community life of the enclosed group and integration of that group in society. The emphasis on religious community for the identity process of groups and individuals in a secular country like Sweden would appear to be a decisive shift from socialization as formerly connected with work and the profession learned in a work place.

However, Thörn's contribution shows that there have always been parallel community building processes, and previously unaddressed histories of space and wealth creation, which are again visible today with the establishment of a more pluralistic society. The investigation by Fridolfsson and Elander proves that the process of site-constructing, in this case involving a religious and cultural Muslim community, in reality follows quite different patterns in different cities. The places as well as the importance designated to basement mosques and new built mosques could be linked to different perspectives on minority rights and the need and willingness of the group itself to interact with the surrounding society.

In other cases, places can be inextricably linked to entire subcultures, something that is particularly evident when talking about youth and music culture. Susanna Nordström analyses the heavy metal scene in Gothenburg, Sweden's second largest city. She demonstrates how place and music create a strong identity link through a youth culture that is spread out across the country. Nordström argues that the heavy metal scene in Gothenburg shows characteristics of a diaspora, in which music becomes a means for people to connect to an imagined place of birth or upbringing.

The spread of values and conducts that originally came from urban conditions can be read in several sectors of society and in medium-sized and small towns as well. Anders Trumberg's chapter shows how economic and ethnic segregation in the Swedish compulsory school also is a reality in medium-sized towns in Sweden after the major school reforms in the early 1990's. Previously, segregation between the primary schools has been treated exclusively as a phenomenon in larger metropolitan areas. Trumberg discusses how the individualization of democratic values has altered the social geography not least in places that have accomplished structural transformation from once industrial production towns to become places of knowledge production.

In the penultimate chapter, Monika Persson also addresses an aspect of urbanization and urban life that long has been associated with metropolitan areas: (un)safety and the perceived dangers of the urban environment. Persson discusses how the differentiation of insecurity by gender, age and social class and urban space as a 'moderator' of social relations is a predominant reality also in small and medium-sized Swedish towns.

A point of departure for several chapters in the book is the *construction* of places; the physical and mental design and their social and economic importance. This may involve selling strategies of houses and homes through marketing and storytelling, as analysed in the final chapter by Maja Lilja and Peter Sundström. The market depiction of people and places associated with imagined locations and their values are a prominent feature of private construction companies and investors. Places are defined by what is emphasized and what is deselected. Lilja and Sundström observe how a number of dichotomies occur frequently for various planned residential areas: history and modernity, nature and city life, people and lifestyle. Several residential areas could be interpreted as projects of self-segregation for an urban, active middle class. At the same time

Lilja and Sundström reflect upon how conceptions of the home are connected to leisure, rather than to work. Moreover, the marketing of residential sites demonstrates a greater awareness of the importance of leisure time spent at the residential area.

As introduced above, this collection presents studies from different disciplines covering a variety of cases. Each chapter takes as its point of departure an existing or imagined place in connection to Swedish empirical material gathered by the authors. It discusses questions of identity related to people's everyday practices in or related to that place. How do people relate individually and collectively to various places? Can we observe socio-cultural developments in this type of relationships? Can everyday practices be explained by studying characteristics of place? But also: how can the identity of a place be produced and instrumentalised in political visions and processes, for example concerning sustainability and policy? This volume addresses these and other questions using an array of place- and identity-related theories and concepts.

Places are historical and geographical, but also subjective entities. They may radically change due to economic and political development. People living in once booming towns and regions that recently have turned to face declining population and stagnating economy interpret their lives differently than before. In other circumstances, culture and society give places new meaning and attractiveness. This is related to the different and often overlapping meanings that the concept of place can have (Castree 2006: 170). This collection sheds a light on these meanings from Swedish rural and urban perspectives. Places make a lasting impression in people's minds and they are thus important components of the (dis)continuities of social life and the formation and values of society.

Due to mobility's increasing impacts on place, place identities have become more fragmented over the past decades. A major challenge in researching place and identity is to overcome this fragmentation and combine increasingly fluid and remaining static interpretations of place, as they emerge in various new contexts among different groups in Swedish and other societies. Combining the contributions presented here, this volume takes a step towards addressing this challenge.

Örebro and Umeå, Sweden, Summer 2014

References

Andersson, Frida, Richard Ek & Irene Molina (2008), 'Introduktion: En regional politik i förändring'. pp. 7–34 in: Andersson, Frida, Richard Ek & Irene Molina (eds), *Regionalpolitikens geografi – regional tillväxt i teori och praktik*. Malmö: Studentlitteratur.

Castree, Noel (2006), 'Place: connections and boundaries in an interconnected world'. pp. 165–185 in: Holloway, Sarah, Stephen Rice & Gill Valentine (2006) (eds), *Key Concepts in Geography*. London: Sage.

Gren, Martin & Per-Olof Hallin (2003), *Kulturgeografi, en ämnesteoretisk introduktion*. Malmö: Liber.

Isacson, Maths, Mats Lundmark, Cecilia Mörner & Inger Orre (2009) (eds), *Fram träder Bergslagen – nytt ljus över gammal region*. Bergslagsforskning 3. Västerås: Mälardalens Högskola.

Koselleck, Reinhard (1992 [1979]), *Vergangene Zukunft. Zur Semantik geschichtlicher Zeiten*. Frankfurt a.M.: Suhrkamp.

Lefebvre, Henri (1979), 'Space: social product and use value', pp. 285–295 in: J. W. Freiberg (ed.), *Critical Sociology. European Perspectives*, New York: Irvington Publishers.

Massey, Doreen (1991), 'A global sense of place'. *Marxism Today* 38: 24–29.

Massey, Doreen (1995), 'The conceptualisation of place'. pp. 46–79 in: Massey, Doreen & Pat Jess (ed.s), *A place in the world?* Oxford: Oxford University Press.

Relph, Edward (1976), *Place and Placelessness*. London: Pion.

— (1996), Reflections on *Place and Placelessness. Environmental and Architectural Phenomenology Newsletter*, 7, 3, 14–16 [special issue on the twentieth anniversary of the publication of *Place and Placelessness*].

Thrift, Nigel (1999), 'Steps to an ecology of place'. pp. 295–323 in: Massey, Doreen, John Allen & Phil Sarre (ed.s), *Human Geography Today*. Chichester: Wiley.

Torkington, Kate (2012), 'Place and Lifestyle Migration: the Discursive Construction of "Glocal" Place-Identity'. *Mobilities* 7: 71–92.

Tuan, Yi-Fu (1977 [2008]), *Space and Place: the perspective of experience*. Minneapolis: The University of Minnesota Press.

— (2005), 'Space and Place: Humanistic Perspective'. pp. 444–457 in: Agnew, John, David Livingstone & Alisdair Rogers (ed.s), *Human geography. An essential anthology*. (Seventh edition) Oxford: Blackwell.

Urry, John (2007), *Mobilities*. Cambridge: Polity Press.

Ageing, Identity and Place
– Senses of Belonging

Christina Hjorth Aronsson

Introduction

This contribution to the anthology about identity and place has to some extent been influenced by the ongoing Swedish media attention during 2011 to what has been called scandals in elder care, especially residential care. This media debate has focused on the fact that private companies make huge profits by having extremely cost-effective care organizations, and that frail elderly persons suffer from this. The cases of deeply disgraceful treatment of older persons that have surfaced are as far from any idea of human dignity as possible. But what is interesting to reflect upon is the fact that the concept of identity is remarkably absent in most discussions about the content and quality of elder care, and not only these current examples. The focus of elder care has been on solutions to bring health care and social assistance to individuals, not on how the help might contribute to the quality of life to ageing persons in terms of their lifelong identities. Scientific knowledge should contribute to better care content, as well as to how to put personnel and financial resources to use in a better and more dignified way.

In the years around 1900, human ageing was not yet something that was regarded as a social policy issue. The great demographic changes during the twentieth century, however, with rising in average life expectancies all over the Western world due to better hygiene, food and health care and medical treatment, forced society to recognize the need to take action to deal with the ageing population. The Swedish average life expectancy is projected to continue to increase until around 2050, for men from the current

78.6 to 83.6 years, and for women from 82.8 to 86.3 years (SCB, 2006:2). The fact that we live for so long has also meant that we live as retired persons for a fairly long period, sometimes more than thirty years. Also, the transition from an active, working life to living as pensioners is far from an abrupt change from one day to next. Many prefer to retire step by step between the ages of 60 and 67, thus keeping in contact with their occupations to some degree. Also, many preserve their good health to a high age and lead active lives travelling, pursuing interests and hobbies, and taking part in social activities with friends.

The argument that will be focused on in this chapter concerns aspects of the connection between the person, social interaction and place as they have been theorized on psychological, social-psychological and social levels in social science and social gerontology. As is asked by Forssell in the introductory chapter, matters concerning dignity, belonging and social interaction, deeply influence identities of older persons and this is especially important when the amount of freedom in action is restricted by bad health and illness. Over the course of their entire lives, individuals develop a deep identification with an environment, be it rural, a small rural town or an urban environment, with the consequence that they either live there for the rest of their life, have resettled during a later part of life, or arrange a mixture of both, all in order to keep in contact with a geographical location that is familiar to them. The places where one lives and has lived during one's life reflect aspects of one's self (Chapman & Peace 2008) and life experiences are connected to certain places which themselves contribute to and influence how identity develops through the life course. Though people may move many times during their lives, all the places where they have lived form a kind of mental map which contributes to their identity and to a sense of belonging as well as of exclusion (Lynch, 1967). The aim of this chapter is to review and discuss some aspects of the concept of identity in terms of how research captures this in connection with human ageing in a social context where social care of older people is of great importance for their daily lives. Places and artefacts as well as relationships, play a vital role in the continuity and change of individual identity. Identity arises in the relationship between one's own and others' definitions of who I am, and identity changes over time as well as according to the social context. The chapter will begin with some notions about the home ideology of Swedish elder care, followed by a theory of personality development and then move on to theories explaining ageing from social and sociological levels and the importance issues concerning place when trying to understand ageing and the life course.

The home ideology

An increasing dependence on health and medical care as well as social care such as home help is often a reality in the life of older individuals. Welfare solutions are based on the idea of remaining at home for as long as possible on the grounds that it is good for the individual to remain in a familiar and comfortable setting. This chapter will discuss the importance of place relations for the individual self throughout the entire course of life. The ideological preference within the Swedish welfare sector for having the elderly remain at home is supported by scientific evidence, although it to some degree also is a case of making a virtue of hard realities in a situation characterized by budget constraints. In formulating the continuity theory, Atchley (1999) concluded that there is a constant internal logic in the thinking, acting and preferences of individuals during their life course. It is important for those responsible for the health and social care of older people to recognize this in order to respect the individuality and personalities of those in their care.

The possibility for elderly persons to remain in their own houses or apartments and receive help in the form of home care from the public social service has been an official goal of Swedish social policy since the 1950s (Hjorth Aronsson, 2007). The concept that underpins this policy and practice has been normalization, the idea that old age as well as various kinds of disabilities in different stages of life are best dealt with through individually adopted assistance in a familiar environment. One's own home is understood to be the place where an individual can feel safe, familiar, and comfortable. Institutions in the form of elder care centres have been and still are regarded as socially excluding and as the final alternative in a late phase of a person's physical and/or mental deterioration. According to the Social Services Act (SFS 2001:453), an ageing citizen has the right, no matter where he or she lives, to social care and services according to his or her particular needs and conditions. According to law, individual preferences and personal decision-making are the factors that should carry the most weight in deciding how to assist a person. Assistance should, as far as possible, be provided where the person lives. The kind and amount of the home care to which a person is entitled – for instance buying food, cleaning, preparing meals, personal help with hygiene – are decided by a social worker after individual assessment. A nurse is responsible for deciding what kind of medical care that may be necessary for the individual in question. A division of labour is thus established between medical treatment performed by a nurse and home care tasks carried out by the home care staff. This division of labour is paradigmatic and is based upon the legally defined areas of responsibility of medicine and social work respectively.

The normalization strategies within Swedish elder care have been created and developed through public efforts in the municipalities under the direction by the state. During the last decade the new public management model of welfare organization has evolved, which stipulates that the care user should have a choice between different private or public providers of care. Hence, the possibility to remain in your own home is associated with the possibility to choose between different private care companies (see also SFS 2008:962). This new situation has raised questions concerning the quality of the care of older people and the media attention on scandals mentioned above is a reflection on this situation within the care of elderly. As a consequence of this the Swedish government has decided to investigate whether there exist systematic differences of quality between private and public deliverers of care to older people (Regeringsbeslut/Government Decision/S2011/11253/FST).

Identity and Place

Self, Social Interaction, Narrative and Life Style
Writing from a social psychological and psycho-analytical perspective, Erik H. Erikson argued that the human self develops through an ongoing interaction between individual and society throughout

the entire life course (1982/2004:135). According to Erikson's theoretical work, there are eight successive and distinct developmental stages, with the ageing period (late adulthood) comprising the last parts of life. He pointed our civilization's lack of a culturally sustainable ideal for human ageing, which means that we have no conceptual notion of human life as a whole (*ibid.* p. 135). Instead of being included in society, older persons are often excluded and neglected. Instead of wisdom, defined as 'an objective, and yet active interest in life until death' (*ibid.* p. 76, my translation), the ageing period is a personification of shame. After Erik H Erikson's death, his wife Joan complemented his developmental theory with a ninth stage comprising the very last part of life, a period characterized by frailty, dependence, and an increasing need for care and medical treatment before death. The end-of-life-period is presumed to be the time when a person concludes his or her life. A good place to live is thus an important part of this period. In this period of life reflections of the personality are mostly expressed through artefacts – memories of lived experiences – such as photos, literature, books, music, art, furniture. An interpretation of this phase in Joan Erikson's augmentation of the general theory is that this development forms a general human development, no matter where an individual has spent the main parts of his or her life. During this end-of-life period, physical and spatial connectedness to a well-known but restricted physical and social context is of great importance. Joan Erikson points out the need for these kinds of well-known artefacts in the familiar environment of older persons (*ibid.* pp. 136–143). The importance of this well-known physical environment at the very end of life is shown in a study by Whitaker (2004). Whitaker studied very old, dying women living in care homes and narrow bounded to their beds and a few personal things that they could regard as their own.

Though the focus is on individual development Erikson's theorizing about the identity formation during the entire life of an individual definitively involves a social interactional perspective. The developmental stages that an individual follows are influenced by experiences on interactional levels. Later, researchers have drawn attention to the importance of regarding the self as composed of narratives, by means of which we express elements of ourselves internally and present the self externally, and argue that this is a process that goes on in dialogue with someone else or in a text, a script (Rubinstein & de Medeiros, 2005: 52).

The life-course perspective within social gerontology, which takes as its starting point the ongoing and dynamic relationship between the individual and the social context, the circumstances and changes occurring at structural levels, has theorized about how older persons within the population live in congruence with the era in which they live. The life-course perspective should be understood as saying that in the modern way of ageing, different life styles and ways of living are challenging ideas of how life and ageing are or should be, namely a series of stages in a life cycle. Daly and Grant (2008) make the following definition of a life course perspective that it

> places an emphasis on understanding the physical, spatial, social and temporal contexts in which people live, as well as the ways in which individuals and their environments shape each other (2008:12).

Daly and Grant (2008), as well as Rubinstein and de Medeiros (2005) take an important step away from regarding human life as a series of developmental stages in Erikson's sense. Instead they emphasize the important idea that human life is culturally embedded and socially contingent (Daly & Grant, 2008: 12) and the self is narratively constructed in dialogue with the context (Rubinstein & de Medeiros, 2005). Different lifestyles within the late modern consumer society are also represented among the elderly population, and market forces which are adapted to specific goals of the consumer population also target them. Commercial forces have long recognized the strong market potential that exists among the ageing population (Vincent 2003), whether it be for general consumption, body-fitness products, fashion or goal-oriented travelling (Öberg, 2005). Conceptions of the elderly as asexual are less prominent nowadays as studies have shown that they establish new partner relationships when their former partners have died or after a separation. Emotions do not diminish with age, although expressions of them might change in character (Öberg, 2003; Öberg & Tornstam, 2003). The concept of intersectionality is important in understanding aspects of ageing and later life

(Cranswick, 2003). Professional works as well as household duties are gendered throughout life, and this will continue regardless of ethnic and socioeconomic belonging. Borell (2003) showed how men and women differed in their efforts to rebuild a new home after divorce or the death of their former partner. Women who had been responsible for caring for their husbands until his death were less inclined to build a new home with a new partner, than were men who had lost their wives. The women studied preferred an intimate relationship that did not involve entering a new role as the one responsible for household duties. The term for this is LAT-relationships (Living Apart Together) and seems to be a trend in countries of the western world. In Sweden there is a special term for this phenomenon of living apart but having a close relationship, namely *särbo* (*ibid.* p. 469). This can be seen as an example of a late modern way of living for ageing women who wish to claim a period of autonomy before the final years of frailty and disease that often follow.

Also of interest is a set of phenomena that have been gathered under the concept of 'elective belonging', by which refers to those aged persons who consciously select where to live as part of their lifestyle and identity (Phillipson, 2007). Phillipson refers to studies of retired, often affluent people who move to rural areas that are favoured by them such as the English Cotswolds, the Welsh Borders and the Peak District. He also cites to studies of those Swedes who migrate to Spain at higher ages (2007:329). Interestingly in the studies of the migrated Swedes is that there is no 'agreed form of belonging to their new community' (*ibid.* 329), but instead they are visitors in the new country, and not seldom are more connected to other Swedes living there than to local residents. I interpret these examples of settling in self-selected and preferred locations at higher ages as expressions of a wish, for those who can afford it, to spend some years of pursuing their interests, or hobbies in a comfortable climate, or living in a beautiful natural setting.

Homes, artefacts, places and neighbourhood

The importance of the home and home environment for the elderly emphasizes its status as a part of identity; at home you have furniture, goods and other things that represent memories of a lived life at the same time as life still continues inside as well as outside the home, in the neighbourhood and beyond. Even if older persons have to adopt their home environment to facilitate their present way of life, this environment is familiar to them, says something about who they are, and is an expression of their identity. Home-decorating, style and furniture express personal tastes and prefer-ences, confirm identity, and keep memories alive, as well as being able to serve as a bridge between generations. People's homes are an expression of the person they have been throughout the experi-ences of life. Daily routines and everyday rituals are connected to the home and contribute to emotions of being at home and feeling safe according to Rubinstein and de Medeiros (2005). As they argue (2005:52–53), the things in a person's home can become one with the self. Of special importance is the familiar character of the home for persons with incipient or fully developed Alzheimer's Disease, for whom the very concept of home has a deep symbolic meaning of belonging, recognition and importance (Frank, 2005). In this case the sense of home might be expressed through a piece of music, a well recognized smell, or a familiar piece of furniture. The meaning of home for a person with dementia might be a special case, but generally speaking, homes for ageing people are places in the sense of 'settings with personal significance' (*ibid.* p. 59).

For the individual, the place, the home and the physical artefacts connected to the home confirm one's personal identity and are expressions of memories (narratives) of a lived life. In total, the home environment includes interests, daily routines and every day rituals which make us feel safe and satisfied in the immediate context. A person has possessions with whom he or she has been connected throughout life and these represent memories of a lived life. Sherman and Dacher (2005), in a critical essay, point out the significance of old persons' cherished objects and how important it is to be conscious of and to respect this when an old person is in need of social care in his or her private home. Respect for the individual in need of personal assistance therefore requires that adaptations of the physical place to simplify the provision of care must not be made against the will of the person (*ibid.* p. 75).

Oswald and Wahl also address the importance of the home environment as people age (2005). They state that a majority of the ageing population in the Western countries live independently in their own home, and not in institutions, either alone or with a partner. This is also the case in Sweden as has been stated above. Even when in need of assistance and care, old people continue living in their own apartments or even houses. Oswald and Wahl refer to studies showing that older people spend more time at home than younger people, and also that there is 'an age-related tendency for environmental centralization inside the house' (*ibid.* 2005:25). This refers both to the home of an older person being comfortably adopted and the person's outside interest needing to be accessible within a close radio from the home. As a result of health changes in later life, older persons must alter their homes or move to new dwellings that meet their needs. The meaning of home is of great significance when a person needs to relocate to a new place of residence because of health impairments and changing social conditions. The process of relocation should ideally be the result of the personal wishes of the older person, and an expression of how he or she prefers to spend the final years of life (*ibid.*). For an older person, the actual process of relocation is often a matter of moving from larger to a smaller dwelling. Whether it be from a house of one's own to a rental property, or from a bigger to a smaller apartment, the relocation process involves decisions to part with cherished objects.

Stepping outside the home we come to the neighbourhood context, which can be regarded as the familiar circle within the home environment which constitutes the link to the surrounding world (Peace, Holland & Kellaher 2005; Svensson, 2006). The neighbourhood, whether urban or rural, is the intimate outer living environment and is an important factor of social life, well-being and self-identity. That important environmental changes must occur with increasing age due to health impairments is shown in an empirical study by Peace, Holland and Kellaher (2011), where they develop the concept of 'option recognition' by means of which they

> describe the consequences for older individuals at points in
> time when, in spite of the importance of personal autonomy
> in establishing a "place of one's own", change occurs that
> requires a new strategy to maintain self-identity (2011:751).

Ageing is an individually experienced process in the life of an individual and the way in which ageing proceeds is influenced by factors on all levels, biological, psychological, and social as well as by gender and ethnicity. In spite of these differences, at some point in life the options for a good place to live during old age becomes more important than before, because they have to do with one's survival during the final period of life.

Research on ageing in rural areas has been conducted from a variety of perspectives. Struthers (2005) studied the wishes of older persons regarding living conditions in American rural areas, and found a strong desire to continue living in these areas, with good housing conditions being an important precondition for this. The need for health care and assistance programs when growing old in rural areas has also been studied by Butler and de Poy (1996) and Butler and Sharland (2003). Butler and Kaye (2003) as well as Butler and Webster (2003) and Butler (2006) have pointed out that social workers need a better understanding of the living conditions among old people in rural areas in order to help them better and have the necessary competence and provide better service. Older persons living in rural areas differ from those in urban areas in important ways. They are generally less educated, poorer, have worse housing conditions and suffer from more chronic illnesses than retired persons in urban areas. In spite of faring worse in terms of those parameters than older people in urban areas, they appreciate the independence they experience in their rural living situation. Although most of the ageing population lives in urban areas, there are older persons who are deeply rooted in rural settings where they have spent most of their lives. The subject of rural ageing has been of interest in Sweden as well as in highly urbanized countries such as England, where the idea of personalization underpins a range of initiatives that aim to give older people, wherever they live, greater choice and control regarding the care and service they receive from the public sector. How these public efforts affect older people in rural areas has been studied by Manthorpe and Stevens (2009). This idea of personalization can be seen as corresponding to the concept of normalization which serves as ideological mantra within Swedish welfare policy. In the Swedish context, normalization has stressed the immediate social, home-like environment of an individual, at the expense of institutional care, whereas in the English context personalization emphasizes the individual preferences in way of life. This is to be regarded as an important difference between fundamental ways of creating welfare communities in liberal vs. social democratic regimes; the personalization emphasizes the individually adapted choice, while normalization emphasizes social and community aspects.

'The living countryside' (*levande landsbygd*) is a slogan used by Swedish politicians and policy makers when arguing in favour of efforts to maintain rural areas as sustainable and viable places to live for people of all ages and socioeconomic levels. Everyone should be able to have a high quality of life in these parts of the country with sufficient public services (preschool, school, health and social care) and commercial services, as well as satisfactory communications. Rural areas are geographically characterized by agriculture and forestry with local centres of public and commercial activity. Goals are formulated for the elderly, stating that they should be able to lead lives of high quality and satisfaction and receive requisite social and medical care. Research and reports have been published documenting the efforts of certain regions to bring care and services to older people in rural areas (Norling, 2007; Svensson, 2006; Socialstyrelsen, 2008). In an opinion article in Sweden's largest daily newspaper, leading members of the Centre Party (*Centerpartiet*) argued for the right of older persons in need of home care to choose between private and public assistance alternatives (*Dagens Nyheter* July 19, 2011). These can be seen as signs of both an awareness of an ageing population living in the countryside and a wish for private alternatives within the care sector. In a yet unpublished paper Hjorth Aronsson (forthcoming) discusses the demographic situation in the biggest rural part of Örebro municipality, characterized by agriculture and forestry. The demographic statistics show a remaining population of persons of high or very high (>90 ys of age) living in this area, many of them in their own homes. The home care services for those in need demand a 24 hours of organization for some of them, which also include a vast travelling in cars n order to deliver the service needed.

The rural environment is not just the opposite of the urban environment in terms of its architectural, social, and dense way of thinking and imagining place, but also involves a way of living as a whole – a life style, a way of organizing everyday life, professional work, outcomes. The availability of public and commercial services differs to a greater or lesser extent than in the urban way of life. Distances are important factors in the organization of every day life as is shown in the studies mentioned above. The urban way of life involves both actually living in an urban environment but also, as Max Weber once stated in his famous essay on *The City* (1911– 13/1987), a kind of mentality; i. e. you are an urban person and bring along your urban way of acting and behaving even when you go to a rural place on vacation. Max Weber regarded the bourgeois way of life as hegemonic for the rest of the population *(ibid)*. Hence, the rural way of life means both to having a deep connection to a rural environment and being forced to have a connection to urban centres. This is the very challenge for the politicians when they talk about the 'the living countryside' for all, and of all ages.

Conclusion

This chapter has discussed some theoretical aspects and empirical evidences of the development of identity in human social life and the importance of place in that process. Individual identity can be seen as the result of an ongoing interaction process where the self, social interaction and physical artefacts located in specific places serve as elements helping to create lifelong experiences that, taking together, create and manifest human identities. Identity and identity formation are regarded as an ongoing exchange between the self, social interaction and the context of place that plays a role in the life of a person. Erik and Joan Erikson (1982/2004) regarded the self as developing through nine stages, with the final stage representing the fulfilment of life. An interactional perspective has been of fundamental importance in their theoretical work. Rubinstein and de Medeiros (2005) and Daly and Grant (2008) discuss the importance of a life-course perspective on life in which the individual life should be regarded as embedded in its social contexts. The self as narratives or as texts is put forward by Rubinstein and de Medeiros (2005). Cranswick (2003) highlights the gendered lifestyle that characterizes the whole course of life in which women, no matter of their ethnic and class-belongings are kept occupied by household duties. When ageing they continue this pattern and bear the main responsibility for an aged husband. The concept of 'elective belonging' has been formulated by Phillipson (2007) and refers to those affluent older persons who choose to live in exclusive areas abroad or in a kind of gated communities in their own country.

An important finding in studies is that older persons do spend more time at home, especially when their ability to move outside is restricted. This means that the home environment becomes even more important and the artefacts of the home increase in importance. The home as a place represents memories and recognitions of past and present and is thus an expression of identity. To respect the home environment of the individual is of great importance when it comes to persons in need of social care due to physical impairments (Sherman and Dacher, 2005). The concept of 'option recognition' formulated by Peace, Holland and Kellaher (2011), expresses a situation where an older individual has to develop a new strategy to maintain self-identity because of disease and disability (*ibid.* 751). By that time life conditions are restricted and the dependence on personal assistance is obvious.

To conclude, the concepts of age, identity and place have been given attention to in many studies and using different perspectives within the social scientific research field. There is a wealth of scientific knowledge that could provide valuable support for how to organize the professional health and social care, whether private or public. The personal dignity of the elderly is protected by law in Sweden (SFS 2001:453, ch. 5), which places a demand on society to develop in this direction. In order to avoid scandals within the elder care sector, it is time to take serious on concepts like need, in connection to place and identity.

References

Anhörigstöd i glesbygd /Family sup-port in Rural Areas/ Stockholm: Socialstyrelsen, Report No. 11/2008.

Atchley, R. (1999) *Continuity and Adaptation in Aging: Creating Positive Experiences.* Baltimore, MD: John Hopkins University Press.

Borell, K (2003) 'Family and Household. Family Research and Multi-Household Families'. *International Review of Sociology*, Vol. 13, No. 3, pp. 467–480.

Butler, S. & de Poy, E. (1996) 'Rural Elderly Women's Attitudes Towards Professional and Governmental Assistance'. *Affilia*, Vol. 11, No. 1, pp. 76–94.

Butler, S. & Hope, B. (1999) 'Health and Well-Being for Late Middle-Aged Lesbians in Rural Area'. *Journal of Gay & Lesbian Social Services*, Vol. 9, No. 4, pp. 27–46.

Butler, S. & Sharland, D.W. (2003) 'Specialized Housing and Rural Elders'. *Journal of Gerontological Social Work*, Vol. 41, No. 3 – 4, pp. 247–263.

Butler, S. & Kaye, L.W. (2003) 'Rurality, Aging and Social Work: Setting the Context'. *Journal of Gerontological Social Work*, Vol. 41, No. 1–2, pp. 3–18.

Butler, S. & Webster, N. M. (2003) 'Advocacy Techniques with Older Adults in Rural Environments'. *Journal of Gerontological Social Work*, Vol. 41, No. 1–2, pp. 59–74.

Butler, S. (2004) 'Gay, Lesbian, Bisexual, and Transgender (GLBT) Elders: the Challenges and Resilience of this Marginalized Group'. *Journal of Human Behaviour in the Social Environment*, Vol. 9, No. 4, pp. 25–37.

Chapman, S. H. & Peace, S. (2008) 'Rurality and Ageing Well: "a Long Time Here"'. In: Keating, N. (ed.) *Rural Ageing: A Good Place to grow Old?* Bristol: The Policy Press.

Cranswick, K. (2003) *General Social Survey Cycle 16: Caring for an Aging Society 2002*. Ottawa, ON: Statistics, Canada.

Daly, T. & Grant, G. (2008) 'Crossing Borders: Lifecourse, Rural Ageing and Disability'. In: Keating, N. (ed.) *Rural Ageing. A Good Place to Grow Old?* Bristol: The Policy Press.

Demografiska rapporter 2006:2, Sveriges framtida befolkning 2006–2050, /Demographic Reports 2006:2, The Swedish Population 2006–2050/ Stockholm/Örebro: Statistiska Centralbyrån.

Erikson, E. H. (1982/2004) *Den fullbordade livscykeln. (The Life Cycle Completed: a Review. Extended Version With New Chapters by Joan M. Erikson.* Stockholm: Bokförlaget Natur och Kultur.

Frank, J. (2005) 'Semiotic Use of the Word "Home" among People with Alzheimer's Disease: A Plea of Selfhood?' In: Rowles, G. D. & Chaudhury, H. (eds.) *Home and Identity in Late Life. International Perspectives.* New York: Springer Publishing Company, Inc.

Hjorth Aronsson, C. (2007) 'The Care of Older People in Sweden'. In: Balloch, S. & Hill, M. (eds)

Care, Community and Citizenship. Research and Practice in a Changing Policy Context. Bristol: The Policy Press.

Hjorth Aronsson, C. (2008) 'Asta, 90 Years: "Now I will stop to visit pensioners". Self, Society, Ageing, some Impressions'. (In Swedish) *Svensk Idrottsforskning (Swedish Journal of Sport Research)* No. 3.

Hjorth Aronsson, C. *Demographic Changes and The Care of Older People in a Rural Area, the Example of Östernärke.* (unpublished material), Örebro University.

Jonsson, A. W. *et al.* (2011) 'Underlätta för vårdvalet i glesbygden'./Enlighten the Possibility to Choose Between Social Care Deliverers in Rural Areas/' *Dagens Nyheter* 2011-07-19, p. 7.

Lag (2001:453) om Socialtjänst /Social Services Act/.

Lag (2008:962) om valfrihetssystem / Act of Freedom to Chose among deliverers of Services/

Manthorpe, J. & Stevens, M. (2009) 'Increasing Care Options in the Countryside: Developing an Understanding of the Potential Impact of Personalization for Social Work with Rural Older People'. *British Journal of Social Work* Volume 40, Issue 5, pp. 1452–1469.

Norling, M. (2005) *Finns det något alternativ? Nya serviceformer för äldre på landsbygden. /Is there any Alternatives? New Kinds of Service Alternatives to Older People in Rural Areas/* Falun: Dalarnas Forskningsråd.

Oswald, F & Wahl, H-W (2005) 'Dimensions of the Meaning of Home in Later Life'. In: Rowles, G. D. & Chaudhury, H. (eds.) *Home and Identity in Late Life. International Perspectives.* New York: Springer Publishing Company, Inc.

Peace, S., Holland, C. & Kellaher, L. (2005) 'The Influence of Neighbourhood and Community on Well-Being and Identity in Later Life: an English Perspective'. In: Rowles, G. D. & Chaudhury, H. (eds.) *Home and Identity in Late Life. International Perspectives.* New York: Springer Publishing Company, Inc.

Peace, S, Holland, C, & Kellaher L (2011) '"Option recognition" in later life: variations in ageing in place'. *Ageing & Society,* 31, 734–757.

Phillipson, C. (2007) 'The "elected"and the "excluded": sociological perspectives on the experience of place and community in old age'. *Ageing & Society,* 27, pp. 321–342.

Regeringsbeslut S2011/11253/FST. *Uppdrag att granska om det förekommer systematiska kvalitetsskillnader mellan offentligt och enskilt driven äldreomsorg. /*Government decision to control the existence of systematic differences between public and private elder care/. Stockholm: Socialdepartementet.

Rubinstein, R.L. & de Medeiros, K. (2005) 'Home, Self and Identity'. In: Rowles, G. D. & Chaudhury, H. (eds) *Home and Identity in Late Life. International Perspectives.* New York: Springer Publishing Company, Inc.

Sherman, E. & Dacher, J. (2005) 'Cherished Objects and the Home: Their Meaning and Roles in Late Life'. In: Rowles, G. D. & Chaudhury, H. (eds) *Home and Identity in Late Life. International Perspectives.* New York: Springer Publishing Company, Inc.

Struthers, C. B. (2005) 'Housing Conditions and Housing Options for Older Residents: a Question of Need, a Question of Acceptable Alternatives'. *Journal of Housing for the Elderly*, Vol. 19, No. 1, pp. 53–78.

Svensson, L (2006) *Mötesplatser på landsbygden. Om äldre människor, gemenskap och aktiviteter. /Meeting Places in the Countryside. Older Persons, Community Spirit and Activities/.* Akademisk avhandling, Institutionen för socialt arbete, Göteborgs universitet.

Weber, M (1911–13/1987) 'Staden/ The City/'. In: *Ekonomi och samhället. Förståelsesociologins grunder, del 3: Politisk sociologi.* Lund: Argos.

Whitaker, A. (2004) *Livets sista boning: anhörigskap, åldrande och död på sjukhem. /The Last Home of Life: Relatives, Ageing and to Die in a Care Home/.* Stockholm: Dept. of Social Work, Stockholm University.

Vincent, J. (2003) *Old Age.* London & New York: Routledge.

Öberg, P. (2003) 'Images Versus Experiences of the Aging Body'. In: Faircloth, C.A. (eds.) *Aging Bodies. Images & Everyday Experiences.* New York: Alta Mira Press.

Öberg, P. & Tornstam, L. (2003) 'Attitudes Towards Embodied Old Age among Swedes'. *The International Journal of Aging and Human Development*, Vol. 56, No. 2, pp. 133–153.

'I Felt Confined'

– *Narratives of Ambivalence among Dutch Lifestyle Migrants in Rural Sweden*

Marco Eimermann

Dutch lifestyle migration to Swedish rural areas in the early 21st century

In recent decades, the majority of European migration research has focused on refugees and the political implications of flows from third countries – *i.e.* from outside the European Union (EU) (Blotevogel & Fielding 1997, Castles & Miller 1998, Castles 2000, Hansen 2008). The main destination areas for these flows are urban centres such as London and Paris (Sassen 2008). The economic and social challenges related to integration of third-country migrants have been described in terms of welfare dependence and high transaction costs for employers (Lang 1986, Rooth & Saarela 2007). In destination countries, segregation (Molina 2008) as well as transnational and imagined communities of everyday life (Vaiou 2010) have also been studied.

Dynamics related to retirement-, student-, and lifestyle-migration within the EU have only gained due attention relatively recently (King 2002, Benson & O'Reilly 2009). Some of these flows consist of affluent urban-to-rural migrants. The migrants' motives may be examined against the background of

> a host of social transformations that have given rise to, or enabled, this type of migration and which explain its emergence as a distinct phenomenon over the last 50 or 60 years. These include, for example, globalisation,

individualisation, increased mobility and ease of movement, flexibility in working lives, and increases in global relative wealth. (Benson & O'Reilly 2009, p. 3)

Within the context of lifestyle migration, this chapter describes and analyses the motives of a group of affluent Western migrants in the rural Swedish municipality of Hällefors. The group consists of Dutch households that have decided to move north, a novel direction within lifestyle migration research. Migration from the Netherlands is illustrated in Table 1 in relative terms. Measured in this way, Sweden's increase as a destination country is among the largest in Europe, Australia, Canada and the United States of America (usa).

Compared to 1995, the number of registered out-migrants from the Netherlands has increased by 43% to 90,067 in 2008 (Statistics Netherlands 2011). In absolute terms, the neighbouring countries of Germany and Belgium are the most popular destinations, with around 11,500 Dutch moving to each country in 2008. These are followed by the usa (4,676) and Spain (4,021) (Statistics Netherlands 2011). In 1995, 494 (0.8%) people were registered as migrants to Sweden (Statistics Netherlands 2011). This figure had increased both absolutely and relatively, to 1280 (1.4%) in 2011 (Statistics Netherlands 2011). According to the Swedish National Rural Development Agency (2008, p. 47), the distribution of the Dutch population in Sweden differs from that of most other migrants. The Dutch seem to prefer rural and sparsely populated areas over urban areas (Eimermann *et al.* 2012).

Against this background, the study at hand focuses in particular on one rural Swedish municipality: Hällefors. The aim of this chapter is to examine the migration process of Dutch lifestyle migrants in Hällefors and their ambivalent attitudes towards returning, and thereby to give voice to the hope, pain, nostalgia, and triumph of lives lived in other places (King *et al.* 1995). Consequently, the empirical question is as follows: 'After migrating to Hällefors, what influences the Dutch households' attitude towards returning?' This question is addressed through narratives of Dutch migrant households, gathered during fieldwork in 2011.

The structure of the chapter is as follows. After this introduction, some background is provided on the history and geography of Hällefors and its collaboration with the migration consultancy agency Placement. The conceptual framework is then presented, and the research design of the study is outlined. After this, a description and analysis of the fieldwork is presented, giving special attention to the households' ambivalent attitudes towards returning. After this empirical section, the concept of the creative class is discussed in relation to Dutch migrants in Hällefors. Finally, in the concluding discussion, the findings are related to the conceptual framework.

Table 1: Destination countries for emigrants from the Netherlands, 1995–2008

Country / Year	1996	2000	2004	2008
Belgium	1.16	1.07	1.26	1.53
Denmark	0.84	1.01	0.81	0.89
Finland	0.95	1.37	1.28	1.31
France	0.99	1.19	1.30	1.37
Germany	1.06	0.96	1.20	1.48
Italy	0.97	1.01	0.98	1.17
Norway	1.15	1.12	1.66	2.61
Portugal	1.07	1.13	1.18	1.58
Spain	1.02	1.28	1.61	1.79
Sweden	0.99	1.32	1.64	2.59
Australia	0.88	0.92	1.01	1.53
Canada	1.13	1.13	1.07	1.22
USA	1.01	1.05	0.82	0.91

Source: Statistics Netherlands 2011 (Index: 1995=1)

Hällefors, Placement, and international rural place marketing

In the contemporary era of globalisation and time-space compression (Janelle 1991), many rural areas in Sweden and Europe have experienced international urban-to-rural migration (Hedberg & Do Carmo 2011). For instance, Müller (1999) studies German second-home owners in Småland. Among population geographers in Sweden, the county of Värmland is well-known for its large Dutch population (Andersen & Engström 2005, Eriksson Robertson 2010). However, rural municipalities such as Hällefors have not been studied in the context of Dutch lifestyle migration to the Swedish countryside.

On the one hand, Hällefors is a typical Swedish small industrial town. The municipality is located in northern Örebro county, in a rural area known as Bergslagen, formerly characterised by forestry as well as iron and steel industry (Braunerhielm 2006, Heldt Cassell 2008, Jakobsson 2009). Over the centuries, the area has attracted labour migrants from Belgium, Germany, Finland, and other countries (Borgegård *et al.* 1998, Åkesson 1998). During the past decades, however, the municipality has suffered from population decline and economic stagnation. The number of inhabitants decreased from 11,723 in 1968 to 7,220 in 2010 (Statistics Sweden 2011). Traditional patriarchal social values in Hällefors (Hedfeldt 2008) may be hampering its adaptation to post-industrial conditions (Boyle & Halfacree 1998, Heldt Cassel 2008, pp. 106–107).

On the other hand, Hällefors is a trend-setter in rural Sweden. In 2003, in an attempt to turn the tide of depopulation, the municipality's executive board formulated three policy profiles: culinary arts, technology, and design (Braunerhielm 2006, pp. 116–117). This shift resulted among other things in collaboration with a privately owned migration consultancy agency based in Norway called Placement (Interview Björklund 2008). According to its director, the aim of Placement is 'to attract Dutch and other families ideally consisting of adults aged 35–45 and children under the age of 10'. Furthermore, 'In order to minimize the risk of remigration, Placement looks for families with pre-existing ties to the destination countries' (Interview Vreeswijk 2008). Between 2004 and 2007, Hällefors participated in an international rural place-marketing campaign, with the purpose of attracting lifestyle migrants from the Netherlands and elsewhere (Eimermann 2013).

Information meetings for prospective migrants are at the core of the campaign. Four meetings in the Netherlands are part of this study: Nordic migration information days in 2008 and 2009; a seminar on entrepreneurship in Sweden in 2009; and the seventh occasion of Scandinavia Day in 2011. The number of visitors to these events varied from about 240 at the general information days to approximately 2,400 at the Scandinavia Day. The purpose of these meetings is for Placement to inform visitors about the projects and about employment and housing conditions, as well as other practical issues in the municipalities. Representations of Swedish versions of the rural idyll (see below) are mediated during those meetings. In general, prospective international migrants' level of knowledge about socio-economic conditions in destination areas cannot match the level of knowledge of domestic target groups (Eimermann 2013). Partly as a result of these rural place-marketing efforts, about 50 Dutch families settled in Hällefors from 2004 onwards.

Conceptual framework

The conceptual framework for this chapter consists of the following interrelated concepts: lifestyle migration, the good life, the rural idyll, the urban-rural continuum, the creative class, ambivalence, and identity shift. Their use in this chapter is elucidated below.

First, lifestyle migration is utilised by Benson and O'Reilly (2009, pp. 2–3) as a conceptual framework for a selection of contemporary intra-EU migration flows. They refer to concepts such as 'modernity and self-identity' (Giddens 1991), 'liquid modernity and the art of life' (Bauman 2000, 2008), 'privileged travel and movement' (Amit 2007), and the 'new mobilities paradigm' (Sheller & Urry 2006). Each of these concepts suggests increasing opportunities for individuals to create their own preferences in a context of diminishing social and practical constraints. In this context, lifestyle migration is understood as 'the spatial mobility of relatively affluent individuals of all ages, moving either part-time or full-time to places that are meaningful because, for various reasons, they offer the potential of a better quality of life' (Benson & O'Reilly 2009, p. 2). In other words, affluent individuals' increased mobility has created opportunities for them both to explore places and to move to a particular place with which they identify.

Second, the concept of the good life contributes to our understanding of the decision of Dutch households to migrate to Hällefors. Benson and O'Reilly (2009, p. 3) argue that 'the good life takes many shapes and forms; narratives articulate ongoing quests to seek refuge from what they [the migrants] describe as the shallowness, individualism, risk and insecurity of contemporary (Western) lifestyles in the perceived authenticity of meaningful places'. A more concise statement of what constitutes the good life sought for when migrating away from a high-income country such as the Netherlands is offered by Van Dalen and Henkens: 'nature, space, and less populated surroundings' (2007, p. 56).

The third concept is the rural idyll, which is closely related to the good life. In Anglo-Saxon contexts, the rural idyll is described by Boyle and Halfacree (1998, pp. 9–10) as 'physically consisting of small villages joined by narrow lanes and nestling amongst a patchwork of small fields [...]. Socially, this is a tranquil landscape of timeless stability and community, where people know not just their next door neighbours but everyone else in the village.' The related discourse of the 'rural childhood idyll' of safety, health, and closeness to nature (Baylina & Berg 2010, p. 287) also serves this chapter's purposes.

Lilja and Sundström (this volume) describe and analyse the use of representations of nature in marketing urban housing projects. Among other things, the authors study people's aspirations to combine vibrant city life with experiencing nature and tranquil environments. Similar dynamics are explored in this chapter. Here, notions of an urban-rural continuum are combined with the concept of the creative class.

Fourth, in contemporary society, it may be difficult to draw a line between 'the rural' and 'the urban' (Woods 2009, p. 4). These concepts are usually distinguished by 'a population size threshold, population density, contiguity of the built up area, political status, proportion of the labour force engaged in non-agricultural work, and presence of particular services and activities' (Champion & Hugo 2004, p. 9). However, as Kūle (2008, p. 9) argues, 'new forms of populated areas are emerging, and they do not correspond to this binary separation. Both rural and urban areas are becoming increasingly multidimensional and interactions between them more intensive.' As a result, 'one is basically accepting the idea of a full continuum of situations lying between the most rural condition that can be conceived and the most urban' (Champion & Hugo 2004, p. 13).

Fifth, within the framework of this continuum, this chapter investigates some notions of the creative class (Florida 2002, 2006).

> The creative class consists of people who add economic value through their creativity. It thus includes a great many knowledge workers, symbolic analysts and professional and technical workers, but emphasises their true role in the economy. [...] Most members of the creative class do not own and control any significant property in the physical sense. Their property [...] is intangible because it is literally in their heads. (Florida 2002, p. 68)

The creative class 'constitutes a significant part of the population of cities that are characterised by diversity and tolerance in terms of ethnic, cultural, religious and sexual orientation' (Nuur & Laestadius 2009, p. 3). Cities, followed increasingly by rural areas, compete to attract members of this class. In Nuur and Laestadius's words (2009, p. 8), 'nonurban contexts at least under certain conditions can contribute to creative processes'. In this context, Jakobsson (2009, p. 79) formulates five categories of creative industries in the Bergslagen area: 'film and media; advertisement, design and fashion; cultural heritage; tourism and meals; and art' (my translation). These categories form the basis for the analysis in the next-to-last section below.

The sixth concept, ambivalence, is related to the migrants' attitude towards returning (or moving elsewhere), once the move to the Swedish countryside is undertaken. Ambivalence (Bærenholdt & Granås 2008, p. 8) may be a particular issue for this type of migration, which is perceived as 'voluntary'. In contrast to refugees, Dutch lifestyle migrants have the possibility to return at any time to their country of origin, or to move elsewhere. Paradoxically, this complicates the decision whether or not to stay.

This decision is studied in connection to a possible identity shift after migration, which is the final concept in this framework. As White (1995, p. 2) describes:

> At any point in our lives we can think of ourselves as relating to a number of identities – in gender terms [...], in terms of a stage in the life course, in terms of age and family sta-

tus, in terms of economic identity [...], in terms of linguistic, religious and other cultural identities and in terms of ethnic identity.

Identity shift may be related to social-scientific perspectives on migration; 'the characteristics of the migrants, the nature of the places of origin and destination and the underlying [...] forces and structures that [...] condition movement' (White 1995, p. 10). The Dutch lifestyle migrants in Hällefors will be described and analysed using these perspectives in the empirical section below. Push-, pull-, and keep-factors are used intermittently in order to frame the migration decisions (Boyle *et al.* 1998, p. 67).

Research design and data

The migrants' unique experiences are central to this research. Hence, data are mainly gathered through qualitative methods. Visiting members of Dutch households at their homes or work-places in Hällefors, observing their immediate surroundings, and conducting in-depth interviews with them resulted in insights that would not have been possible to achieve using quantitative research methods (see Appendix for an interview guide). As King *et al.* (1995, p. x, original italics) argue, aggregative approaches often 'fail to capture the essence of what it is like to *be* a migrant; and be, or not be, part of a community, a nation, a society – cut off from history and from a sense of place.' The fieldwork for this chapter emphasises migrants and the 'realities' of their situation in Hällefors (Halfacree & Boyle 1993).

The interviews are about three hours in length, usually with both adults simultaneously. Children are usually not present during the interviews, except for the part of the visits that is combined with a family gathering around the dinner table. This less formal setting facilitates an interactive-relational approach, in which 'the particular qualities in the interaction and relationship that emerged fuelled our encounters' (Chirban 1996, p. xiv). Contacts with the interviewees have been established through meetings prior to the actual interview.

In 2011, around 50% of the originally 50 Dutch households in Hällefors had left the municipality. Some of them returned to the

Netherlands, others moved to another country, while still others moved to neighbouring municipalities. Hence, out of the original 50 households, approximately 25 remain. Contrary to the definition of lifestyle migration above, I focus not on people of all ages, but rather on those economically active migrants, who usually also have children. This study draws on data gathered from twelve households.

Table 2: Household composition and age structure

Migration	Household	First visit	Adults	Children
April 2005	Van Leeuwen	2005	♂1958, ♀1961	1999, 2000
April 2005	Storm	2002	♂1964, ♀1964	1997, 1999
July 2005	Monnee	± 1970	♂1957, ♀1958	1990, 1994
May 2006	De Geer	2001	♂1954, ♀1974	2002, 2005, 2008
June 2006	De Caluwé	1987	♂1962, ♀1966	1995
April 2007	Swanenburg	2004	♂1965, ♀1967	1997, 2000
May 2007	Landers	2006	♂1970, ♀1971	1996, 1997, 2006, 2009
July 2007	Louwerens	± 1976	♂1960, ♀1963	1994, 1996, 1999
Aug 2007	Lochtenberg	± 1990	♂1970, ♀1969	1998, 2002
Jan 2008	Mansveld	1996	♂1968, ♀1967	1997, 1999
May 2008	Korevaar	2007	♂1957, ♀1959	-
July 2010	Ouwehand	2005	♂1971, ♀1979	1999, 2001, 2006

Source: Eimermann, fieldwork 2011

Two households refused to participate. It may be interesting to briefly reflect on their reasons for not participating. One household stated 'private reasons', which appeared to be a divorce. This is an example of how aspirations, expectations, and contrasting migration experiences may put pressure on family life. The other household stated that they might be moving to Canada the following year, and therefore their participation would not be of any benefit to the research. Unfortunately, this ambivalence is exactly what this chapter focuses on, but they could not be convinced.

The composition and age structure of the households included in this study are presented in Table 2 (for reasons of integrity, names are fictitious). All the families have thought about returning to the Netherlands or moving elsewhere. However, two households expressed their ambivalent attitudes towards returning most explicitly: the Landers and Van Leeuwen families. The Landers family stayed in Hällefors; the Van Leeuwen family moved. Hence, these households are highlighted in this study.

The households presented in Table 2 can be analysed socio-demographically. In general, all households arrived between 2004 and 2011. A distinction can be made between 'planners' and rather spontaneous movers. The Monnee and Louwerens families first visited Sweden 30 to 35 years before actually moving there, whereas the Van Leeuwen, Landers, and Korevaar families visited Sweden one year or less before their move. The adult family members were mainly born in the late 1950s or the 1960s. They were aged 31 to 52 when they moved. The children were born in the 1990s and early 2000s and were between one and fifteen years old when they moved. In two households, a child was born in Sweden (after the move). Including demographic figures for the two families that are not part of the interview study, six out of fourteen families have three children or more, six have two children, one has one child, and one has none. The households are thus comparable regarding composition and age structure.

'I woke up this morning, screaming 'I want to go back, I want to go back!''

> Just an example: we met some of our Dutch connections who live here in Hällefors the other day. They asked us how we were doing and we said 'so-so'. Their situation was similar. We chatted for a while and concluded that most of us Dutch here pretend to live a good life, but that it simply is not true. We all miss things we used to do and have in the Netherlands. (Interview Van Leeuwen 2011)

Here, it becomes clear that Dutch lifestyle migrants in Hällefors experience social difficulties comparable to those studied by King *et al.* (1995). Addressing the empirical question ('After migrating to Hällefors, what influences the Dutch households' attitude towards returning?'), these difficulties are examined in the remainder of the chapter using the concept of identity shift (indirectly) and the three social-scientific perspectives on migration presented above.

Characteristics of the migrants

In relation to the first perspective, Table 2 presents the composition and age structure of the Dutch households in this study. This is complemented in Table 3 with an overview of the places of residence prior to moving and the migrants' occupations prior to and post migration. Statistics Netherlands (2012) defines five degrees of urbanisation, depending on surrounding address density. As all five categories are inhabited by approximately a quintile of the Dutch population, they are comparable in size.

Table 3 shows that six households moved from moderately, strongly, or extremely urbanised municipalities, whereas three households moved from non-urbanised areas and two from hardly urbanised places. However, even the hardly and non-urbanised areas in the small and densely populated country of the Netherlands can be argued to have an urban character, as they are all situated close to urban centres. The Ouwehand family (2011) illustrates this as follows: 'where we lived in Friesland, you could call that rural. But there, on an average day 20,000 vehicles passed by on the main road. Here, on the same kind of road, it is about 1,400 a day.' This reinforces the thesis that for people living in the Netherlands, moving to a 'real' rural area requires emigration (Eimermann et al. 2012). Moreover, the above quote reveals both physical and social characteristics of a perceived rural idyll.

The age of the migrating adults, as well as social and physical consequences of urbanisation in time and space, appears to play a significant role in the decision to migrate. In other words, many migrants grew up in rather small Dutch villages that became urbanised during the migrants' early adolescence. Related to this, nostalgic sentiments and discontent are expressed in the following quotes:

When we were children, H. was a village. We lived among farmers, and I could hear the cows in the barn. Of course, these surroundings have all been urbanised, swallowed by the largest Dutch agglomeration called the Randstad. (Interview Korevaar 2011)

I lived on the edge of the village of V. During my youth,
V.-West was developed. For us, that was heaven on earth
as we could play and build our own hide-outs there. It was
fantastic, but after a while a new neighbourhood was built,
and another one, and another one. Soon, the population
of Veenendaal had increased from 25,000 to 65,000. The
municipality grew fast, resulting in crime, among other
things. And traffic congestion. We lived 10 km from our
workplace; it took 1½ hours to commute. Everyday!
(Interview Mansveld 2011)

The nostalgic sentiments above relate to growing up in a perceived
rural idyll that no longer exists. The discontent that is expressed
is due to social and physical disadvantages of urbanisation and
densely populated areas, such as criminality and traffic congestion.

The nature of the places of origin and destination

In relation to the second social-scientific perspective on migration, the nature of the place of destination is compared with the
nature of the place of origin within social and physical contexts.
These contexts (*e.g.* property, nature, landscape, and less populated
surroundings) may develop into keep-factors after the migration.
On the other hand, friends, relatives, and cultural aspects in the
Netherlands are pull-factors for a possible return. This may partly
explain the ambivalent attitude towards returning. To begin with,
property prices differ greatly between the urban areas of the
Netherlands and the sparsely populated Swedish rural areas. The
Landers family live in a former church (Figure 1). Their sense of
triumph is expressed thus:

One reason for moving to Hällefors was that we can own
something here that you could never own in the Netherlands
– a larger house. One of our sons has always wanted to live in
'a house you can walk around' [*i.e.* a detached home, instead
of a row house or semi-detached home]. Even when we didn't
have any plans to migrate at all... And when we had decided
to migrate, we told the children that we would be living in a

Table 3: Place of residence prior to moving and occupations of the migrants

Household	Place of residence[a]	Pre-migration occupation	Post-migration occupation
V. Leeuwen	Strongly urbanised	♂ Producer * ♀ Artist	♂ Producer * ♀ Project leader *
Storm	Hardly urbanised	♂ Road construction ♀ Designer	♂ Road constr., self-employed ♀ Owner of shop
Monnee	Moderately urbanised	♂ Entrepreneur (safety)* ♀ Entrepreneur (safety)*	♂ Entrepreneur (safety)* ♀ Entrepreneur (safety)*
De Geer	Extremely urbanised	♂ Freelance illustrator ♀ Teacher (prim. school)	♂ Freelance illustrator ♀ Teacher, self-employed seller
De Caluwé	A rural area outside the Netherlands	♂ Employed at holiday resort ♀ Employed at holiday resort	♂ Manager of a hostel * ♀ Manager of a hostel *
Swanenburg	Hardly urbanised	♂ Truck driver ♀ Owner of restaurant	♂ Truck driver ♀ Nurse
Landers	Strongly urbanised	♂ Manager * ♀ Manager (day-care centre)	♂ Carpenter ♀ Nurse, owner of shop *
Louwerens	Not urbanised	♂ Civil servant ♀ Teacher (sec. school)	♂ Self-employed, forestry ♀ Manager, food company*
Lochtenberg	Not urbanised	♂ Industrial designer ♀ Employed at florist shop	♂ Entrepreneur * ♀ Employed at employment agency
Mansveld	Strongly urbanised	♂ Teacher (sec. school) ♀ Employed as electrician	♂ Teacher (sec. school) ♀ Nurse
Korevaar	Strongly urbanised	♂ Editor, Motion designer * ♀ Director at a post-production company *	♂ Editor, Motion designer * ♀ Director at a post-production company *
Ouwehand	Not urbanised	♂ Emp. (insurance company) ♀ Employed at cleaning firm	♂ Employed at a factory ♀ Unemployed

*Source: Eimermann, fieldwork 2011, * = running an own enterprise*
[a] degrees of urbanisation are based on Statistics Netherlands 2012.

house that you can walk around. This house feels like a palace! (Interview Landers 2011)

This sense of living in a palace is combined with notions of the good life and the rural idyll, as vividly described during the interviews. Some of the following quotes illustrate how impressed the migrants in this study are by social and physical aspects of the Swedish landscape and nature:

We used to go on holiday to France, and then some friends recommended that we visit Sweden; so we decided to give it

a try. And when we got here, we thought 'wow, this is actually what we have been looking for in France' – the same
abundance of wilderness, but with the right of public access.
In France, everything is gated. And here, you have access and
can enjoy the forests and the lakes. We were sold instantly! So
tranquil and beautiful. (Interview Landers 2011)

The first years we took our holidays in Sweden, we were
particularly impressed by the tranquillity of the Swedish outdoors. Where we lived in the Netherlands, there were forests
as well. But when you go picking berries there on a Sunday
afternoon, there are 200 people on a single square kilome-
tre. Here, you don't run into anyone, and that is so brilliant!
(Interview Mansveld 2011)

We've visited Norway, but I wouldn't want to live there. The
landscape is too rugged, and people live packed together in the
valleys. The Swedish landscape has more gentle slopes. And
lakes. Everywhere, there is wilderness. You can encounter rare
birds and wolves in the woods. (Interview Louwerens 2011)

The above quotes illustrate both social and physical perceptions of
the rural idyll in and around Hällefors. These perceptions function
as pull-factors for the move and as keep-factors after the move.
However, the migrants in this study also reflect on a number of
pull-factors for a possible return. In the words of Mr Van Leeuwen
(2011): 'We all miss Dutch-style out-door terraces at pubs, happy
faces, and people greeting each other merrily.'

Underlying forces and structures that condition movement

In relation to the third social-scientific perspective, the migrants'
narratives are used to study forces and structures that condition
movement. In addition to sentiments and memories of their own
childhood, the adult migrants see the discourse of the 'rural childhood idyll' as promising safety, health, and closeness to nature for
their children (Baylina & Berg 2010, p. 287). During the interviews, this discourse was both affirmed and denied. The Louwerens

Figure 1. Residence of the Landers family. Photo: Marco Eimermann.

family consider activities for children such as music classes, various kinds of clubs, and theatre to be 'affordable and accessible, certainly compared to the Netherlands' (Interview Louwerens 2011).

On the other hand, because of a perceived lack of education opportunities for children aged sixteen years and over (who study at the Swedish *Gymnasium*) and the fact that public transport is not optimal in this part of the Swedish countryside, children are forced to move to larger towns such as Örebro and find an apartment there at a relatively young age. This is contrasted to the situation in the Netherlands, and it plays a significant role in the migrants' attitude towards moving. The Van Leeuwen family explains:

We've had our moments of hesitation, but our original plan for moving here was that we would evaluate the situation after three years. Now that we've lived here for three years, we've decided to move to southern Sweden. In the village we're moving to, there are good educational facilities up to and including *Gymnasium*. And afterwards, there are good possibilities for studying not far away from where we will be living. We moved to Sweden partly to be able to spend more time with our family, not to see the children moving far away at the age of sixteen-seventeen. (Interview Van Leeuwen 2011)

Mrs Landers (2011) talks about the decision process and the attitude towards returning:

> We moved to Hällefors four years ago, but we only actually decided to stay two weeks ago. How can I explain this decision to you? Initially, we lived in another house and we bought this property (Figure 1) to open a shop. The property is inhabited by two more tenants and the rent they pay to us seemed to cover our costs. That way, I could run this shop without the pressure of making a profit. Just run a shop because I like it.
> It went quite well until winter came. Heating expenses were too high and owning both a house and this property became too costly. We decided to sell the house and move to this property. But as we were in the process of packing, a couple from Stockholm showed an interest in the shop. We told ourselves 'now that we're packing anyway, we might as well return to the Netherlands.'
> These questions come up regularly anyway: do we like it enough here? Don't we miss our relatives too much? Coming over to drink a cup of coffee together. A chat with other parents at the schoolyard. Social contacts are much easier to establish in the Netherlands, and we keep missing that.
> We could live in my parents' house in the Netherlands and we started looking for jobs there. But due to the financial crisis, it proved very hard to find a job or even return to the jobs we had before we moved. Then we decided not to take the risk of giving up everything we have here in Hällefors – which we can only dream of in the Netherlands – for so much uncertainty. So two weeks ago we really decided to stay and live here. (Interview Landers 2011)

Ambivalent attitudes towards returning are illustrated in the above quote. The quote exemplifies complex and shifting post-migration identities that are related to the nature of the places of origin and destination, social contacts, and returning. Family relationships are also considered, both in the above quote (about Mrs Landers' parents) and in the previous one (about the children in the Van Leeuwen family). The ambivalence may perhaps best be described as a sense of being in-between, as when Mrs Landers analyses her scream, quoted in the title of this section:

> Well, I did not really scream; I dreamed that I was screaming. I was in a concrete box, floating on water, surrounded by hundreds of thousands of similar concrete boxes. There was almost no space between the boxes. This is how my mind pictured the Netherlands in my dream. I felt confined. I wanted to go back, back to Sweden! (Interview Landers 2011)

A Dutch creative class in Hällefors?

The policy profiles formulated by Hällefors's executive board (culinary arts, technology, and design) may have been responsible for attracting a relatively large proportion of migrants employed in these sectors. Applying the concept of the creative class to the Dutch migrants in Hällefors, the pre- and post-migration occupations of the migrating households (Table 3) can be studied here. The households can be divided into two groups: those who maintained their pre-migration occupation after migration, and those who changed occupation. Maintained occupations are often in the creative industries (Jakobsson 2009), such as a freelance illustrator, a producer, an editor, a motion designer, and entrepreneurs in media or a CE marking company. These members of the creative class (Florida 2002) are often engaged in projects in both the Netherlands and Sweden, and often travel between them.

On the other hand, those who changed occupation often changed from a white collar office job (civil servant) or a job in the public sector (teachers) to being an entrepreneur or self-employed in outdoor occupations such as forestry or an organic food enterprise. Still others combine different employment statuses, for instance working part-time as a teacher and starting up an enterprise in toys or a website selling motorcycle parts, thus attempting to make a living from their hobbies. These changes of occupation may be related to lifestyle migration motives (Benson & O'Reilly 2009, pp. 2–3).

However, this can be an exhausting activity, as the De Geer family illustrate in retrospect:

> We have three young children, the youngest of whom was born here in Sweden. I combine working as a part-time sub-stitute teacher with selling toys on a self-employed basis. At times it felt like every time I got going with selling toys, the telephone would ring and I had to work as a teacher. At the same time, we were working with one or two websites for our activities with illustrating and running a B&B. I also wanted to spend some time at home with the children, so in the end it simply became too much and I forced myself to take a time-out from the jobs. (Interview De Geer 2011)

It is apparent that the migrants' actual experiences do not always meet their expectations. Especially in an economically stagnating small industrial municipality, one needs to keep many balls in the air to earn an adequate income. Moreover, finding time for family life may be a challenge. In particular, when people are entrepre-neurs or self-employed, social and economic interests may overlap. In this context, those migrants who are not active in the creative industries (exemplified by the Landers family, who stayed) made more creative efforts in Hällefors than the members of the creative class (exemplified by the Van Leeuwen family, who left).

Concluding discussion

The aim of this chapter has been to examine the migration process of Dutch lifestyle migrants in Hällefors and their ambivalent atti-tudes towards returning to the Netherlands, and thereby, to give voice to the hope, pain, nostalgia, and triumph of lives lived in other places (King *et al.* 1995). The empirical question of this chap-ter is as follows: 'After migrating to Hällefors, what influences the Dutch households' attitude towards returning?' In order to address this question, a conceptual framework was briefly introduced con-sisting of seven interrelated concepts: lifestyle migration, the good life, the rural idyll, the urban-rural continuum, the creative class, ambivalence, and identity shift.

The chapter has examined the migrants' ambivalence regarding returning and shifting identities (White 1995) in relation to the migrants' characteristics, the nature of the places of origin and destination, and the forces and structures that condition moving to a new country. The sentiment of longing back to things in the country of origin, expressed by Landers (Interview 2011) and Van Leeuwen (Interview 2011) above, are perhaps the clearest indications of such identity shifts.

As far as the characteristics of the migrants are concerned, this study suggests that the degree of preparation before the move may also be decisive for the households in this study, as long-term planners show less ambivalence than spontaneous movers. Moreover, the migrants' attitude towards returning is related to age structure and household composition. As illustrated in Table 2, the adults of the van Leeuwen family were born about ten years earlier than the adults in the Landers family. As the Landers family has four children, this may imply that the family is more rooted in Hällefors. Compared to the Landers family, the children in the van Leeuwen family are closer to *Gymnasium* age, which may have contributed to their decision to move to a place with more possibilities.

The nature of the places of origin and destination is essential to take into account when studying the forces and structures that condition moving. The rural childhood idyll is important in two ways. It plays a role in the adult migrants' nostalgic sentiments and sense of discontent related to rapid urbanisation of the rural areas of their childhood. Related to this, it creates the adults' aspirations to find an idyll for their own children to grow up in.

Social and physical aspects of nature, space, and less populated surroundings (*i.e.* the good life) initially stimulate the Dutch migrants to move from their urbanised areas of origin to Hällefors. After the move, the migrants' experiences of this perceived good life are contradictory. Ultimately, some migrants may long back to the conditions they were eager to leave behind in the Netherlands. As lifestyle migration is voluntary, the migrants' attitude towards returning is paradoxically more ambivalent than they expected.

Florida's (2002) thesis concerning the creative class may have stimulated Hällefors and other rural municipalities in the developed world to engage in place-marketing efforts. The purpose of these efforts is to attract inhabitants, enterprises, and investments to the municipality (Eimermann 2013). Hällefors thus competes for the creative class with other stakeholders across the developed world.

However, as illustrated in the previous section, members of the creative class may not be as creative as expected. Their economic activities may not benefit the local economy as hoped for by the municipalities. Moreover, as members of the creative class in this study are engaged in projects in the Netherlands, Sweden, and elsewhere, they have fewer constraints hindering them from moving away from Hällefors. Hence, both the concept of the creative class and rural place-marketing campaigns to attract migrants with low 'transaction costs' for employers (Lang 1986, Rooth & Saarela 2007) may require further elucidation in future research.

ACKNOWLEDGEMENTS – The fieldwork for this study was funded by the Swedish Society for Anthropology and Geography (SSAG; *Svenska Sällskapet för Antropologi och Geografi*). I am grateful for the hospitality and enthusiasm of the migrants who participated in this study. Many thanks go to commentators on previous drafts.

References

Amit, Vered (2007), 'Structures and Dispositions of Travel and Movement'. pp. 1–14 in: Amit, Vered (ed.), *Going First Class? New Approaches to Privileged Travel and Movement*. Oxford: Berghahn Books.

Andersen, Ulrika & Hans-Peter Engström (2005), *Ett holländskt fenomen i Värmland, faktorer bakom och effekter av en holländsk inflyttning*. [A Dutch phenomenon in Värmland: Factors underlying and effects of Dutch immigration.] Karlstad: Karlstad University.

Bærenholdt, Jörgen & Brynhild Granås (2008), Places and Mobilities Beyond the Periphery. pp.1–10 in: Bærenholdt, Jörgen & Brynhild Granås (eds), *Mobility and Place: Enacting Northern European Mobilities*. Aldershot: Ashgate.

Bauman, Zygmunt (2000), *Liquid Modernity*, Cambridge: Polity Press.

— (2008), *The Art of Life*. Cambridge: Polity Press.

Baylina, Mireia & Nina Gunnerud Berg (2010), 'Selling the countryside: Representations of rurality in Norway and Spain'. pp. 277–292 in *European Urban and Regional Studies* 17(3).

Benson, Michaela & Karen O'Reilly (eds) (2009), *Lifestyle Migration – Expectations, aspirations and experiences*. Farnham, Surrey: Ashgate Publishing Ltd.

Blotevogel, Hans & Anthony Fielding (eds) (1997), *People, jobs and mobility in the new Europe*. Chichester: John Wiley and sons.

Borgegård, Lars-Erik, Johan Håkansson & Dieter Müller (1998), *Concentration and Dispersion of Immigrants in Sweden, 1973–1992*. pp. 28–39 in: *The Canadian Geographer* 42(1).

Boyle, Paul J. & Keith Halfacree (1998), *Migration into rural areas*. Chichester: John Wiley and sons.

Boyle, Paul, Keith Halfacree & Vaughan Robinson, (1998), *Exploring contemporary migration*. Singapore: Longman Singapore Publishers Ltd.

Braunerhielm, Lotta (2006), *Plats för kulturarv och turism: Grythyttan – en fallstudie av upplevelser, värderingar och intressen*. [A place for cultural heritage and tourism: Grythyttan – a case study of experiences, values and interests.] Karlstad: Karlstad University.

Castles, Stephen (2000), 'International migration at the beginning of the 21st century; global trends and issues'. pp. 269–81 *International Social Science Journal*, 52 (165).

Castles, Stephen & Mark Miller (1998), *The age of migration – International Population Movements in the Modern World*. (2nd edition). London: Macmillan Press limited.

Champion, Tony & Graeme Hugo (2004) 'Introduction: Moving beyond the urban-rural dichotomy', in: Champion, Tony & Graeme Hugo (eds), *New Forms of Urbanization. Beyond the Urban-Rural Dichotomy*. Aldershot: Ashgate. pp. 3–24.

Chirban, John T. (1996), *Interviewing in depth – The*

interactive-relational approach.
London: Sage Publications.
Dalen, Hendrik van & Kène
Henkens, (2007), 'Longing for
the good life, understanding
emigration from a high-income
country'. pp. 37–66 *Population
and Development Review*, 33 (1).
Eimermann, Marco (2013),
'Promoting Swedish countryside
in the Netherlands: international rural place marketing to
attract new residents'. *European
Urban and Regional Studies,* DOI:
10.1177/0969776413481370.
Eimermann, Marco, Mats
Lundmark & Dieter K.
Müller (2012), 'Exploring
Dutch migration to rural
Sweden – International
Counterurbanisation in the EU'.
pp. 330–346 *Tijdschrift voor economische en sociale geografie*, 103 (3).
Eriksson Robertson, Ing-Gerd
(2010), *Livsstilsmigration till
landsbygden och transnationella
företagare – Nederländsk bosättning
och turistföretagande i mellersta
Klarälvdalen under 2000-talet.*
[Lifestyle migration to rural
areas and transnational entrepreneurs – Dutch settlements
and tourist business in the
central Klarälven Valley in the
2000s.] Stockholm: Stockholm
University.
Florida, Richard, (2002), *The rise of
the creative class.* New York: The
Perseus book group.
— (2006), *The flight of the creative
class.* New York: HarperCollins.
Giddens, Anthony (1991) *Modernity
and Self-Identity: Self and Society in
the Late Modern Age.* Cambridge:
Polity Press.

Halfacree, Keith & Paul J. Boyle
(1993), 'The challenge facing
migration research: The case
for a biographical approach'.
pp. 333–48 *Progress in Human
Geography*, 17 (3).
Hansen, Peo (2008), *EU:s
migrationspolitik under 50 år.
Ett integrerat perspektiv på en
motsägelsefull utveckling.* Malmö:
Studentlitteratur. [In Swedish]
Hedberg, Charlotta & Renato
Miguel Do Carmo (2011),
*Translocal ruralism – mobility and
connectivity in European rural
spaces.* Dordrecht: Springer.
Hedfeldt, Mona (2008), *Företagande
kvinnor i bruksort: arbetsliv
och vardagsliv i samspel.* [Self-
employed women in small
industrial towns: the interaction
between work life and everyday
life.] Örebro: Örebro University.
Jakobsson, Max (2009), *Från industrier till upplevelser – En studie av
symbolisk och materiell omvandling
i Bergslagen.* [From industries to
experiences – a study of symbolic
and material restructuring in the
Bergslagen area.] Örebro: Örebro
University.
Janelle, Donald (1991), 'Global
interdependence and its consequences'. pp. 49–81 in: Brunn,
Stanley & Thomas Leinbach,
(eds), *Collapsing space and time:
geographic aspects of communication and information.* London:
HarperCollins.
King, Russel (2002), 'Towards a new
map of European Migration'. pp.
89–106 *International Journal of
Population Geography* 8 (2).

King, Russell, John Connell & Paul White (eds) (1995), *Writing across worlds – Literature and migration*. London: Routledge.

Kūle, Laila (2008), 'Concepts of rurality and urbanity as analytical categories in multidimensional research'. pp. 9–17 *Proceedings of the Latvian academy of sciences*, Section B 62.

Lang, Kevin (1986), 'A language theory of discrimination'. pp. 363–382 *The Quarterly Journal of Economics*, 101 (2).

Molina, Irene (2008), 'Segregation – eller den svenska bostadsförsörjningens paradoxer'. pp. 151–169 in: af Geijerstam, Jan (ed.), *Industriland: tolv forskare om när Sverige blev modernt*. Stockholm: Premiss.

Müller, Dieter K. (1999), *German second home owners in the Swedish countryside*. Umeå: Umeå University.

Nuur, Cali & Staffan Laestadius (2009), 'Is the 'creative class' necessarily urban? Putting the creativity thesis in the context of non-urbanised regions in industrialised nations', *Debate June 2009*, *European Journal of Spatial Development*.

Rooth, Dan-Olof & Jan Saarela (2007), 'Selection in migration and return migration: Evidence from micro data'. pp. 90–95 *Economic Letters* 94.

Sassen, Saskia (2008), *Territory, authority, rights – From medieval to global assemblages* (4th edition). Princeton and Oxford: Princeton University Press.

Sheller, Mimi and John Urry (2006), 'The new mobilities paradigm'. pp. 207–226 *Environment and Planning A* 38 (2).

Statistics Netherlands (2011), *Statline*. Available at www.cbs.nl (latest access 25-07-2011).

Statistics Netherlands (2012), *Degree of urbanisation*. Available at www.cbs.nl/en-GB/menu/methoden/toelichtingen/alfabet/d/degree-of-urbanisation.htm (latest access 05-11-2012).

Statistics Sweden (2011). Available at www.scb.se (latest access 17-11-2011).

Swedish National Rural Development Agency (2008), *Sweden's sparsely populated areas and countryside 2008* [Glesbygdsverket (2008), Sveriges Gles- och landsbygder 2008.] Östersund: Glesbygdsverket.

Vaiou, Dina (2010), Gender, migration and socio-spatial transformations in Southern European cities. pp. 470–482 in: Pike, Andy, Andres Rodríguez-Pose & John Tomaney (eds), *Handbook of Local and Regional Development*, London: Routledge.

White, Paul (1995), Geography, literature and migration. pp. 1–19 in: King, Russell, John Connell & Paul White (eds), *Writing across worlds – literature and migration*. London: Routledge.

Woods, Michael (2009), *Rural Geography*. London: Sage.

Åkesson, Åke (1998), *Invandrare i Bergslagen, Tyskar, Finner, Valloner*. Fellingsbro: Affärstryckeriet AB.

Interviews: (pseudonyms)

Björklund, development officer in
   Hällefors, October 2008.
De Geer, Dutch migrants in
   Hällefors, March 2011.
Korevaar, Dutch migrants in
   Hällefors, March 2011.
Landers, Dutch migrants in
   Hällefors, March 2011.
Van Leeuwen, Dutch migrants in
   Hällefors, April 2011.

Louwerens, Dutch migrants in
   Hällefors, April 2011.
Mansveld, Dutch migrants in
   Hällefors, April 2011.
Ouwehand, Dutch migrants in
   Hällefors, June 2011.
Vreeswijk, director of Placement,
   September 2008.

Appendix – interview guide

Aspirations and expectations prior to moving

General socio-demographic characteristics of the household members
☐ Year of birth
☐ Education prior to moving
☐ Swedish language course in the Netherlands
☐ Occupation prior to moving
☐ Previous places of residence (place of birth, last place before moving to Sweden and other significant places, possibly lived in a third country)

Visits to Sweden prior to the move
☐ First time in Sweden (month and year)
☐ Subsequent visits
☐ Frequency of the visits
☐ Duration of the visits
☐ Purpose of the visits
☐ Mode of transport to and from Sweden
☐ Possible role of visiting other countries (experiences in third countries compared to Sweden)

The initial 'spark'
☐ When and why did you first consider a possible move to Sweden (during a particular event)?
☐ Why did you decide for this Northern direction (opposed to Southern destinations)
☐ Why this region in Sweden?

- Why this (part of the) municipality?
- Why this property?
- What information has played a role in your decision?
- Where have you obtained this information?
- Did you know of any fellow-countrymen living in the municipality before your move?
- What aspirations and expectations did you have prior to moving considering living and working in (this part) of Sweden?
- What kind of preparations have you made prior to moving? (*e.g.* attending Swedish language courses in the Netherlands)

Experiences after moving

General socio-demographic characteristics of the household members

- Current and previous places of residence in Sweden (property and address)
- Current and previous occupations in Sweden
- Education / (language)courses in Sweden

Specific experiences after moving

- Experiences considering the current occupation compared to the aspirations and expectations prior to moving
- Experiences considering living in the current property
- Experiences considering the current everyday life in this municipality in general
- The degree of progress considering the process of social integration in this community
- The role of the Swedish language in this process of social integration in the local community
- An estimation of the number of Dutch households living in this municipality
- Particular contacts with (some of) these households, reasons for this
- Differences between contacts with Dutch, Swedes or others

Mobility

- Frequency of journeys to the Netherlands
- Duration of journeys to the Netherlands
- Purpose of journeys to the Netherlands

- ☐ Mode of transport used for journeys to the Netherlands
- ☐ Members of the household that undertake journeys to the Netherlands

- ☐ Frequency of friends or relatives visiting in Sweden
- ☐ Duration of friends or relatives visiting in Sweden
- ☐ Purpose of friends or relatives visiting in Sweden
- ☐ Mode of transport used by friends or relatives visiting in Sweden

- ☐ The purpose of keeping contact with friends and relatives elsewhere (predominantly but not exclusively in the Netherlands)
- ☐ The frequency of use of different devices (internet, mobile phone, satellite TV) in keeping contact with friends and relatives elsewhere (predominantly but not exclusively in the Netherlands)
- ☐ The effects of using different devices (internet, mobile phone, satellite TV) in keeping contact with friends and relatives elsewhere (predominantly but not exclusively in the Netherlands) on social integration in the local community

Attitudes towards the future
- ☐ The short term future (coming three years) and long term future (more than three years) considering place of residence
- ☐ The short term future (coming three years) and long term future (more than three years) considering occupation
- ☐ The short term future (coming three years) and long term future (more than three years) considering social integration and everyday life
- ☐ The short term future (coming three years) and long term future (more than three years) considering mobility

Multiplying the Unique

The Place Identity of a Rural Swedish Landscape

Charlotte Fridolfsson

This is how the story goes

In 700 BC, people began heating the red soil to prepare iron for the first time in the known history of the territory presently known as Sweden. This happened in a mineral-rich area today called Bergslagen.[1] This region defies precise geographic definition, but is located in a mountainous region in central Sweden (see Figure 1). Renowned since the middle-ages for its mining and metallurgical production, Bergslagen is sometimes referred to as 'the cradle of Swedish industry' (Central Sweden 2011), and can as such alledgedly be credited for the modern wealth of the country.

Bergslagen was a victim of the global steel crises in the 1970s and onwards, with depopulation following the closing of steel-related industries and widespread unemployment lingering among those who stayed (Berger 2009; Jakobsson 2009; Lundmark 1988). In the mid 1980s, abandoned industrial sites like the copper works at Riddarhyttan or the blast furnace of Lienshyttan, and mining remnants like the Red Soil forest [Röda Jorden] were converted into tourist attractions that together formed Ecomuseum Bergslagen, an outdoor museum with a focus on the history and culture of iron manufacturing (Skinnskatteberg municipality 2011).[2] The extra-

---

1   Bergslagen literally means 'Mountain Law'. The metallurgic production in the area was highly regulated from the 1300's and onward.

2   This open-air museum was founded in 1986 as a joint venture by two council museums and seven local authorities. It includes 60 local heritage sites run by volunteers form local-heritage associations. Twelve of these are situated in Skinnskatteberg municipality (Ecomuseum Bergslagen 2011).

Figure 1. Map of
Bergslagen. Source:
Intresseföreningen
Bergslaget.

linguistic moment of establishing Ecomuseum Bergslagen, was an
institutional articulation reproducing/constituting Bergslagen as a
mining and metallurgical cultural-heritage site.

Social anthropologist Karin Norman (1993) has interpreted
Ecomuseum Bergslagen's focus on varying techniques of iron
production and the skilled work associated with it, as a projection
of modern values and interests onto the past. In these times of
economic uncertainty, she reasons, concerns about controlling the
future are a central motivation for the museum to turn to history
in search of continuity.

Kolarbyn – From a cultural-heritage site and labour-market measure to a globetrotters' eco-lodging

Around the lake of Skärsjön, just outside Skinnskatteberg municipality in Bergslagen, people have manufactured charcoal from
wood in charcoal stacks for more than a thousand years, as evi-
denced by the many charcoal pile bottoms left in the ground of this
area. Commercial charcoal production ceased in Sweden after the
Second World War, but enthusiasts have preserved the knowledge
and skills associated with the practice.

As a labour-market measure in the mid-1990s, twelve forest huts, modelled after the charcoal workers' lodges, were constructed by the lake Skärsjön, at a site containing the remains of a charcoal stack bottom (see Figure 2). The Swedish university of Agricultural Sciences had continued using this very spot for burning charcoal piles up until the 1960s. Skinnskatteberg municipality initiated the project and the National Labour Market Board funded the construction. The initiative came from charcoal-burner enthusiasts, who would be able to stay overnight in the huts while building and burning the charcoal piles. In this way the cultural heritage of old-fashioned iron making and charcoal burning could live on and be passed on to future generations. The site received the name Kolarbyn, which literally means 'charcoal-burner village'. Apart from its historical links, this particular piece of land was chosen for its picturesque setting and easily accessible location (Carlsson 2011).

Figure 2. Charcoal burner's hut in Kolarbyn, Bergslagen. Photo: Mona Hedfeldt.

At first, Skinnskatteberg municipality rented out the huts to tourists. The overnight guests were often older people from the area who themselves had experienced charcoal burning long ago.

After a few years the municipality looked for a commercial actor who could operate Kolarbyn more efficiently (Carlsson 2011). An entrepreneur who had already started commercial moose safaris in Bergslagen a couple of years earlier took over the huts in 2004 and opened a hostel with an eco-friendly profile at the premises in cooperation with STF.[3] The overnight visitors at Kolarbyn have thus changed over the years and the operation now reaches broader masses. Kolarbyn has until now had guests from 73 countries around the globe (Ahlsén 2011, Carlsson 2011, Eldh 2011). The operation has become an incredible asset to the region according to the civil servants at Skinnskatteberg municipality. 'It's the best thing we have, it's crazy!' says the tourism coordinator, celebrating the global success of Kolarbyn.

Around half of the tourists come from other countries, mostly in Europe, and the other half from Sweden. There are no 'typical visitors' to Kolarbyn, according to the owner; they can be 'Stockholmbrats' or wildlife enthusiasts. However, middle-aged couples are overrepresented (Ahlsén 2011). Many of the tourists at Kolarbyn come from larger cities. 'Differences between a person from a Swedish city and some other European city are marginal. People come here to experience something different.' (Eldh 2011), says the former proprietor of Kolarbyn.[4] Country of origin is deemed less significant here than the common denominator of living a city life and frequenting eco-lodgings.

Global influences come not only from the well-travelled foreign guests. The first commercial owner of Kolarbyn utilises his own travel experiences when developing ecotourism in a Swedish context. The following story summarises how his business in Bergslagen was set in motion:

3   STF is the abbreviation of *Svenska turistföreningen* [Swedish Tourist Association]. STF is one of the largest popular movements in Sweden with around 300,000 members. Besides helping tourists with their journeys across Sweden, they also advise the Swedish government on issues pertaining to infrastructure, environmental protection, and other matters regarding tourism (http://www.svenskaturistforeningen.se/en/).
4   A new manager took over in 2010. The first private proprietor of Kolarbyn has a close collaboration with the current owner, and Kolarbyn's guests often go on the tours that are offered by his business WildSweden. Joint package tours are also offered (Eldh 2011, Ahlsén 2011).

It all began when I was travelling in Indonesia back in 2002.
I had an interest in nature and I joined several Orangutan
jungle trekking tours during my travels in Sumatera. The
Sumateran [sic!] jungles were impressive but what inspired me
the most were the hard working tour guides. They all seemed
to enjoy their profession as they hosted guests from all over
the World who came to see orangutans and other wildlife. I
told to myself: "This could be done in the Swedish forests...
Why not offer wildlife watching tours in Sweden!"

Once I returned back in Sweden, I went straight to the local
tourist information center in the town of Västerås. While I
was there I overheard an Austrian couple who asked where
they can see wild Moose and was surprised to hear that they
were recommended to go to "Skansen" – the Stockholm Zoo!
The forest is full of Moose, why send them to the zoo? That's
when I decided to begin to offer Moose watching tours in the
nearby forest. (Eldh 2009a)

Here it is apparent that Bergslagen's abundance of wildlife does
not in itself generate ecotourism. In this case, the professional and
inspiring behaviour of guides halfway around the world made a
lasting impression on the Swedish entrepreneur and motivated his
undertaking. Sumatran orangutan trekking tours are thus being
disseminated and iterated in a global ecotourism discourse as
Swedish moose-safari tours.

Kolarbyn could here be read as an empty signifier, to use
Ernesto Laclau and Chantal Mouffe's anti-foundational discourse
theory (Laclau & Mouffe 1985). This means that the landscape of
Kolarbyn, like that of any other place, is considered discursive. As
such it possesses no inherent or final meaning and is intrinsically
subject to possible renegotiation.

Hence, we have so far seen that the meaning of Kolarbyn has
shifted away from being articulated as a cultural heritage conservation site related to the mining industry. A global discourse on
ecotourism now organises the meaning of the landscape instead.
In the following, I will show how new articulations constitute
Kolarbyn ideologically, but also how selected articulations from the

contested hegemony[5] have been negotiated and now sutures the new ideological organisation of Kolarbyn. Still other subjectivities, historical positions and conditions are silenced through the logic of difference or are impossible to articulate through contemporary hegemonic discourse. Some identities and relationships between people thus remain foreclosed possibilities in the present.

A Unique Place

The coining of the term 'ecotourism' can be traced to the Mexican architect and environmentalist Héctor Ceballos-Lascuráin, who at the time (1983) was also Director General of Standards and Technology of the Mexican Ministry of Urban Development and Ecology.[6] A wide range of meanings and uses are now ascribed to the term, and it is also sometimes confused with broader concepts such as sustainable tourism (Mader, 2000). A revised version of Héctor Ceballos-Lascuráin's original definition was, however, officially adopted by the International Union for Conservation of Nature, IUCN, at its 1st World Conservation Congress:

> Ecotourism is environmentally responsible travel and visita-
> tion to relatively undisturbed natural areas, in order to enjoy
> and appreciate nature (and any accompanying cultural features
> – both past and present) that promotes conservation, has low
> negative visitor impact, and provides for beneficially active
> socio-economic involvement of local populations. (Ceballos-
> Lascuráin, 1996)

The identity of Kolarbyn is no longer just about the history of the charcoal stacks; it also borrows elements from other stagings of unique places. The global ecotourism discourse organising

5   The contestation of the mining heritage hegemony has not been loud or open, but is nevertheless ideological and political in the sense that power relations change, both directly and indirectly, as new meanings emerge.
6   By using the word 'ecotourism' he could describe how tourists would become essential in boosting local rural economy, creating job opportunities, and preserving the natural habitats of the American Flamingo of the wetlands in northern Yucatan, Mexico (Mader, 2000).

Kolarbyn is recognised by the visitors, as can be illustrated with the following quote reinforcing the discourse:

> It was a familiar ambiance. I had a feeling that I had experienced something similar before ... somewhere in the world. [...] This could have been at many places, in many countries and with many different themes. Almost all countries that have wildlife, and wilderness possible to stay in, could create something similar. It would be possible to make a local variation of this, using the local histories and local traditions. [...] But it requires a certain kind of personality to pull this off, because the experience was so dependent on the owner's personality. So if they don't have that, it would be difficult. (Visitor 3)

The local natural assets and customs are mentioned here, both of which are important ingredients in any definition of ecotourism. Furthermore, the unique personality, skills, knowledge, and enthusiasm of the owner or wildlife adventure guide were mentioned by all visitors interviewed, without any direct questions being asked on the topic. The unique human response or introduction to the place therefore seems to be as significant as the historical account or the natural setting itself.

The current proprietor of Kolarbyn is often asked by journalists 'what makes this place unique?' to which he says there are several answers:

> There is a history behind it, which makes it exciting. There are the charcoal burners' huts, and every summer we build a charcoal pile. Charcoal burning has been done here for 400 years. That in itself makes it mysterious in a way. There is a lovely feeling, and a lovely mystique to everything out here. And it is calm, and one is able to go out in the woods. I think it is a mixture of a little bit of history, the thrill, the woods ... I think there is something of an enchanted feeling [trollkänsla] about this place. Something like that is what makes it unique. (Ahlsén 2011)

Soon another important ingredient for the construction of the unique place is touched upon. The mystique associated with the place is here placed alongside the natural and historical conditions, as factors contributing to making the place unique. When asked what constitutes the most important thing about Kolarbyn, the current owner responds:

> The wilderness is the most important thing here. We have it all here in the woods. It is the best thing we have. So being able to use this, and at the same time preserve it, is essential for this to work. [...] Working locally is also important. We aspire to buy local produce or local services whenever possible, to develop the community. If the local community is strong, that benefits me, and vice versa. (Ahlsén 2011)

Again the values embedded in the global ecotourism discourse are articulated, namely supporting the local community and caring for nature. There furthermore exists an entire infrastructure of institutions that are devoted to the cause of ecotourism and that issue certifications and awards. Kolarbyn has won several prestigious national and international awards since its start in 2004. Among other prizes, Kolarbyn has been nominated for a Grand Travel Award and a World Travel Award in the category 'leading European green hotel'.

Kolarbyn is also featured in a number of renowned international tourism guides and in coffee-table books about 'unusual hotels'. The former owner stresses Kolarbyn's authentic relationship to the past, which makes it stand out from similar objects in other parts of Sweden:

> There is the ice-hotel and another tree-hotel up north. But many of these other places have been built in order to be different, so it is a bit artificial. Kolarbyn feels more genuine. The huts were here, of course, before there was any touristic activity in them. (Eldh 2011)

When asked how significant the charcoal burning was for Kolarbyn's particular attraction, as opposed to other scenic places in the area, he brought up yet another motive as to why people visit it:

> I would say that an even greater reason to go there [to Kolarbyn] now is because so many others have been there. People want to see why this place has had visitors from 73 countries. Because I think that has affected this place almost more than the charcoal-burning has. I think people read about Kolarbyn in the newspaper, and about how popular it is, and then they say "let's go up there". Almost everyone who goes to Kolarbyn has travelled much around the world; many Swedes have. They realize that there are great things to discover nearby too. And if they see that people from many other countries go there, they do too. (Eldh 2011)

As a guest, looking for the unique while at the same time gravitating towards places that are already proven to be worth visiting is ironically self-defeating. Stefan Jonsson (1993) calls this phenomenon 'imperialistic nostalgia' – meaning that one mourns the loss of something pristine (nature/culture), while at the same time contributing to its destruction.[7]

The institutions of eco-branding and the publication of guides to interesting and unique places also introduce something of a paradox regarding place and identity, namely that what renders a place unique simultaneously makes it part of something else. In the process of constructing the unique place, elements of other unique places are included, in order that it can be recognised, sanctioned, and used as precisely a unique place. Through the very invoking of singularity, the place becomes multiplied as it becomes identifiable as one among many unique hotels.

Primitive Luxury

Kolarbyn does not put time or money into marketing. Instead, web-sites, newspapers, and magazines find Kolarbyn, and this serves as a much more efficient way of spreading information about what the businesses connected with the site have to offer. Word of mouth has proven to be the best way of marketing their services. People go there because they want to do something out

---

7   As in 'you *simply must* go before it gets ruined!'

of the ordinary, such as getting away from civilisation for a short while.

Kolarbyn proclaims itself 'Sweden's most primitive hotel'. There is no tap water or electricity at the premises. The guests sleep in the forest huts or a log cabin, fetch drinking water in a fresh forest well, cook food over an open fire, wash their dishes under a small waterfall in a nearby creek, and bathe in the lake. There is also a canoe, a rowboat, and a sauna for the guests to use. Moose safaris, wolf howling tours, and other wildlife adventures are available to the visitors.

One of the visitors says he first read about Kolarbyn in the Swedish Tourist Association's magazine, which is distributed to all its members, and that he instantly fell for the place. The historic ties were not important to this guest who calls the past charcoal burning practices 'curiosities' and says that the experience would have been just as good without them.[8] Instead the visitor refers to the wilderness, its exotic disposition, and its location close to the city, as the main attractions:

> It looked exotic yet was still a hostel; I liked that combination. It didn't have water faucets or electricity. It was nice to get away from everything, if only for one night. (Visitor 3)

The appeal of the primitive life in the Swedish woods is also identified by the municipality: 'Not everyone knows how to chop wood. It is quite exotic to some,' says one civil servant (Carlsson 2011). A reviewer going by the name 'Starmist' from Devon, England, gives this venue the highest possible score on Tripadvisor, an online forum for holidays, tourism, and travel. She also writes in her review:

> Obviously it's not to everyone's taste, but if you enjoy being outdoors, experiencing wildlife and getting back to basics, you should definitely consider staying here! (Starmist 2007)

Starmist acknowledges that 'getting back to basics' is not for

---

8 The visitor's indifference to the charcoal burning history was emphasised by his accidently, without correcting himself, saying he spent the night *in* the charcoal stack [kolmilan].

everyone, but at the same time recognises that 'less is more' is an exclusive choice, which nevertheless makes it appealing.

One of the visitors, with extensive wildlife experience and know-how, said the best thing about staying in Kolarbyn was the sense of being able to get by in the woods:

> We fetched our water, and started a fire. This went very well. The facilities were conveniently located. There was a fresh-water well. It was rather unproblematic to manage. (Visitor 2)

Another visitor mentions how time-consuming all the practical tasks were, but nevertheless also appreciated the slow pace at the venue (Visitor 1).

Throughout the research, I encountered no signs of anyone asking for modern facilities at the premises, only the opposite: 'If I were to change anything about this place, I would remove the road. There were not that many cars that drove by, but I would rather be without them' (Visitor 3), one visitor says, wishing the traffic away. It seems as if Kolarbyn's humble past has played well into the ecotourism discourse of what is considered attractive living.

Ideological Interpellation and Performing Ecotourism

Kolarbyn's pronounced historical heritage becomes manifest in, and is embodied by the visitors' chopping firewood, washing dishes in the nearby creek, fetching water from the well, and cooking over an open fire.

There is magic to this place, according to most people I met during this research. This could be expressed through paying respect to nature. The former owner says:

> I want everyone to feel a sense of reverence as they finish a tour with WildSweden. At the end of a tour I often say, "now take a moment to think about the moose that we spotted for a few seconds; think about how they live their entire lives in the woods". They can identify 200 different kinds of plants using

their nose. We think they are stupid, but we could not survive a winter in the woods. I wonder, who is stupid? (Eldh 2011)

Magic is also reproduced in special rituals, with visitors being encouraged not to speak while fetching water in the well (with reference to a supernatural being), and to knock three times on the spring's lid before drinking.

Mythic tales also circulate about previous dwellers at the location. However, the spiritual dimension is also present in stories told by tourists about things they have experienced at the hostel. These could take the form of light phenomena they have observed or other mysterious occurrences.

Upon the arrival of overnight guests, a moose antler is passed around among the visitors who are seated in a ring by a lit campfire. As they are handed the antler, they are each encouraged to share a story about why they have come to Kolarbyn. The narrations have a confessional character and are strikingly similar. They are variations on the theme that one loves nature, spent a great deal of time in the woods during childhood, but now lives a hectic city life and wishes one had more time to spend outdoors. The ecotourism discourse does not merely organise the place's identity, but also the peoples' identity at this place. Through their unique outdoor experience in the woods, the tourists also construct a busy city person on a merely temporary visit to the countryside. Not every visitor comes from a big city, though. The dichotomy between wilderness and civilisation, which is frequently used, functions also among rural residents and marks the difference between everyday life and the adventure in the woods.

Nostalgia Incorporated

'It is not the absence of electricity itself that attracts people; it becomes attractive because this is how people used to live', the former owner says (Eldh 2011). Historic and past times are incorporated into the current uses of the Kolarbyn premises. It is precisely Kolarbyn's historic past that sets the place aside from other unusual hotels, treehouse types of hotels or design hotels set in the woods, the current owner says:

I think the historic link makes it strong and authentic;
one gets to go back and relive the past in a way. It makes
it a strong brand. We try to preserve it, keep it primitive.
Chopping the firewood ... fetching the spring water ... we try
to keep it like this. Doing the dishes in the creek is not that
common. We will always keep it like this. (Ahlsén 2011)

The entrepreneurs running Kolarbyn acknowledge the importance that charcoal-burning used to be performed at the location,
although the mining heritage rather takes the form of a backdrop,
or even commercial branding, in the ecotourism discourse.

Speaking about Kolarbyn's changing clientele over the years, the
municipality's tourism coordinator says:

From the beginning it was mainly older guests who wanted
to spend the night in the huts; there was a little nostalgia
involved; they remember what it was like; they themselves
used to follow along [to work] out in the woods. Now it is
younger people who really do not know what is going on
[regarding the former use of the place], but want to experience
the wildlife. It is the wildlife that appeals to them. The
charcoal-burning history is more of an extra. (Carlsson 2011)

The nostalgia or authenticity described in this quote does not refer
to a collective memory of the mining heritage, but refers directly to
the visiting tourist's personal memories of working in the woods.
Similar incorporations of the private past into the overnight experience at Kolarbyn are also adhered to in the ecotourism discourse,
as one visitor explains how the charcoal burners' huts were remi-
niscent of the shelters the visitor used to build in the woods as a
child (Visitor 3).

Furthermore, the acknowledgement that Kolarbyn's past was
not merely a façade reinforces the importance of the cultural heritage for the meaning of Kolarbyn also in the ecotourism discourse:

I thought it felt genuine. It did not feel contrived: the huts or
fetching water. It felt rather genuine. But what we did there
was not related to the charcoal burning history. We could have
barbequed ... we could have rowed a boat ... much of what we

did we could have done anywhere else in the woods. But it felt
genuine ... the way the place appeared. (Visitor 1)

This is also articulated on Kolarbyn's official webpage, under the
heading 'Sweden's most primitive hotel':

At STF Kolarbyn neither electricity nor running water disturb
your wilderness experience. Here you can happily fall asleep in
front of the crackling fireplace and awaken to beautiful birdsong. (Kolarbyn 2011)

The wildlife-watching tour company WildSweden has a similar
description of Kolarbyn:

Kolarbyn consists of twelve little forest huts located in a glade
by the beautiful lake Skärsjön. Many guests choose to come
here for lodging in one of the huts – just like a normal hotel,
only more primitive and much more adventurous! There is no
electricity, but candles and a crackling fireplace will lull you
to sleep. After a silent night you slowly wake up to birdsong
and a fresh swim in the lake. Kolarbyn is undoubtedly a true
nature experience for both family and friends. (Eldh 2009b)

The contrast is stark, when Kolarbyn is compared to grimmer stories in the realist literature and testimonials from the charcoal piles,
here exemplified in a verse by the poet Dan Andersson:

Black the night sneaks, around rock strewn county –
fall not asleep, do not drift off!
If you go to sleep, you could be woken by an infernal fire
and the sorrow of the hungry shall be yours.
(Andersson 1913/1990, p.11)[9]

The brutal comparison may seem unjust, but then again, this is
exactly the point – to show the signifying effects of the ideologi-

9   Original: [Svart smyger natten kring stenströdda land – somna ej, somna icke in!
     Om du somnar kan du väckas av en helvetesbrand och den brödlöses sorg skall
     bli din.]

cal inscriptions of Kolarbyn into a global ecotourism discourse.[10] Articulations commemorating or identifying the charcoal burners' work and way of life cannot be pronounced within the ecotourism discourse, but are instead constructed as part of history, safely secluded from present time.

If the establishment of Ecomuseum Bergslagen in the 1980s was a projection of modern values onto an imagined past (Norman 1993), perhaps the discursive shift regarding the meaning of Kolarbyn tells us something about a contemporary imaginary. The place identity of Kolarbyn is not especially a product of the historical and natural assets of this particular piece of land, but instead acquires meaning from distant places mediated through institutions such as eco-branding, genre-specific publications, and networks of social relations. It could of course be argued that iterating a romantic charcoal-burning culture, while only acknowledging the positive features, hides poor working conditions and other less attractive features of the charcoal-burning life. However, I would argue that this failure to identify certain subjects in the past also tells us something about the possibilities to acknowledge similar contemporary positions. Perhaps there is an absent referent, a non-determined/impossible identity hiding in the ecotourism hegemony.[11]

Conclusion

One can note a shift in the inscription of the ground, soil, trees, logs, and cabins in Kolarbyn. From having constituted a spatial memory of a charcoal-burning culture, they now rather carry the meanings of a global discourse on ecotourism. Stories constituting Kolarbyn no longer primarily involve the iron manufacturing history, even though it remains an important backdrop to Sweden's most primitive hotel. Current accounts sometimes contain anecdotes about former dwellers at the location, and sometimes also mythical tales involving phantom-like characters.

---

10   Which in essence is a discourse sustaining a neo-liberal imaginary (Fridolfsson, forthcoming).

11   Compare to Carol Adams (1990/2000).

Now, instead, visitors' individual histories are key, their positive memories of spending time in the woods during childhood and other positive experiences of nature or a current lack thereof. An essential part of the ideology shaping this place is now media exposure, such as feature stories in major newspapers or specialised travel magazines that reflect an authentic experience of unspoiled nature. However word of mouth and the creation of 'this is the place to go' are also important for the popularity of Kolarbyn. The appeal to a contemporary audience involves the anticipation of genuine adventures and wildlife in the woods – something which simultaneously establishes the civilisation, still there, secure and convenient upon return.

The hegemonic global ecotourism discourse establishing Kolarbyn as first and foremost an eco-lodge is articulated through institutions (NGOs and associations) and key concepts such as 'authenticity', 'local', 'sustainable development', and 'magical'.

One could easily imagine other stories being told about Kolarbyn, stories of deprivation, hard work, poor working conditions, injustices, and sacrifice; however, these connotations are almost certainly less prolific. The charm is not so much in the destitution, disease, loneliness, work-related injury, or death prevalent in the lives of the charcoal workers. Nevertheless, even the charcoal burners' simple living conditions have to some extent been rearticulated and have become part of the current attraction in the hegemonic account of this place. The lack of conveniences is used in the marketing of the venue, and the lack of facilities also functions as a reason for visitors to travel to Kolarbyn. Ordinarily discouraging phrases, such as 'primitive kitchen facilities', 'no fancy toilets', 'sleeping on wooden boards lined with sheepskin rugs', and 'no electricity or running water' have undergone a change and become part of the desirability of this place. The moss growing on the roofs of the huts does not signal poverty, but closeness to nature instead, and simple living in a positive sense. The search for an authentic connection with nature, or an imagined past with only basic living conditions, becomes attractive in this discourse and a sought-after and scarce luxury for the modern city dweller.

The ideological reinscription of Kolarbyn and the surrounding landscape finds new meanings in old symbols. The simple becomes luxurious and the primitive an exciting experience. As the present meanings characterising this place prevail, others fade away or are forgotten, while possible future ones remain hidden or unheard of. Selective historical reproduction of a place does not only tell us that people would like to experience a pleasant time[12] while on holiday. Forgetting about a past landscape with hardships that could not merely be enjoyed on demand, perhaps not only serves to conceal large parts of life in olden days. The present day exclusive use of Kolarbyn may also tell us something about current inabilities to recognise vulnerability elsewhere. Poor people residing in Sweden today[13] do not stay in these cosy huts, in the modest charcoal burners' primitive shelters.

12 The definition of a pleasant time has obviously changed over time here.
13 Poverty in terms of monetary, social, or cultural capital.

References

Adams, Carol (1999/2000) *The sexual politics of meat.* New York: Continuum.

Ahlsén, Andreas (2011) Interview with current owner of Kolarbyn, July 15, 2011.

Andersson, Dan (1913/1990) 'Visa vid kolvakten' in: *Samlade dikter visor och ballader.* Stockholm: Wahlström & Wistrand.

Berger, Sune (2009) 'Vem tror på bruksorten?' in: Isacson, Maths, Lundmark, Mats, Mörner, Cecilia and Orre, Inger (red.) *Fram träder Bergslagen: Nytt ljus över gammal region.* Bergslagsforskning III. Västerås: Penta Plus och Mälardalens högskola.

Carlsson, Marlene (2011) Interview with tourism coordinator, August 5, 2011.

Ceballos-Lascuráin, Héctor (1996) *Tourism, Ecotourism, and Protected areas: The state of nature-based tourism,* Gland, Switzerland/ Cambridge, UK: International Union for Conservation of Nature and Natural Resources (IUCN) in collaboration with the Commission of European Communities.

Central Sweden (2011) http://www.centralsweden.se/ Retrieved 2011-08-02

Ecomuseum Bergslagen (2011) http://www.ekomuseum.se/, Retrieved 2011-08-05

Eldh, Marcus (2011) Interview with tourism coordinator, August 5, 2011.

Eldh, Marcus (2009a) 'About us' on WildSweden's web-page http://www.wildsweden.com/about/

ecotourism/ Retrieved 2011-08-02

Eldh, Marcus (2009b) 'Kolarbyn Eco-lodge' on WildSweden's web-page http://www.wildsweden.com/accommodation/ kolarbyn-ecolodge/ Retrieved 2011-08-02

Fridolfsson, Charlotte (forthcoming) Working title: 'Essentialist assumptions in ecotourism'

Intresseföreningen Bergslaget (2014), http://www.bergslaget.se Retrieved 2014-11-06

Jakobsson, Max (2009) *Från industrier till upplevelser. En studie av symbolisk och materiell omvandling i Bergslagen.* Örebro Studies in Human Geography 3. Örebro: Örebro universitet.

Kolarbyn (2011) Official web-page, http://www.svenskaturistforeningen.se/en/ Discover-Sweden/Facilities-and-activities/Vastmanland/ Vandrarhem/STF-Hostel-KolarbynSkinnskatteberg/ Retrieved 2011-08-01

Jonsson, Stefan (1993) *De andra: amerikanska kulturkrig och europeisk rasism,* Stockholm: Norstedts

Laclau, Ernesto & Mouffe, Chantal (1985). *Hegemony & socialist strategy.* London: Verso.

Mader, Ron (2000) 'Ecotourism Champion: A Conversation with Hector Ceballos-Lascurain' in: http://www.planeta.com/ecotravel/weaving/hectorceballos.html, Retrieved 2011-08-01

Lundmark, Mats and Malmberg, Anders (1988) *Industrilokalisering i Sverige – regional och struk-*

turell förändring. Geografiska regionstudier nr 19. Uppsala: Kulturgeografiska institutionen, Uppsala universitet.

Visitor 1 (2011).Interview with former overnight guest at Kolarbyn and Moose Safari participant (MH), July 18, 2011.

Visitor 3 (2011) Interview with a previous Kolarbyn overnight guest, (ML) August 4, 2011.

Visitor 2 (2011). Interview with a previous Kolarbyn overnight guest and Moose Safari participant, (DL) July 26, 2011.

Voluntary worker 1 (2011) Student from France, July 15, 2011.

Voluntary worker 2 (2011) Student from France, July 15, 2011.

Skinnskatteberg municipality (2011) http://www.skinnskatteberg.se, Retrieved 2011-08-04

Norman, Karin (1993) 'Controlling a future by admiring a past: An ecomuseum in Sweden' in Ethnos, 58 (1-2).

Starmist (2008) http://www.tripadvisor.com/members-reviews/starmist, Retrieved 2011-08-04

Stephenson Shaffer, Tracy (2004) 'Performing Backpacking; Constructing "Authenticity" Every Step of the Way' *Text and Performance Quarterly*, vol. 24, No 2. April 2004.

Greenest of them all?

Climate Change Mitigation And Place-Branding In Three Swedish Towns

Eva Gustavsson & Ingemar Elander

Introduction[1]

'Cities market themselves to create or change their image with the intended goal of attracting business, tourism and residents', writes John Rennie Short, opening the chapter 'The Competitive City' in his book *Urban Theory: A Critical Assessment* (Short 2006, p. 111). Indeed, the literature on competitive cities has become voluminous, although the research overview offered by Short shows that this literature has mainly focused on world cities, 'wannabe' world cities, or former industrial cities. Similar results are reported in a comprehensive review of the state of the art of city branding (Lucarelli and Berg 2011, p. 14). There has been less interest in smaller cities and towns, which are the particular focus of this chapter.

Two principal themes identified when cities use marketing to try to 'sell' themselves are 'the city as a place for profitable business' and 'the city as a good place to live', and these lead to subthemes such as 'the global city', 'the fun city', 'the cultural city', 'the pluralist city', 'the post-industrial city', or 'the green city'. In this article we turn to three small cities, or rather towns,[2] in Sweden, to show

1   A slightly different version of this chapter was published as Eva Gustavsson and Ingemar Elander (2012) Cocky and climate smart? Climate change mitigation and place-branding in three Swedish towns. *Local Environment: The International Journal of Justice and Sustainability* 17 (8): 769–82.

2   The legal term for the basic local self-governing level in Sweden is 'municipality' (Sw. *Kommun*). There are 290 municipalities in the country ranging from

that even small places are drawn into the discourse of global city competition (*cf.* Andersson 2010). One of these towns, Växjö, has become renowned for its willingness and capacity to reduce emissions of greenhouse gases (GHG), thereby becoming less dependent on fossil-based energy. Växjö has also used this as a marker of identity both inwardly, towards its own residents, and outwardly, towards other towns and cities, even on a global scale. In the other two towns, Askersund and Laxå (which, like Växjö, are both situated in forested areas), climate mitigation is not at the top of the agenda, although the EU has sponsored a project – the Climate Pilots – to change attitudes and behaviour among their residents in a more climate-friendly direction, and potentially make climate mitigation a marker of place identity.

Climate change mitigation has become an urgent matter for governments at all levels, and many nations, cities, and municipalities are committing themselves to contributing to the decrease of GHG emissions, as has been exhaustively illustrated in the Global Report on Human Settlements 2011: Cities and Climate Change (UN Habitat 2011). One argument sometimes heard in the global battle against global warming is that climate change mitigation may threaten economic growth and the competitiveness of a nation or a city. Mitigation is thus connected with stagnation and backwardness. However, sometimes mitigation has been ascribed the opposite effect, *i.e.* contributing to long-term economic prosperity. It such cases it has created a positive image of the city as a forerunner in climate work, *i.e.* as a place whose identity is associated with the catchword 'smart growth' (Ingram *et al.* 2009). This is also perfectly in line with the popular notion of eco-modernisation, signalling efforts to marry economic development to ecological sustainability (Krueger and Gibbs, 2007; Milanez and Bührs 2007). However, Maheshwary *et al.* (2011) write that 'the link between place branding and its relationship with sustainable development has received little attention [...] there is a dearth of research and very little evidence that the place brand and place marketing activities are essential drivers of sustainable growth', and they therefore point to a need to explore the relationship between sustainability

cities like Stockholm, Göteborg, and Malmö to small countryside towns or villages like Bjurholm, Malå, and Dorotea, each of the latter having no more than 2000–3000 inhabitants.

and place branding strategies (Maheshwary *et al.* 2011, p. 202). This speaks in favour of this article's focus on climate mitigation and place branding in three Swedish towns.[3]

The aim of the article is to analyse and compare climate mitigation as an ongoing, or potential policy of place-making and place-branding in three Swedish towns: Växjö, Askersund, and Laxå. Växjö was an early starter in deciding on a local climate policy, whereas the other two only recently began the process of developing climate goals and strategies. Växjö is known as 'the Greenest City in Europe', while the climate policies of Askersund and Laxå are barely known outside the town halls. Whereas in Växjö the climate profile is a conscious strategy on the part of the city leadership, the climate change initiatives in the other two municipalities are originally a bottom-up attempt, supported by the EU, to transform the local/regional identity of the municipalities in a green direction.

Like a number of similar small-scale local projects, the Climate Pilots project in Askersund and Laxå aims to explore the everyday habits and attitudes of the participants and transform them in a more climate-friendly direction; and in a second step to make the participants role models for other residents. The expectations placed on these projects are threefold: (i) to change the consciousness and behaviour of the participants; (ii) to influence residents on a broad scale to change their behaviour; and (iii) to create dialogue between residents and local government on sustainable climate policy formulation and implementation. Thus, by establishing dialogue, the expectations and long-term aim is to increase residents' involvement in climate-change mitigation. Another aim is to identify opportunities and barriers in national politics in order to reduce greenhouse gas emissions, *e.g.* by developing cooperation between local government, residents, firms, and organisations. There is also an explicit ambition, written into the project plan, that the two municipalities should become forerunners in climate-

3 One city often mentioned in this context is Portland, Oregon, which has 'the reputation of America's leader in smart growth and sustainable development: the Mecca for U.S. planners, both academic and professional' (Richardson and Gordon 2004, p. 132). The city of Curitiba, Brazil, is another city often mentioned in this context, especially with regard to public transport (Macedo 2004).

change mitigation. Arguably, this would yield the potential for future place branding in terms of sustainability and 'climate smartness'.

The theoretical framing of our empirical study draws upon the scholarly literature on place-making and place identity, though without being caught up in the strong attachment to economic growth commonly associated with this literature. The focus will be on the local government rhetoric and its relationship to the geographical basis of each town in terms of location, demography, and natural resources, as well as on pinpointing the relationship between official policies and citizen support. The article poses three main questions. (i) Why has climate change mitigation become a marker of local/regional identity in Växjö but not in the other two towns? (ii) How does the local government in Växjö advertise its climate-friendly image to its residents and to other towns and cities? (iii) How great is the potential to make climate change mitigation an identity marker also in Askersund and Laxå, for example through projects like the Climate Pilots? The last question would arguably also be of interest with regard to climate mitigation as a potential marker of place identity more generally.

The article is based on documentary studies and interviews with participants in the Askersund and Laxå projects (Gustavsson 2010, 2011). As for Växjö it largely draws on an earlier in-depth study (Gustavsson 2008) supplemented by information about the municipality's later climate-mitigation activities. With reference to the two towns that so far have been more passive regarding climate mitigation (Askersund and Laxå) the rationale of the article could briefly be formulated in the words of one 'climate pilot', *i.e.* participant in a local climate dialogue project: 'It would be great if the municipality could be a little bit more cocky [Sw. *kaxig*, overly self-assured] – that would help to strengthen the municipality's self confidence' (Gustavsson 2010).

Following this introduction is a section on the conceptual framework, centring on the concepts of place-making and regional identity. The third section contains a brief description of the three towns followed by an analysis of their climate-mitigation efforts with regard to how these efforts are used as a strategy of place-marketing and place-branding. In the concluding section, the various observations will be summarised, the questions will be answered, and some reflections will be presented in relation to the conceptual framework.

Place Identity and Branding: A Conceptual Framework

The growing role of regions as instruments for economic growth and competition in a globalising market has attracted attention from numerous researchers. For example, when discussing the position of the 'local' in relation to the supra-local transformations, such as globalisation and the intensification of interspatial competition, Neil Brenner and Nik Theodore state that 'In the recent decades, the notion of a 'revival of the local' has attracted widespread attention from academics and policy-makers' (Brenner and Theodore 2002, p. v). This partly new role of regions could be explained as a consequence of the ongoing rescaling of the nation-states' power upwards to international institutions, downwards to actors on the local and regional scales, and horizontally to non-governmental actors (Brenner 2004). The huge number of interurban networks is also a striking trait, for example with regard to climate-change mitigation (Betsill and Bulkeley 2006; Gustavsson *et al.* 2009). Leitner and Sheppard (2002, p. 167) conclude that the structure of interurban networks is often hierarchal; *i.e.* these networks have 'to a large extent, been driven and shaped by top-down state-initiated actions', thereby facilitating 'the top-down spread of the neoliberal gospel of competitiveness and flexible governance'. However, they also point out that these networks 'have created new collaborative possibilities and new political spaces for cities to challenge extant state structures and relations'; *i.e.* they are 'governance networks' with intent and powers of implementation. In this revival of the local, concepts like 'place making', 'place marketing', and 'place branding' have become commonplace when it comes to creating a more or less unique identity of a place (Lucarelli and Berg 2011). Although the three concepts partly overlap, and sometimes are used more or less interchangeably in the literature, in this article we will use 'place-making' as an umbrella term and, depending on the particular context, sometimes specify it as 'place marketing' or 'place branding'.

Notably, the marketing of cities or places at a national or global scale is not a new phenomenon. As shown by Brusman (2008), Dannestam (2009), Holgersson *et al.* (2010), Mukthar Landgren (2009), Strömberg (2005), and others, Swedish cities like Norrköping, Malmö, Göteborg, and Örebro have a long record of more or less successful efforts at place branding and place-marketing. With the growing tourism of the 19th century onward, place marketing also became commonplace in smaller cities and towns, from the 1970s onward, more broadly established in public planning and policy, as illustrated by the proliferation of catchy slogans (Heldt Cassel 2008, Jakobsson 2009).[4]

Ek (2003, p. 29) identifies four types of place development strategies: physical upgrading of the territory, exploitation of local history and local culture, spectacles, and marketing. Andersson (2010, p.199) highlights a number of marketing themes, such as creativity, cosmopolitanism, and sustainability, which have recently acquired global impact. He also notes that globalisation has had an impact on local development not only in large cities, but also in rural regions. This is underscored by Hanna and Rowley (2008, p.63; *cf.* Anholt 2005) who state that 'To be precise, place branding, both as a necessity and a phenomenon, is mainly provoked by globalization processes where the market place for ideas, culture, reputation, in addition to products, services and funds are fusing into a single global community'. However, place marketing is not a one-way, top-down homogenising process. Even in small towns and rural municipalities, local actors such as politicians and planners strive to implement independent initiatives to brand and market their towns.

> Local policy-makers are more often on the receiving end of globalization than the initiators of flows and movements. In spite of that [...] Global discourses are not mediated passively through local policy-makers. They are decoded (interpreted) and thereafter appropriated and practiced – encoded – in a locally adjusted form. (Andersson 2010, p. 206)

4 An early example is 'When in Europe, don't miss Skurup' (Rune *et al.* 2011). A later one, 'Hällefors – from steel to meals', refers to the replacement of the traditional steel industry by food related enterprises, including the recently established academic programme in gastronomy (Braunerhielm and Blom 2007).

As concluded by Short (2006, p. 76), the city should be regarded 'as an arena of globalization, rather than simply as an outcome', thus highlighting 'the active process of globalization rather than the passive impacting of global forces'.

Places become loaded with symbolic values. This can be done by using discursive components, such as slogans, or material components, such as spectacular buildings. Based on an extensive review of the place branding literature, Hanna and Rowley conclude that branding at different levels of government is as much 'a way of planning development policies as branding in the private is about business strategy'. Thus, 'branding has transcended into a composite construct that not only encompasses tourism but also economic, socio-political and historical prospects' (Hanna and Rowley 2008, pp. 63–64).

Andy Pike (2009) has developed a multi-dimensional framework for elucidating 'the geographical entanglements of brands and branding' in terms of different themes, characteristics, and practices. An example of a branding theme could be ecology, bringing green values to the fore and including practices such as fair trade and organic certification (Pike 2009: 638). In line with this, Nyseth (2007, p. 151) observes that the competition between places has been 'partly forced and stimulated by new indexes produced by researchers and consultants, *e.g.* creativity indexes, sustainability indexes, urban indexes, and so on'. In the context of our empirical study, we find climate policy indexes that have been constructed by the Swedish Society for Nature Conservation (SSNC 2010) [Naturskyddsföreningen] and the journal *Miljöaktuellt*. In the latter, Växjö is ranked fourth, Askersund 58th, and Laxå 125th of 288 municipalities compared (*Miljöaktuellt* 2011). The ranking criteria include issues concerning climate change mitigation and adaptation, transport policies, energy efficiency, waste disposal, etc. Together these criteria give a broad picture of the municipalities' environmental ambitions and efforts. As will be demonstrated in the following section, the local government in Växjö has been very eager to use its high environmental ranking in its place branding.

In the 1990s place marketing became an integral part of European city planning (Jakobsson 2009). Many local and regional authorities tried to package and brand their 'products' to be competitive in the marketplace, and thereby attract jobs, a qualified workforce, and tourists. The Finnish geographer Aansi Paasi makes a distinction between 'regional identity' and the 'identity of a region'. The identity of a region is about features distinguishing one region from another in terms of nature, culture, and inhabitants that 'can be *used* in the discourses of science, politics, cultural activism or economics to distinguish a region from others' (Paasi 2002, p. 140). Regional identity, on the other hand, is about the residents' identification with their region, and is also called regional consciousness. Thus, what constitutes the identity of a particular region is basically a question of interpretation. In other words, attempts by a local or regional government to create regional identity may not always correspond with the residents' view of what constitutes a region. As stated by Paasi (2002, p. 140), 'delimiting, naming and symbolising space and groups of people' is a matter of power.

In line with Paasi (2002, p. 140) we conceptualise identity construction as a three dimensional process including: (i) a (socially constructed) territorial space, and borders that distinguish one region from other regions; (ii) a symbolic space 'that manifests itself in practices such as the economy, culture/media and governance and is used to construct narratives of identity. This shape includes the name of the regions and numerous other symbols'; (iii) a number of institutions within and outside the territorial borders, which maintain and reproduce the territorial and symbolic forms and differences between the regions, implying the presence of 'us' and 'them'. Together these dimensions or processes constitute an identity of a region that 'can be used by social groups and movements as a medium in a struggle over resources and power, or – at the other extreme – against the other. Actors involved in these struggles often use the identity among their arguments' (Paasi 2002, p. 140). The following two sections on climate-change mitigation as a potential marker of place identity in three Swedish municipalities are inspired by Paasi's conceptual model and the analytical framework proposed by Pike (2009).

Creating Climate Mitigation Identities

The three municipalities differ in size and character, and when it comes to climate change they exhibit obviously different levels of ambition concerning mitigation policies and goals. Askersund and Laxå are two adjacent rural municipalities with approximately 11,400 and 5,900 inhabitants respectively. Each municipality is dominated by a small town centre, where most of the public services are located, and, in the case of Laxå, also most of the industrial workplaces.

Laxå advertises itself as a green municipality, based on its natural surroundings. The convenient accessibility of the vast nature reserve Tiveden, a popular area for outdoor recreation, is explicitly communicated on Laxå's official webpage with the slogan 'Laxå, the Tiveden-municipality, situated as close to the wilderness as possible' (Laxå kommun 2011a). Otherwise, Laxå is usually looked upon as an industrial municipality in decline. Its population has halved since the 1960s and over 1,000 industry jobs have been lost during the last ten years.

Askersund municipality has had a more stable rate of employment, as well as a fairly stable population. The town itself is beautifully situated on the shore of Lake Vättern, and a number of smaller villages are spread throughout the more rural parts of the municipality. On its official web page, the municipality describes itself as the idyllic archipelago town (Askersunds kommun 2011a) and draws the potential visitor's attention to its small-town charm, and the attractive qualities of the surrounding countryside (Askersunds kommun 2011b).[5] The most important businesses, however, from an economic perspective, are related to mining and the production of wood pulp, which might be perceived as disturbing the idyllic picture. Farming is also a significant activity in the region.

It was not until 2008 that efforts began to formulate a more structured environmental policy in the two municipalities. Before

---

5   In the mid-1990s there was an attempt to market the municipality with the slogan 'The Global Small Town. Work in the World – Live in Askersund'. The slogan was placed on a huge billboard along the highway passing the town, but after internal criticism and discussion among politicians as well as other residents the slogan was dropped. The argument for this was that it might appear ridiculous in the eyes of external spectators (*Nerikes Allehanda*, March 12, 1996).

that, the local government in Laxå had adopted a climate policy in 2005, and Askersund had followed suit, adopting the same policy in 2009. The policy aim is to take into consideration factors that have an impact on climate change when developing the municipal comprehensive plan [översiktsplan]. The local government and its publicly owned companies should also serve as good examples, and stimulate the inhabitants, businesses, and industries to reduce their impact on the climate.

Because of Laxå's situation (with depopulation and unemployment), one would expect its primary political focus to be on economic and labour issues, and this is in fact the case. In Laxå, the policy was followed by a climate strategy in 2006, one that not surprisingly focused on energy use and transport. Quite a large number of commuters travel every day from Laxå to the larger town of Örebro, 50 km away, and large amounts of goods are transported to and from the industries. The town's location, along one of Sweden's main railways and the E20 highway, is used in marketing the town. Addressing representatives of trade and industry, the municipality's webpage exclaims: 'Laxå municipality is perfectly situated! This makes us an attractive place for establishments and investments' (Laxå kommun 2011b).

Askersund's climate policy underscores how important it is that knowledge about climate change reach individuals, as well as industry and local businesses. When it comes to the local climate mitigation work, the policy mentions that the rural character of the municipality offers possibilities in the form of local production of food and fuel.

In 2009 both Askersund and Laxå signed the Covenant of Mayors, which aims to support European local governments in their work to reduce the effects of climate change and reach the EU objective of a 20% reduction of CO_2 emissions by 2020 (EU Mayors n.d.). In this process, both Askersund and Laxå reformulated their climate goals, which are now to reduce their climate impact by 25% between 2009 and 2020 and, in Laxå, to increase the share of organic, locally produced, and/or climate-smart groceries used in schools and day care to 25% by 2014.

Recently the two local governments have taken steps to introduce a more active climate and environmental policy. In 2011, after implementing a new environmental management system,

Laxå received an 'environmental diploma' from the organisation
'Svensk miljöbas' [Swedish environmental base] (n. d). That means
that the municipality's standards meet the requirements of the
organisation. Askersund is now introducing the same standards in
its administration.

Växjö is an old trade centre 'in the middle of the woodshed'
['mitt i vedboden'], as the municipality describes itself in its climate
policy document (Växjö kommun n.d.). With its 75,000 inhabitants, the city is situated in an area where forestry has long been
the main industry. Timber and wood products are commercially
successful regional products for the international market, as is, to
a growing extent, bio fuel for the local and national markets. The
region is known for its strong spirit of entrepreneurship, and many
local industries are related to forestry and bio fuel. Obviously, this
has been an advantage when building the city's 'trademark' as a
forerunner in combining advanced knowledge for economic development and a radical climate change mitigation policy.

Concerns about air quality and the economic risks of oil
dependency led the local government to introduce bio fuel as early
as 1980 as a complement to oil in its district heating plant. This
makes Växjö an early starter in reducing GHG-emissions, despite
global warming not having been high on the environmental agenda
at that time. Climate-change mitigation came into focus in 1996,
when Växjö formulated the overriding climate goal of becoming a
fossil fuel free municipality. The city has not missed any opportunities to market itself as green or climate friendly. 'Växjö is a prime
mover on climate protection', a pamphlet from Växjö municipality
boasts (Växjö kommun n.d.). The climate profile of the city has
attracted international attention, and won three international
awards.[6] The city's growing international renown is illustrated by
the following quotation from Associated Press:

> When this quiet city in southern Sweden decided in 1996 to
> wean itself off fossil fuels, most people doubted the ambitious

6   In 2000 ICLEI (International Council for Local Environmental Initiatives)
     recognised Växjö for its project 'Fossil Fuel Free Växjö' which encompassed
     activities in the energy and transport sectors. In 2007 Växjö received the EU
     commission's Sustainable Energy Europe Award, and the Union of Baltic
     Cities' environmental award.

goal would have any impact beyond the town limits. A few melting glaciers later, Växjö is attracting a green pilgrimage of politicians, scientists and business leaders from as far afield as the United States and North Korea seeking inspiration from a city program that has allowed it to cut CO_2 emissions 30 percent since 1993. (Ritter 2007).

Inspired by the awards and the attention, the local government have decided to use the slogan 'Växjö, the Greenest City in Europe'. In addition to the introduction of bio fuel, the city has successfully applied for national grants to stimulate environmental and climate investments, and has carried out projects mainly in the transport and energy sectors. One example is the construction of a new residential area consisting of eight-floor, energy-efficient wooden buildings, something that has attracted wide attention. The city is also keen to participate in transnational networks on the climate and environmental arena.

Despite their differences, the three municipalities have something in common: they all have taken part in local projects aiming to get households to change their behaviour in the direction of a climate-friendly lifestyle. For six months in spring 2010, seven local celebrities participated in a Växjö project called 'The Climate Idols', while in Askersund and Laxå, ten households called 'Climate Pilots' took part in a twelve-month project (November 2009 to November 2010). The main aim of both projects was to show that changing one's lifestyle required little effort and could even be fun and rewarding. The idols or pilots were then expected to be role models and a source of inspiration for the local residents. The Växjö project was initiated by the local government, and was related to the 'Greenest City in Europe' slogan, whereas in Askersund and Laxå the initiative came from one environmentally engaged resident.

For Växjö, the Climate Idols were just another component of the city's already green trademark. The stated ambition of the Climate Pilots project (though not of the municipalities themselves) in Askersund and Laxå was for the two municipalities, by the conclusion of the project, to have established themselves as national forerunners in climate mitigation work. There is an explicit belief that climate change mitigation work has the power not only to save the planet, but also to give small, rural, and sometimes even declining towns a possibility to survive with a new identity as environmental forerunners. However, leaving aside the similarities, there are striking differences in how the municipalities used climate smartness as a marker of identity. Let us therefore turn to the three research questions raised in the introduction.

First, why has climate change mitigation become a marker of place identity in Växjö but not in the other two towns? In Växjö there is a strong link between the municipality's forestry context, its climate policy, and its local/regional identity. Växjö has a long history of using the climate issue as a local/regional identity marker, both in material and symbolic terms, and there is a strong political consensus around this strategy. In the two smaller municipalities, the climate has not really been acknowledged as a policy issue, despite the fact that, like Växjö, both are situated in regions with plenty of forests. The Climate Pilots project in Askersund and Laxå is just an attempt by a few climate activists to use support from the EU to raise the awareness of local government and residents and put the issue onto the policy agenda. Notably, the small-town, green profile advertised by both municipalities does not include anything about the climate, but only speaks in terms of the natural setting's suitability for recreation and tourism. The massive marketing of Växjö as 'The Greenest City in Europe', on the other hand, has been accompanied by the implementation of several tangible measures related not only to the climate but to the environment in a broad sense as well (for an extensive review of this see Gustavsson 2008 and Gustavsson *et al.* 2009).

Second, how does the local government in Växjö advertise its climate-friendly image to its residents and to other towns and cities inside and outside the country? For the municipality the slogan 'The Greenest City in Europe' is an outstanding trademark. By making use of the international networks in which the municipality takes part, Växjö has succeeded in becoming internationally renowned as a town at the forefront of climate-change mitigation. On its webpage, the municipality gives examples of recent publications where it promotes itself, *e.g.* a one-page article in the French newspaper Le Monde in April 2011 focusing on its energy conservation achievements, and on the CSR (Corporate Social Responsibility) Newswire website (based in the US) where a journalist begins an

article with the words 'Växjö, Sweden has been able to slash its car-
bon footprint by a third while nearly doubling its GDP' (Rheannon
2011). The latter is a message that Växjö is eager to spread to media
and to anyone interested, in a diagram published on the municipality's official website. Even in the US, NBC News has noticed this.
In a television flash titled 'Sweden holds key to going green' King
Carl XVI Gustaf and the city of Växjö are chosen to symbolise
Sweden's prominent climate and environmental work (nbc no
date). However, the city does not only address an international
audience, it also addresses its own residents and offers them advice
and appreciation on its website:

*Figure 1. Thank you, Växjö Residents, for your contribution to a fossil fuel free
Växjö. Source: Växjö municipality website, November 2007.*

The guide book 'Växjös lilla gröna' [Växjö's little green book] contains a list of shops, restaurants, hotels, etc. in the city where you
can shop in a sustainable way. Another webpage, 'Du och miljön'
[You and the environment], offers advice on several subjects,
from stain removal to how to heat your home. Information on the
municipality's participation in several environmental and climate
networks and projects are easily accessible on the website. Växjö's
participation in international networks and projects also proves
to be an excellent platform for marketing the city as a showcase in
climate change mitigation and adaptation.
    In Askersund and Laxå, the link between climate policy and
local identity is very weak or almost non-existent. From the

websites of the two municipalities, one gets the impression that the Climate Pilots project is the only component of their climate-mitigation work. Actually, Askersund is a Fair Trade City (as is Växjö), and all three have signed the Covenant of Mayors, by which European mayors promise to meet or exceed the European Union's 20 percent CO_2 reduction objective by 2020 (EU Mayors, no date). Both Askersund and Laxå are members of the Swedish Eco-municipalities network. All this information, however, lies hidden deep in internal documents on the municipalities' websites, if it at all is possible to find.

Third, how great is the potential to make climate-change mitigation an identity marker also in Askersund and Laxå, for example through projects like the Climate Pilots? The signing of the Covenant of Mayors has obviously generated some discussion on climate and energy in the local governments and resulted in climate-mitigation strategies. However, this seems to have been more of an internal discussion within the municipal organisation than something that is advertised to the public. Nor has the environmental diploma attracted any special attention apart from an article in the local press (Svensson 2010), despite the diploma's logo being visible on the front page of Laxå municipality's website.

The stated goal of the Climate Pilots project, that both munici-palities should become prominent climate actors, seems to be unrealistic, due to insufficient interest from the leading politi-cians as well as the administration. Interviews with participants in the Climate Pilots project reveal a positive attitude towards the municipality's capacity, especially as expressed by one pilot, employed in one of the municipalities.[7] This person appreciated the municipality's efforts to educate its employees about environ-mental issues and how to employ the knowledge in different areas of the organisation. However, others had a more pessimistic (or realistic?) approach. The respondents said it is difficult to uphold services in rural municipalities like these, with small, scattered villages, and mention cancelled bus lines and closures of recycling spots as examples that show how the municipality sends a dual message: 'as a resident you should behave in a climate-friendly way,

---

7   Detailed information about the interviews and the respondents is documented in Gustavsson (2011).

however, we will not make it easier for you'. Some respondents even have doubts about the local government's interest in climate change mitigation and environmental politics when it comes to practice – there is a difference between writing and adopting a climate policy and implementing it.

When launching the project, the members of the municipal councils were invited to apply to be 'shadow pilots', *i.e.* to try to do the same exercises as the pilots and become climate smart. One respondent describes the disappointing result: 'The municipal council had decided that all its members should be shadow pilots, but none of them, or maybe just one, ended up applying. They just stood there nodding their heads. I wonder why they make a decision and then ignore it'.

Conclusion

Relating our findings to the conceptual model inspired by Paasi, we first notice the fact that all three municipalities are located in forest regions with a great potential for supplying bio fuel and related industries. However, this has only been substantially utilised as a place identity marker by one of them, Växjö. In other words, only in Växjö has 'the identity of the region' been transformed into 'a regional identity' in terms of consciousness and action. This brings us to the second dimension of identity marking, the symbolic one. Thus, based on material climate mitigation practices, and skilfully using its own website as well as national and international media, Växjö has successfully constructed a narrative depicting it as 'The Greenest City in Europe'. Notably, this is not just a fairy tale. There is also an institutional stronghold of governance behind it, comprising not only the local government but also businesses, the university, the political parties, and other civil society organisations. This governance structure also has external links through networks with other cities nationally as well as globally.

Although there is always a risk of exaggerating success by taking the symbols of place-making too literally, there are enough tangible facts to support the conclusion that the case of Växjö is an example of successful place marketing and place branding, using climate mitigation and ecological sustainability as distinctive markers of place identity. A lesson to be learned from the Växjö case is the importance of having a long-term strategy in which material, as well as symbolic, institutional, and personal components work together in order to establish a place brand with internal as well as external legitimacy. In terms of the place branding framework developed by Andy Pike (2009) Växjö's ecologically flavoured branding strategy has a firm material basis in an economy that makes clever use of the forest surroundings – 'in the middle of the woodshed' – and also incorporates architectural (wooden multi-family housing blocks), historical, cultural, and other characteristics.

The Växjö case also highlights the importance of a dedicated network of influential actors that must step forward and make visible the intention of the municipality to become 'a little bit more cocky', as a way to 'strengthen the municipality's self confidence'.[8] The two other municipalities studied, on the other hand, fall short on the symbolic, as well as the institutional, and personal dimensions, though they still have the potential to go the way of Växjö. Although current institutions and networks are far from offering such a framework, projects like the Climate Pilots may function as triggers, as well as models and drivers of future change in the direction of more sustainable policies and everyday practices; and these latter may also become assets for place branding in the two towns. However, it remains to be seen whether the seeds sown by the Climate Pilots project will grow or just fade away.

8   As stated by one of the 'climate pilots', i.e. participant in a local climate dialogue project (Gustavsson 2010).

References

Andersson, Magnus (2010) 'Provincial globalization. The local struggle of place-making'. *Culture Unbound: Journal of Current Cultural Research* 2, 193–214.

Anholt, Simon (2005) Editorial: 'Some important distinctions in place branding'. *Place Branding* 1, 116–121.

Betsill, Michele and Bulkeley Harriet (2006) 'Cities and multilevel governance of global climate change'. *Global Governance* 12, 141–159.

Braunerhielm, Lotta and Blom, Thomas (2007) *From steel to meal: The birth of a destination*. Paper to the conference Re-Thinking Cultural Economy. ESRC Centre for Research on Socio-Cultural change (CRESC), University of Manchester, 6–8th September 2007.

Brenner, Neil (2004) *New State Spaces: Urban Governance and the Rescaling of Statehood*. Oxford New York: Oxford University Press.

Brenner, Neil and Theodore, Nik, eds. (2002) Preface: From the 'new localism' to the spaces of neoliberalism. *Spaces of Neoliberalism: Urban Restructuring in North America and Western Europe*. Malden, Mass.: Blackwell.

Brusman, Mats (2008) *Den verkliga staden? Norrköpings innerstad mellan urbana idéer och lokala identiteter* [The real city? The inner city of Norrköping between urban ideas and local identities] Linköping: Linköpings

universitet, Institutionen för studier av samhällsutveckling och kultur.

Dannestam, Tove (2009) *Stadspolitik i Malmö. Politikens meningsskapande och materialitet* [Rethinking Local Politics in Malmö. Towards a Discursive-Material Analysis of Politics] Lund Political Studies 155. Lund: University of Lund.

Ek, Richard (2003) *Öresundsregion – bli till!*: de geografiska visionernas diskursiva rytm. [Öresund region – come into being! The discursive rythm of the geographical visions] Diss. Lund: Lunds universitet.

Ekblom, K-G (2011) 'Kommunen tittar tio år framåt'. *Nerikes Allehanda* 2011-07-15, part 2, p. 5 [Accessed 2012-01-23]

EU Mayors (n.d.). Covenant of mayors. Committed to action. http://www.eumayors.eu/index_en.html. [Accessed 8 August 2011]

Gustavsson, Eva (2008) *Mellan det lokala och det globala – klimat, kommuner, nätverk* [Between the local and the global – Climate, municipalities, networks] Örebro Studies in Human Geography. Örebro universitet.

— (2010) *Tid, pengar eller ett personligt klimatsamvete – vad kan inspirera 'vanligt folk' att ändra sitt vardagsliv i en mer klimatvänlig riktning?* [Time, money or a personal climate consciousness] www.lamf.se/download/18.../Rapport+klimatpiloterna+2010_final.pdf [Accessed 8 August 2011].

— (2011) 'Det här var det roligaste jag har gjort' ['This was my most fun experience'] Slutrapport projekt Klimatpiloterna i Askersund och Laxå.

Gustavsson, Eva and Elander, Ingemar (2012) Cocky and climate smart? Climate change mitigation and place-branding in three Swedish towns. *Local Environment: The International Journal of Justice and Sustainability* 17 (8): 769–782.

Gustavsson, Eva, Elander, Ingemar and Lundmark, Mats (2009) 'Multilevel governance, networking cities, and the geography of climate-change mitigation: Two Swedish examples'. *Environment and Planning C: Government and Policy* 27 (1), 59–74.

Hanna, Sonya and Rowley, Jennifer (2008) 'An analysis of terminology use in place branding'. *Place Branding and Public Diplomacy* 4, 61–75.

Heldt Cassel, Susanna (2008) 'Trying to be attractive: Image building and identity formation in small industrial municipalities in Sweden'. *Place Branding and Public Diplomacy* 4 (2), 102–114.

Holgersson Helena, Thörn, Catharina, Thörn, Håkan and Wahlström, Mattias, eds. (2010) *(Re)searching Gothenburg Essays on a Changing City*. Göteborg: Glänta production.

Ingram, Gregory K., Carbonell, Armando, Hong, Yu-Hung and Flint, Anthony (2009) *Smart Growth Policies*. Cambridge, MA: Lincoln Institute of Land Policy.

Jakobsson, Max (2009) *Från industrier till upplevelser: en studie av symbolisk och materiell omvandling i Bergslagen*. [From industries to experiences: a study of a symbolic and material transformation in Bergslagen] Diss. Örebro: Örebro universitet.

Krueger, Rob and Gibbs, David (2007) *The Sustainable Development Paradox: Urban Political Economy in the United States and Europe*. New York: Guilford Press.

Leitner, Helga and Sheppard, Eric (2002) 'The city is dead, long live the net' Harnessing European interurban networks. In: Brenner, Neil and Theodore, Nik, (eds.) *Spaces of Neoliberalism: Urban Restructuring in North America and Western Europe*. Malden, Mass.: Blackwell. pp. 148–171.

Lucarelli, Andrea and Berg, Per Olof (2011) 'City branding: a state-of-the-art review of the research domain'. *Journal of Place Management and Development* 4 (2), 9–27.

Macedo, Joseli (2004) 'City profile. Curitiba'. *Cities* 21 (6), 537–549.

Maheshwary, Vishwas, Vandewalle, Ian and Bamber, David (2011) 'Place branding's role in sustainable development'. *Journal of Place Management and Development* 4 (2), 198–213.

Milanez, Bruno and Bührs, Ton (2007) 'Marrying strands of ecological modernization: a proposed framework'. *Politics* 16 (4), 565–583.

Miljöaktuellt (2011) Kommunranking [ranking of municipalities] http://miljoaktuellt. miljobarometern.se/ [Accessed 3 August 2011]

Mukhtar Landgren, Dahlia (2009) 'The city (as) exhibition: Urban restructuring and place marketing in Malmö during two Fin de Siécles'. In: Frank Eckardt and Ingemar Elander, (eds.) *Urban Governance in Europe*. Berlin: Berliner Wissenschafts-Verlag. pp. 249–274.

Mumford, Lewis (1938) *The Culture of Cities*. London: Secker & Warburg.

NBC, (no date) Sweden holds key to going green. News video published on http://www.msnbc.msn.com/id/22425001/vp/24243707#24243707 *[Accessed 8 August 2011].*

Nerikes Allehanda (1996) 'Löjets skimmer över Askersund? Delade meningar om "Global småstad"' [An air of ridicule over Askersund? Divided opinions about 'Global Small Town'] 12th June.

Nyseth, Torill (2007) 'Towards an understanding of place reinvention'. In: Torill Nyseth and Brynhild Granås, (eds.) *Place Reinvention in the North*. Stockholm: Nordregio.

Paasi, Anssi (2002) 'Bounded spaces in the mobile world: deconstructing "regional identity"'. *Tijdschrift voor Economische en Sociale Geografie*, 93 (2), 137–148.

Pike, Andy (2009) 'Geographies of brands and branding'. *Progress in Human Geography* 33 (5), 619–645.

Rheannon, Francesca (2011) Zero net emissions with economic growth? Europe's greenest city shows the way. Published 2011-07-06 on *CSRlive Commentary*.

http://www.csrwire.com/csrlive/commentary_detail/4785-Zero-Net-Emissions-With-Economic-Growth-Europe-s-Greenest-City-Shows-the-Way [Accessed 8 August 2011].

Richardson, Harry, W. and Gordon, Peter (2004) 'Sustainable Portland? A Critique, and the Los Angeles Counterpoint'. In: André Sorensen, Peter J. Marcotullio, and Jill Grant, (eds.) *Towards Sustainable Cities. East Asian, North American and European Perspectives on Managing Urban Regions*. Aldershot: Ashgate.

Ritter, Karl (2007) NCities take the lead on climate changeM. *The Boston Globe*, 14 October. Available from http://www.boston.com/news/world/articles/2007/10/14/european_cities_fight_climate_change_at_home/ [Accessed 8 August 2011].

Rune, David, Ekberg, Svante and Koutfood, Daniel (2011) *Var femte invånare är en häst: svenska kommunslogans* [Every fifth inhabitant is a horse: Swedish municipality slogans]. Sundbyberg: Kartago.

Short, John Rennie (2006) *Urban Theory. A Critical Assessment*. Houndmills, Basingstoke: Palgrave Macmillan.

SSNC (2010) 'Sveriges bästa klimatkommuner [The best climate municipalities in Sweden] [online]. Available from: http://www.naturskyddsforeningen.se/natur-och-miljo/klimat/lonsamt-klimatarbete/klimatindex-2010/ [Accessed 8 August 2011].

Strömberg, Thord (2005) 'New Logo. Industristaden byter skinn' [New Logo. The industrial city changes its coat]. In: Mats Berglund. (ed.) *Sakta vi gå genom stan: City strolls*. Stockholm: Stockholmia förlag. [e-book] pp. 280–309.

Svensk Miljöbas (n.d.) Föreningen

Svensk Miljöbas (http://svensk-miljobas.se/)

Svensson, Tove (2010) 'Laxå tar nya steg för att minska sin miljöpåverkan'. *Nerikes Allehanda* 2010-03-12, p. 10.

UN-Habitat, 2011. *Cities and Climate Change — Global Report on Human Settlements 2011.*

Municipal documents

Askersunds kommun, 2011a. http://www.askersund.se/byggaochbo.4.1703484105148c66e08000284.html [Accessed 11 May 2011].

Askersunds kommun, 2011b. http://www.askersund.se/turismoche venemang.4.1703484105148c6 6e08000279.html [Accessed 11 May 2011].

Laxå kommun, 2011a. http://www.laxa.se/ [Accessed 11 May 2011].

Laxå kommun, 2011b. http://www.laxa.se/naringsliv.12.html . [Accessed 11 May 2011].

Växjö kommun, n.d. *Fossil Free Växjö*. http://gmf.fcm.ca/files/Program_Docs/2004_Sweden_Mission/fos-fuel-free-_Vaxjo.pdf [Accessed 11 May 2011].

Group Identity and Church Buildings

– The Philadelphia Church in Stockholm 1930

Andreas K. G. Thörn

The Philadelphia Church (*Filadelfiaförsamlingen*) in Stockholm emerged in the early 20th century from a renewal movement (the Pentecostal revival) primarily within the Baptist denomination, which in Sweden was part of the Free Church movement. The movement was long an object of criticism within influential segments of the established churches, and at times also in the secular press. The group of barely thirty people who founded the Philadelphia Church grew, despite the external pressures from other churches and the press, and by the middle of the 20th century the Philadelphia Church was one of the world's largest Pentecostal Churches and remains one of Europe's largest Free Churches (Anderson 2006:96). In 1930, when the congregation had about four thousand members, they opened Sweden's largest assembly hall, the newly built Philadelphia Church (Junggren 1992).

The relationship between groups of people and buildings/spaces has been studied in many different ways. One example is to examine the building's or the space's importance for people sharing the same ideas, worldview, and interests who come together and form various communities (Nylund 2007, Karlsson 2009). In this perspective, there is an empirical focus on the relevance of the space as a basis for the group to meet and constitute itself.

The relationship between the building and the group has also been studied with a focus on the building's symbolic meaning. These studies have surveyed and analysed the architecture and decoration of various groups' or movements' buildings. The aim of this analysis has been to study how different groups' ideological

Figure 1. The Philadelphia Church at Rörstrand 1930. Photo from Evangelii Härold.

and religious orientations are communicated through buildings and other material objects (Hellspång, 1991; Schnell, 1999; Brodd, 2001; Kieckhefer, 2004). In this perspective the empirical material primarily consists of the buildings' architecture and interior decoration. The emphasis is mainly on what the building can reveal about the group's ideas and/or practices, but also what the group may be communicating through the building. One area that has received particular attention within this perspective is religious buildings, mainly churches (Brodd, 2001; Kieckhefer, 2004; Kilde, 2008; Bergmann *et al.*, 2009).

The ethnologist Mats Hellspong also uses this perspective in my opinion. In his ethnographic study of early popular movements' buildings, he explores the themes of architecture and decoration in relation to symbolic meaning. He states among other things that revivalist movements' churches lacked clear religious symbolism, having in their simplicity no clear symbolic function, but primarily a practical one (Hellspong 1991). The architect Göran Lindahl discusses this in a similar way in his analysis of the Free Church movement's architecture, but takes it further when writing of the Pentecostal movement's buildings: 'The same applies with regard to the interior design. There are no religious or church-political reasons to decorate the meeting halls or give them a form that can be associated with a church building. Their function is simply to be a modest and functional shell surrounding the congregation as it waits for the baptism in the spirit' (Lindahl, 1955:163).

This chapter does not adopt any of the above-mentioned empirical perspectives, and hence it is not the buildings as such that are the main object of study. Instead, it is the *agent's* perspective on the buildings that will be in focus. By studying the group leaders' ways of giving meaning to the building through rhetoric, it will be possible to see the function that place has in a group's self-image or group identity.

The aim is to show how the church building was constructed as a place in the Philadelphia Church's official *story* about its history and thus became a part of the group's collective identity. The aim is also to show how the congregation's leaders viewed an uncompleted church building, which was built under the auspices of the Pentecostal movement, and how that affected the story/picture of the movement. Location is thus studied through the lens of narrative. Did the building have any other meaning for the group than, as architect Lindahl writes, to be a 'modest and functional shell'? That is the question I attempt to answer in this chapter by focusing on agents and how they saw their building. The examples are taken from the 1930s.

Identity, narrative, place, and material

What is meant by group identity? In this study, the term will be understood and studied in terms of narrative. With the concept of narrative I am not referring to a literary genre, but a fundamental way for humans to structure their experiences. The term implies that social life – identity and action – is constructed through narratives (Ricoeur, 1981; Eakin, 1999, Brunner, 2002; Robertson, 2005). Identity is therefore not essential, but socially constructed. Events and experiences in the story are linked together in a way that gives meaning. It is therefore something more than a description; it is an interpretation and valuation that makes events comprehensible and meaningful (Rüsen, 2008; Straub, 2005; see also Wiklund, 2006). The term narrative, according to theorists, comprises the changeability and fragmented condition of the subject and life, as well as the individual's understanding of identity as coherent and relatively constant (Ritivoi, 2005). Identity, in this perspective, is constructed of events and experiences and the ability to merge these into a meaningful unity. However, it is not only the past that is connected to the present through identity, but also expectations of the future (Rüsen, 2008; Straub, 2005).

Just as narrative gives context and meaning to an individual, collective narrative gives a foundation in time and space to a group, and meaning to the common work. It also positions the group in relation to other groups (Rüsen, 2008; Straub, 2005). The group's self-image, for example that of the Philadelphia Church in Stockholm, will then be expressed through its story about itself.

In a group as large as the Philadelphia Church, it must be assumed that there were a number of ways to tell the congregation's history – a variety of narratives, each of which strived for a coherent structure and yet always held internal tensions. One of those was the congregation leaders' official story. It is this narrative that will be studied in this chapter.

What kind of group was the Philadelphia Church in Stockholm? During the first twenty years, that is, between 1910–1930, the group showed traits that characterize a sect in Ernst Troeltsch's sense. The group was made up of members who had joined of their own free will, who were 'true' believers, and who were critical of other churches and society at large (Troeltsch, 1992; Sahlberg 1977). The group can also be described as Biblicist (considering the Bible the norm for doctrine and life), apocalyptic (emphasising Jesus' second coming and the end of the world), and apolitical (uninterested in social change) (Sahlberg, 1977). Despite its size – the group grew from 28 to 4,000 members in twenty years – it can be described as a face-to-face group, *i.e.* a group whose members meet face to face (in contrast to, for example, imaginary groups). The many meetings in which members could take part underpin such a description; both private and public meetings were held several times a week. In the Pentecostal movement's congregations in Sweden, members were expected to actively participate in these meetings (Kennerberg, 1996). A loyal membership also characterized the group. The individuals who joined the congregation usually stayed for a long period of time, and member circulation was thus rather low.

Since the Philadelphia Church was a face-to-face group, it was closely related to a place or, in the words of human geographer Lily Kong, experienced 'locatedness into a place' (Kong 2001:221). Place is created by the meaning that is linked to a particular space through language, feelings, and practices (Cresswell 2004). Because place consists of more than just a physical dimension, it is usually studied in relation to three aspects. These can be defined in slightly different ways but often involve a physical dimension, a planning/conceiving/meaning dimension, and a practical dimension (Cresswell 2004, see also Fridolfsson & Elander's chapter, this volume). Given this theoretical distinction, the focus in this chapter is on meaning (the narrative). However, the stories refer to specific construction projects associated with specific sites. In the case of the Philadelphia Church, the place's physical dimension is a construction project initiated in 1926. The actual construction began in 1928 and was completed during 1930. In the case of the chapel in Flen, the physical dimension is the shell a building of which has been raised, but which has not been completed.

What about the history of the Philadelphia Church's buildings before 1930? Ever since the congregation was founded in 1910 the group had access to a regular meeting space. The first location was the Philadelphia Hall at Uppsalagatan 11, in Stockholm. It was located in the basement of an apartment building and had room for about 500 visitors. Due to lack of space, it was replaced in 1921 by new facilities at Sveavägen 45. These were planned and built as the ground floor of an apartment building. The premises held not only a meeting hall with seating for about 1,500 visitors, but also office space and a bookstore. However, the building was from the outset too small to accommodate the entire congregation, which by that time had grown to encompass almost 2,000 members. Only nine years later, in 1930, the Philadelphia Church opened on Rörstrandsgatan. The building's main hall held 3,500 visitors. In addition to meetings, the building was also used for a large part of the congregation's other work. Activities were also held in a 17th-

century palace located on the site purchased for the church building
(Junggren 1992:174–178).

Where do we find the congregation leadership's official story of
the Philadelphia Church's buildings? It may have been expressed
in various ways, for example in annual reports, the congregation's
weekly *Evangelii Härold* (Gospel Herald), and anniversary publications, but also in sermons at the worship services and discussions in
the congregation's private meetings. In this study the story will be
drawn primarily from the Philadelphia Church's anniversary book
from 1930, the year the church was completed. This book describes
the congregation's twenty-year history and can therefore be said
to describe 'what' the Philadelphia Church is. Parts of the story are
also gathered from the group's annual reports and *Evangelii Härold*.
The material for the study of the approach to the construction
project that was not completed is taken from the *Evangelii Härold*.
Chronologically the study is limited to the 1930s.

The building in the story

In the story found in the Philadelphia Church material, I find five
themes related to the Philadelphia Church at Rörstrandsgatan.
These themes are: supernatural reality, diligence, expansion,
finances, and the outside world's reactions. This part of the chapter
is structured around these themes.

Supernatural reality

A recurring theme in the story is that the Philadelphia Church's
work has been characterized throughout its history by the special
participation or influence of God – that it was blessed. This divine
support is found in relation to various parts of the story, such as
the Congregation's founding and critical decisions (Söderholm,
1930:5–8, 11). The 'blessing' is manifested as supernatural inspiration and as a force that makes the work successful. This spiritual
influence was considered to be particularly noticeable in the meeting activities aimed at reaching new people with the group's message, as the following quotes exemplify:

And God has since made his presence felt at these meetings. They have continued to be frequented by many people, and the presence of God has been especially apparent, and many souls have been saved at these meetings. Praised be the Lord's name! A wonderful revival spirit has rained down upon the public meetings in our church during all of these 20 years. (Söderholm, 1930:36)

In the congregation's 1930 Annual Report, the church building functions as something that could be termed a materialization of several themes, one of which is supernatural aid. By materialization, I mean a concrete material expression of their understanding of life – that is, elements of their activities or their worldview that are not always visible to the world outside the congregation. At the end of a passage relating to the handling of the meeting-hall question over the course of twenty years, the author writes that it is 'wonderful evidence of God's faithfulness and of what faith and prayer can do' that 'this great church is now ready to be used' (Söderholm, 1930: 32). In this example the building functions as an empirically observable reality. According to the author, this shows that God is active and that faith and prayer associated with this god are relevant. Such links between the church building and the Christian faith are made repeatedly in the story.

The text talks about God's influence already at the idea stage of the building project. The congregation building fund received a large donation from an anonymous man who was not a member of the congregation. This was seen as an encouraging sign from God that the project was God's will. The financial side of the project is similarly related to the Christian worldview by being regarded as a type of miracle. The miracle, according to the text, is that a group of 'mostly poor church members' were able to defray the financial expenses related to the construction project. The actual construction process was also understood, in various ways, as being under the influence of God (Söderholm, 1930:27–32). Considering that the building's progress from idea to erected church was closely interwoven with divine intervention of various kinds, the building becomes in the story a kind of proof; supernatural existence materializes and takes the form of a building.

That God is closely involved in Philadelphia's activities is related not only to the church as a project but also as building. In the 1930 annual report, the year the church was completed, the building was referred to with the word 'temple'. In the Old Testament, the temple is described as a place where, compared to other places, God is present in a unique way. The contact between man and God, between earth and 'heaven', took place there. Using the term 'temple' implies a strong link between the church and what in the anniversary book is called 'the presence of God' (Söderholm, 1930). This theme is not developed in the Annual Report for 1930. The church leader and poet Sven Lidman, however, developed it when he wrote about the newly opened church in *Evangelii Härold* under the heading 'Temple Inauguration' (an article that probably had inspired the writer of the annual report). In the article, Lidman connects the building with 'God's presence' and thereby distinguishes it from other places of assembly. He writes:

> Few things have given me such an overwhelming sense of God's presence and grace in this revival as the idea and vision of that miracle, which day by day [...] has been constructed [...] at the corner of Bråvalla and Rörstrand streets.
>
> On more than one occasion, when I stood in the room and saw the work, I was permeated by a nameless fear and a trembling question: 'Who are You really, You strange and incomprehensible power.' (EH 1930-10-30:743)

When the anniversary book from 1930 speaks of experiences in relation to buildings or places, these experiences seem to have been related to the activities performed there, such as revival meetings (Söderholm, 1930). In this case, however, no other activities had taken place there than the construction work. Therefore, the experience of holiness seems to be more directly linked to the building/place. The connection between the building and a spiritual presence is also found in Lidman's parallel between the church and the 'cleft in the rock' from Exodus. According to Exodus, Moses wanted to see God's glory. God replied that he would place Moses in a cleft in the rock and that from there he would see God's back (Exodus 33:18–23). 'Such a gap in the mountain, God has opened for us in our new temple in Stockholm' writes Lidman.

Diligence

As noted above, the story describes the building as explicit proof of the group's connection with God, but other themes are linked to the building as well. One is diligence, or being hardworking. In the story, the idea of God's activity is always closely tied with the group's own work. On some occasions, the emphasis on one or the other aspect is so strong that it seems to create a tension between them:

> It is not human wisdom and ability that made the Philadelphia Church what it is now. It is God's wonderful power, revealed through what is weak and insignificant in the world. (Söderholm, 1930:6)
>
> Behind this rapid development, described in the previous chapter, there naturally lies intense work and the warmest life of prayer. The same applies in the kingdom of God as in the world in general: nothing comes of its own accord – nothing is gained without toil and work. (Söderholm, 1930:33)

Another example of the close relationship between supernatural intervention and the group's own work in the story is when the author concludes the section about the buildings with the words, 'His [God's] wellspring never runs dry, as long as we remain faithful in prayer and in work' (Söderholm, 1930:32). Thus, not only is the Philadelphia Church described in the story as a manifestation of abstract beliefs, but the fact that the building was practically finished confirms that the congregation is diligent.

However, diligence should not be interpreted as meaning that each and every member worked concretely with the construction of the church. Some certainly were involved in the project in various ways, but in this case, diligence was above all a matter of praying and donating money to the project.

Expansion

Expansion is a recurring theme in the anniversary publication. In the story, the work also comprises diverse and extensive activities that involve and address a large number of people inside and outside the church. Several of these areas of activity have grown steadily during the congregation's twenty-year history. Statistics reported in the story describe an increase from just under 30 to 3500 members. A metaphor used for the congregation and its growth is that of a small seed becoming a large tree (Söderholm, 1930:5–6).

The theme of expansion is connected with the building through an increased need of space for the activities.

> A few years after the facility at Sveavägen [Philadelphia's previous church, before they built the church at Rörstrand] was opened, it began to become too crowded during the public meetings. Both newspapers and police have over the years busied themselves with the long queues outside the Philadelphia Church's premises before the public meetings. [...] It became quite clear to everyone that the construction of a large church in Stockholm with the associated facilities necessary for such extensive work as ours would, due to the current high prices, cost millions. (Söderholm 1930:27).

What frequently is called 'the meeting-hall question' might just as well have been termed 'the lack of space issue'. The search for suitable premises, according to the story, concerns resolving the problem of a near-constant lack of space. With the Philadelphia Church, the meeting-hall question had reached a 'final, and happy solution'. Since such a statement implies that growth will cease, the author adds that the meeting-hall question may become a pressing issue again if God continues to favourably influence the activities (Söderholm, 1930:22). The Philadelphia Church therefore functions in the story, along with all the people who are members, as a concrete piece of evidence of their expanding work.

Finances

Above it was noted that supernatural intervention was, among other things, described as being related to economic issues. It is only in relation to the construction work, for example, that figures for project-specific costs are mentioned in the anniversary book. In the story it is mentioned that the project was regarded as financially impossible right from the start, if one only evaluated it in terms of human reason. Despite this, there are no problems with the finances:

It [the cost of building the Philadelphia Church] must be in the millions. And where should a crowd of mostly poor church members be able to summon up such sums? Most have, from a human point of view, no more than their low pay, and many are even unable to fulfil their basic needs.

At the turn of 1929–1930 we were busy roofing. The congregation was unsure whether it could raise funds to continue the work. They decided to proceed with the work as money flowed in. But miraculously God provided funds, little by little, so that the work could continue without any interruption, work that in addition required a workforce amounting to as much as 80 men. (Söderholm 1930:27, 30).

According to the story, it is God who made it possible to raise the necessary funds, and who thus made the impossible possible. However, this did not occur without human effort; apparently the members contributed financially. The divine and the human are woven together. By explicitly putting economic issues in relation to the Philadelphia Church, the building becomes symbolically charged with the group's financial determination and strength.

The outside world's reactions

Above it was noted that the story of the building contained an expectation that the Philadelphia Church should communicate the congregation's faith or be a concrete expression of their beliefs and aspirations. Despite this expectation the congregation appears to be surprised when it receives positive feedback on the building in the press:

However, it may be mentioned that the daily press, which often were unsympathetic to our affairs, have given the most favourable reviews of this construction. Being Sweden's, and perhaps Scandinavia's largest meeting hall, it was quite natural that it would attract attention. But that not one of the press representatives had any complaint to make against it, but instead praised it in the highest terms, is more than we could have expected. (Annual report 1930:8).

Perhaps this surprise says more about the congregation's experiences of the press than about the leaders' expectations regarding the building's ability to facilitate communication. Although the question of how the press symbolically charged Philadelphia Church is not the topic of the chapter, it may still be interesting to mention some examples as a contrast to the congregation's story.

When the church was opened the major newspapers in Stockholm and local newspapers in large parts of the country wrote about the event. A theme that occurs in the longer articles in particular is the building's architecture. They describe the architecture as modernistic and different from church architecture in general. Innovative solutions for the acoustics of the large assembly hall are also addressed (*Svenska Dagbladet*, 1930-11-01). Other themes frequently occurring in both longer articles and short items are the size of the church – that it is the nation's largest assembly hall – and the high cost of construction (*Stockholms-Tidningen*, 1930-11-01). Earlier, during the construction work, these two themes were already present. For example, newspapers expressed surprise that the Philadelphia Church, whose members come from the 'poorer classes', could build such a large and costly church. This was described as a sign of the movement's strength (*Stockholms-Tidningen*, 1926-09-10).

In two papers the issue of financing was discussed. *Social-Demokraten* mentioned the members' 'great will to sacrifice'. According to the newspaper they had paid 'one tenth of their earnings to the church activities. [...] It is probably thanks to this excellent system for collection, that the new Philadelphia Church [...] is expected to be the largest church alongside Uppsala Cathedral' (*Social-Demokraten*, 1927-09-30). *Folkets Dagblad Politiken* says that the question of the Philadelphia Church's economic strength must be understood in the light of the leaders' threats about hell and promises about heaven:

> What is more natural than for the very poor, plagued by all sorts of earthly troubles, to long intensely for heaven and fear hell. ... And they threw themselves into the arms of the very agents of salvation, who are capable of the most ardent eloquence. (*Folkets Dagblad Politiken* 1926-09-11).

Because they had such a grip on the poor, the leaders were able to push them to donate to the construction of the church, continues the writer. It is the same as when the popes built St. Peter's Basilica with funds that the poor provided for 'the sake of their souls'. The activity is also conducted, according to the article, in a business-like way, and is called a 'salvation enterprise' (*Folkets Dagblad Politiken*, 1926-09-11). In the press, the building was thus described as both a symbol of the innovative and the modern and as a symbol of strength, primarily economic strength.

Given the interest in the church's architecture that existed in 1930, it is interesting to note that the form of the building was not emphasized in the Philadelphia Church's official story. The architecture is not commented on at all in the anniversary book, despite the fact that the history of the church buildings is treated as a specific theme in the text. The annual report for 1930 mentions ventilation and good acoustics, but not the exterior.

In Sven Lidman's article 'Temple Inauguration', some comments on the architecture can be found. He claims to see connections between what he calls the Pentecostal revival's 'spirit' and 'essence' and the design of the church. These links can be summarized as two pairs of dichotomies. The first speaks of closeness/immanence and grandeur/transcendence. Lidman writes: 'What an exceptional building; it is rising to heaven in a steady ascent, which no obstacle bars – the room inside having something of a rare and mighty cave's mystical loftiness [...] and yet it is so spiritually and intimately enclosed around the pulpit' (EH 1930-10-30:743). The related themes of grandeur and transcendence are clear parallels to the above-mentioned themes of supernatural reality and growth.

The second dichotomy consists of modern/contemporary and traditional/past. 'This construction and this revival are conspicuous by their fresh innovations, and the impression of bustling modernity is at the same time inextricably and intimately linked with the past. A few steps from one side of the gallery you can step back 300 years in time into a gentleman's residence of the 17th century' (EH 1930-10-30:743). In the three texts that essentially constitute the material for the study of the Philadelphia congregation's story, it is only here that the building is explicitly mentioned as being modern.

The above-discussed themes – supernatural reality, diligence, expansion, finances, and the surrounding world's reactions – are to be interpreted in the light of the church leadership's world view and their ideas about the group. The leaders regarded the church as directly linked to the biblical story of the world. The congregation was thus seen as a result of God's action and the human response to this action. One of the aims of the church leadership's stories was to link all of the congregation's activities, including the building projects, to that biblical system of meaning.

The themes are not, however, only related to a biblical system of meaning. Turning beliefs and visions into practical action (for example in a construction project) does not take place in a vacuum; it occurs in relation to structures and other actors' beliefs. The practical action thus bears traces of this diversity. This makes it impossible for a group to talk about such things as a construction project without relating them to different systems of meaning. In the case of the Philadelphia congregation, this becomes visible in the focus on financial issues. However because the Philadelphia Church, according to the leaders, is a positive example, it is possible to ascribe economic success to God's influence. In the light of another case, described below, that the leadership characterised as a negative example, it is clear that other systems of meaning may take precedence over the biblical one.

The place that threatens to create a different story

Since a successful building project is emphasised as a sign of God's influence it seems logical that a failed building project is a sign of the opposite. Such way of reasoning can be found in *Evangelii Härold*. The Philadelphia Church's senior pastor Lewi Pethrus writes about a chapel in the village Flen that the local congregation could not complete because the building costs exceeded the group's financial capacity.

According to the article, Pethrus, with the help of a builder, has investigated what options best could sort out the problem. The solution that is considered both most economically viable and practically efficient is to finish the chapel and rent out an apartment that is part of the building. The congregation members

Figure 2. The chapel in Flen. Photo from Evangelii Härold.

cannot, however, raise the money to complete the construction on their own. Pethrus therefore urges readers to donate funds to the project. To demonstrate the relevance of the project, he points to various effects that an uncompleted chapel could have.

According to Pethrus, the stopped construction adversely affects the movement's 'spiritual work' and its economic credibility. Regarding the spiritual work, Pethrus writes (among other things):

> The case of Flen will be a welcome topic of conversation and oppositional argument in the mouths of those who wish defeat upon the free work [the Pentecostal movement's activities]. Opponents of this wonderful work of God have often used less effective arguments than this might be, when wishing to prove that Pentecostals are unreliable and that their work is in decline. (EH 1936-06-04:462).

According to Pethrus's argument, the chapel in Flen, in contrast to the expanding Philadelphia Church, symbolises decline. The author assumes that a Christian faith that is real and relevant leads to concrete action. Lack of success in the work thus seems to imply, or at least could be interpreted by others as implying, that the group's or the movement's views on God and life were not true. This line of reasoning is not only ascribed to the opponents of the movement, but also to those who 'are close to the movement'. Such a negative sign could also, according to Pethrus, demoralise the congregation in Flen and the entire movement (EH 1936-06-04:462).

Just as the texts about the Philadelphia Church linked economic issues to the meeting-hall, making it a positive symbol, this text links economic limitations with the unfinished construction project, also making it a symbol, but a negative one.

> A failure to complete the chapel in Flen would, with regard to the Free Church's economic credibility, have the same effect that a rejected bill of exchange would have on a businessman's reputation. The best and most detailed explanations, and decades of faithful work, may not suffice to erase the impact of such an event. (EH 1936-06-04:462).

In the text the chapel is a symbol of a weak credit rating, and is thus a sign for banks and other credit institutions.

The idea of supernatural intervention is, in Pethrus's text, not related to the financial aspects of the problem. In this, a difference can be discerned between how the anniversary publication / annual reports and Pethrus's article respectively discuss finances and buildings. Instead of discussing the failure in relation to (the absence) of God's blessing, he writes about the movement's reputation in the banking world, a reputation that was at stake because of a stranded building project (EH 1936-06-04:461–462).

More than a shell

Did the buildings have no other function than, as the architect Lindahl (1955) writes, to serve as a 'simple and functional shell'? To sum up, one should note that the agents charged the buildings symbolically. In the case of the Philadelphia Church the symbolism was related to the themes of an active and true God, a diligent congregation, economic strength, and a positive image in media. This symbolism was already linked to the church during its construction, but similar links were made when the building was taken into use (annual reports for 1930, 1936; Trettioårshögtiden, 1940). The chapel in Flen is also given symbolic meaning, but unlike the

Philadelphia Church, it is about failure in relation to the work and fund-raising.

Who is the intended recipient of this symbolism? Although the texts on which the story draws are primarily directed at the movement's members, they are also written in relation to other existing stories or pictures of the Philadelphia Church, stories that do not necessarily come from the congregation. Sometimes those 'narrators' are made visible, though most often in general terms such as 'human reason'. Many times it is necessary to read between the lines to discern them.

One 'group' that occurs in the story, and which the church's leaders likely had in mind, is those Christians who did not believe that the Pentecostal movement was from God, and who in some cases therefore opposed the movement. The Philadelphia Church and the congregation's growing membership in general are used to prove to this group that the achievements of the Philadelphia movement were only possible with the help of God, and that the opponents are therefore wrong. Given that the explicit purpose of all the congregation's work is to reach new people with the group's message, it is likely that non-Christians as well were intended addressees of what the church was communicating. To them the church should testify to a living and powerful God.

Intellectuals such as journalists, doctors, and academics might also be possible recipients. Throughout the congregation's history a great deal of criticism had appeared in the press, which also is emphasized in the story. Articles, letters to the editor, opinion pieces, and dissertations described the Pentecostal movement as something sickly and intellectually deficient that did not belong in the modern age (Nyberg Oskarsson 2007:60–62). The congregation leaders' account of the Philadelphia Church as the largest assembly hall, and thus a product of diligence and financial capacity, can be interpreted as a counter-narrative to the intellectuals' descriptions. By creating a story in relation to such 'groups' they form a group identity – a 'we' arises in relation to 'the others'.

When it opened, the church was Sweden's largest assembly hall, which was something that the church leaders emphasized along with its cost of construction. The building's size and cost also indicated a desire to demonstrate presence and power, a position of power sought not only with regard to other congregations and denominations, but also society at large. During the 1920s other agents also marked their presence in Stockholm. Seven years before the Philadelphia Church was taken into use, the City Hall of Stockholm was inaugurated, and in 1926 the Swedish Trade Union Confederation (LO) purchased the property that came to be called the LO-castle (LO-borgen).

The conclusion is that the Philadelphia Church not only served as an outer shell, but was ascribed meaning as early as during its construction. Hence it became part of the group's official story and thereby helped form the group identity. It should also be noted that the symbolism was primarily linked not to the architectural design and trimmings but to the building's size, cost, and 'supernatural origin'. The form/architecture is not crucial in Philadelphia's story. This can be compared with the importance of form/architecture in relation to the mosque discussed in Fridolfsson and Elander's chapter in this volume.

Epilogue

What do the Pentecostal churches symbolize today? In the spring of 2011, 75 years after Pethrus's article on the chapel in Flen, the Pentecostal congregation sold the building. The buyer is a Muslim congregation that will use the premises as a mosque. According to an interview in the newspaper *Dagen* with pastor Martin Björnler, the sale was preceded by discussions within the congregation about what uses of the church that would be acceptable. One factor that spoke against allowing the church to be used as a mosque was the conflicts that, in an international perspective, exist between Muslims and Christians. Björnler relates the decision to Jesus' example and message:

> What would Jesus have done? I find it hard to think that he would have closed the door; the message of love must reason-ably also apply to Muslims. We are trying to build good rela-tions with everyone and eventually I think that this could lead to something better than if we had said no. (*Dagen.se*, 2011)

Perhaps today the church sold in Flen can be said to symbolize love for one's neighbour, from the congregation's perspective. The question is whether it symbolizes something more. What does the building say about blessing and growth, or for that matter about the position of Islam? These questions are not answered in the article cited above.

References

The Philadelphia Church's archive
Annual report 1930, 1936.

Periodicals and newspapers

Dagen.se [The Day – Swedish daily on Christian foundation], 2011-05-10, Gammal pingstkyrka blir moské [Old Pentecostal church becomes mosque]. http://www.dagen.se/dagen/article.aspx?id=259762, access 2011-07-27.

Evangelii Härold (EH) [The Gospel Herald], Stockholm 1930-10-30, s. 743–744, Tempelinvigningen [The temple inauguration].
— 1936-06-04, s. 462 Kapellbygget i Flen. En förtroendesak för hela svenska pingstväckelsen [The chapel Construction in Flen. A matter of credibility for the entire Swedish Pentecostal revival].

Folkets Dagblad Politiken, Stockholm 1926-09-11, De fattigas palats [The poor people's palace].

Social-Demokraten, Stockholm 1927-09-30, Filadelfiabyggnaden på Rörstrand Sveriges näst största kyrka [The Philadelphia building at Rörstrand, Sweden's second largest church].

Stockholms-Tidningen, Stockholm 1926-09-10, På tapeten: Stockholms största kyrka [In the news: Stockholm's largest church].
— 1930-11-01, I Filadelfias väldiga sal [In Philadelphia's vast hall].

Svenska Dagbladet, Stockholm 1930-11-01, En originell kyrkobyggnad [An unusual church building].

Literature

Anderson, A. (2006). The Pentecostal and Charismatic movements. In McLeod, H. (ed.), *The Cambridge History of Christianity. Vol. 9, World Christianities c. 1914–c. 2000.* Cambridge: Cambridge University Press.

Bergmann, S. (ed.) (2009). *Theology in built environments: Exploring religion, architecture, and design.* New Brunswick: Transaction Publ.

Brodd, S-E. (2001). Hörsal och mötesplats [Auditorium and meeting place]. In Bergman och Brodd (ed.), *Ett mångtydigt*

rum [An ambiguous room].
Skellefteå: Norma.

Brunner, J. (2002). *Making stories.*
Cambridge: Harvard University
Press.

Cresswell, T. (2004). Place: A short
introduction. Malden, MA:
Blackwell Pub..

Eakin, P. J. (1999). *How Our Lives
Become Stories: Making Selves.*
Ithaga: Cornell University Press.

Hellspong, M. (1991). *Korset, fanan
och fotbollen* [The cross, the flag
and the football]. Stockholm:
Carlsson.

Junggren, H. (1992). *Hyddor och
helgedomar i huvudstaden* [Huts
and shrines in the capital].
Stockholm: Stockholms stad.

Karlsson, L. (2009). *Arbetarrörelsen,
Folkets Hus och offentligheten
i Bromölla 1905–1960* [The
Labour Movement, the People's
House, and the public sphere
in Bromölla 1905–1960]. Diss.
Växjö: Växjö universitet, 2009.
Växjö.

Kennerberg, O. (1996). *Innanför
eller utanför: en studie av för-
samlingstukten i nio svenska
frikyrkoförsamlingar* = [Inside
or outside: A study of church
discipline in nine Swedish free
churches]. Diss. Uppsala: Univ.
Örebro.

Kieckhefer, R. (2004). *Theology in
stone: Church architecture from
Byzantium to Berkeley.* Oxford:
Oxford University Press.

Kilde, J.H. (2008). *Sacred power,
sacred space: An introduction to
Christian architecture and worship.*
Oxford: Oxford University Press.

Kong, L. (2001). Mapping 'new'
geographies of religion: poli-

tics and poetics in modernity.
Progress in Human Geography 25,2,
211–233.

Lindahl (1955). *Högkyrkligt,
lågkyrkligt, frikyrkligt i svensk
arkitektur 1800–1950* [High
church, low church and free
church in Swedish architecture].
Stockholm: Diakonistyrelsens
bokförlag.

Nyberg Oskarsson, G. (2007). Mer
än 340 församlingar ordnade
under tio år [More than 340 congregations founded during ten
years]. In Alvarsson, J.-Å. (ed.),
*Pingströrelsen. D. 1, Händelser
och utveckling under 1900-talet*
[The Pentecostal movement (in
Sweden). Part 1, Events and
developments during the 20th
century]. Örebro: Libris.

Nylund, K. (2007). De religiösa
samfundens betydelse [The
significance of the religious com-
munities]. In Nylund, K. (ed.)
*Periferin i centrum: gränsöver-
skridande praktiker i Stockholms
offentliga rum* [Periphery in the
centre: Cross-boundary practices
in Stockholm's public spaces].
Göteborg: Daidalos.

Ricoeur, P. (1981). Narrative Time.
In Mitchell, W.J.T. (ed.) *On
Narrative.* Chicago: Univ. of
Chicago press.

Ritivoi, A. (2005). S.v. 'Identity and
Narrative'. In Herman, D., Jahn,
M. & Ryan, M. (ed.). *Routledge
encyclopedia of narrative theory.*
London: Routledge.

Robertson (2005). S.v. 'Sociology and Narrative'. In Herman, D., Jahn, M. & Ryan, M. (ed.). *Routledge encyclopedia of narrative theory*. London: Routledge.

Rüsen, J. (2008). *History. Narration, Interpretation, Orientation.* Oxford: Berghahn Books.

Sahlberg, C. (1977). *Pingströrelsen och tidningen Dagen: från sekt till kristet samhälle 1907–63* [The pentecostal movement and the newspaper Dagen: From sect to Christian society, 1907–63]. Diss. Uppsala: Univ.

Schnell, J-B. (1999). Folkrörelsernas byggnader [The buildings of the People's Movement]. In Riksantikvarieämbetet [The Swedish National Heritage Board] *Svenska hus: landsbygdens arkitektur, från bondesamhälle till industrialism* [Swedish houses: rural architecture, from peasant society to industrialism]. Stockholm: Carlsson i samarbete med Riksantikvarieämbetet och Sveriges radio.

Straub, J. (2005). 'Telling Stories, Making History: Toward a Narrative Psychology of the Historical Construction of Meaning'. In Straub, J. (ed.), *Narration, Identity, and Historical Consciousness*. New York: Berghahn Books.

Söderholm, G. E. (1930). *Tjugu år under Guds trofasthet: Filadelfiaförsamlingens i Stockholm tjuguårsberättelse åren 1910–1930: På församlingens uppdrag avfattad* [Twenty years in God's faithfulness: Philadelphia Church in Stockholm's twenty-year Annual Report 1910–1930: Written on the mandate of the Church]. Stockholm: Filadelfia.

Trettioårshögtiden: tal, hållna vid Filadelfiaförsamlingens i Stockholm jubileumsmöten den 30 aug.–2 sept. 1940 (1940) [The thirtieth anniversary: speech, held at the Philadelphia Church in Stockholm, anniversary meetings Aug. 30–Sept 2. 1940]. Stockholm: Filadelfia

Troeltsch, Ernst (1992). *The social teaching of the Christian churches.* Louisville, Ky.: Westminster/ John Knox Press

Wiklund, M. (2006). *I det modernas landskap: historisk orientering och kritiska berättelser om det moderna Sverige mellan 1960 och 1990* [Inside the landscape of modernity: Historical orientation and critical accounts on modern Sweden between 1960 and 1990]. Diss. Lund: Lunds universitet.

Place and Religion
Swedish Muslim Identity Formation

Charlotte Fridolfsson & Ingemar Elander

Introduction[1]

Migration is one, though not the only reason for the alleged post-secular turn in western societies. Many immigrants find religion to be an important marker of identity in new surroundings, and seek out spaces and places to share and express their faith together with fellow believers (Sjödin 2012; de Haardt 2010; Kinnvall & Nesbitt-Larking 2010; Ley 2008). However, depending on the contextual circumstances, expressions of faith among migrants may manifest in different ways at the individual level. According to Orlando Mella (1996) one way is to adapt one's religious culture to the new country, another is for the group to consolidate and isolate itself, and a third is to develop a fundamentalist counterculture.

Sometimes adaptation to the new society may even result in secularisation, as has been the case, for example, among Chilean immigrants in Sweden since 1973 (Nordin 2004: 146). As described

1   The chapter draws largely on research pursued within the context of FACIT – Faith-Based Organizations and Exclusion in European Cities – a European research project funded by the European Commission's Seventh Framework Programme. A detailed presentation of the research framework, methods, and sources is provided in two reports (Elander & Fridolfsson 2011; Dierckx et al. 2009). Based on a common research agenda, researchers from seven European countries investigated the present role of faith-based organizations (FBOs) in tackling different forms of social exclusion in urban contexts. A slightly different version of the chapter was earlier published as Fridolfsson, Charlotte & Elander, Ingemar (2012) Faith and place: constructing Muslim identity in a secular Lutheran society. *Cultural Geographies* 20(3): 319-337; first published on October 25, 2012. Available online: DOI: 10.1177/1474474012464024.

by a young male immigrant who escaped from Bosnia with his family and came to a Swedish town in 1992, the approach one takes to religion in a new country is strongly related to one's previous experience:

> There are Muslims from many countries here. Many newly established groups. What you bring with you from your homeland and your culture influences how you practise your religion. (*Nerikes Allehanda* 2011)

The quotation nicely corresponds to the argument presented by Bäckström and Davie (2011: 170), referring to David Martin's work, that the 'interactions of the religious and secular should [...] be seen in the long-term [...] they work themselves out differently in different places [...] the shorthand of 'God is back' does not, indeed cannot, do justice to this urgent and complex agenda.'

Immigrants with Islamic faith arriving in Sweden encounter something of a paradox: a strongly secularised society with a strong Lutheran heritage, as physically symbolised by the more than 3 500 Church of Sweden buildings spread throughout the country. In addition there are thousands of small free-church buildings used in the same manner for mass, prayer, baptisms, weddings, funerals, or other religious ceremonies – signposts of place identity in a seemingly religious landscape. Although Sweden is sometimes considered one of the least religious societies in the world (Norris & Inglehart 2004: 90; Gallup 2009), about 70% of Swedish citizens are nevertheless members of the Church of Sweden. Today, both joining and leaving the Church requires a deliberate action, and most Swedes currently alive became members before 2000; they are members by tradition, and do not actively practise Christianity.

Although Church membership and attendance are declining in Sweden, as in other European countries, shifting post-war values and belief systems, commonly conceptualised as modernisation and secularisation, have made people rediscover religion, though in the more pluralistic and less institutional form of 'patchwork religion'; in other words, religion is becoming more 'invisible', yet remains 'a steady part of people's lives' (Pickel & Müller 2009: 8). In addition, religion is not just a matter of evangelisation, saving people's souls, or individual and invisible beliefs, it can also be about meeting people's needs in a fundamentally social sense: helping poor people find shelter, defending their legal rights, or simply helping them to survive. Thus, we agree with McLennan (2010: 41–62) that 'post-secular' is a very crude term that covers a broad spectrum of intellectual stances, and certainly does not exclude the simultaneous presence of secular as well as post-secular tendencies in different real-world contexts.

About one percent of Church of Sweden members relinquish their membership every year, whereas Muslim congregations and the Catholic and Christian Orthodox Churches are increasing their memberships. The free churches face declining membership and are trying to handle this through, among other things, mergers between congregations (*Dagens Nyheter* 2011a; Svenska Kyrkan 2011). Despite these and other signs of secularism in Swedish society, Muslim immigrants arrive in a landscape of Christian landmarks, which has very few visible physical spaces linked to Muslim identity. Imams and other Muslim leaders try to find financial resources and suitable places to build mosques, or at least premises that can serve as provisional spots for ceremonies and worship.

The aim of this chapter is to assess the religious and cultural significance that Muslims in Sweden ascribe to the presence of a mosque – its proximity, visibility, and utility – when it comes to forming a Swedish Muslim identity. What meanings in terms of place and identity are connected to the mosques, the land on which are (or will be) built, and the discourses on Muslim identity as expressed by Muslims in Sweden? How is a Swedish Muslim identity constructed and negotiated in surroundings characterised by mixed attitudes towards Muslim immigrants and Islam as such? Drawing upon the conceptual distinction between physical, mental, and social space, we describe the places where the mosques are built in terms of visibility and proximity for Muslims in Sweden, draw attention to the various social activities organised by the mosques, discuss their social utility, and ascertain whether they are predominantly religious and proselytising, or address a broader audience and thus indicate an intention to develop a Swedish Muslim identity.

The Swedish Context

Officially starting with the King Olof Skötkonung's baptism around year 1000, Sweden has a millennium-long Christian tradition. In Swedish elementary schools pupils are taught that the French Benedictine monk Ansgar first preached the Christian gospel in 829 AD to the pagan Vikings residing in the area now called Sweden. Pagan sacrifices were performed alongside Christian ceremonies for a long time, but in 1210 Erik Knutsson became the first king to be crowned by a Christian bishop. The event also marked the union between Church and State, an alliance that would last until the year 2000. This officially sanctioned story suggests a smooth and slow conversion from the Aesir faith to Christianity. However it excludes possible power struggles between different faiths and other interpretations of Sweden's religious past, as hinted at, for example, by the arrival of a Muslim follower at the Viking trading centre of Birka 150 years before the arrival of Ansgar (Gardell 2010: 6).

In the 1530s, King Gustav Vasa joined the reformation and proclaimed Sweden an evangelical kingdom. For a long time thereafter, confessing to the evangelical faith was compulsory in Sweden. Foreigners who wished to practise another faith, or even another form of Christianity, were required to do so behind closed doors. During the 18th and 19th centuries, the less hierarchically organised low church and free church movements began paving the way for freedom of religion in Sweden, which, however, was not formally established until 1951.

Far into the 20th century Sweden was considered culturally, ethnically, and religiously homogeneous, although there has also been considerable diversity in the past. Besides the indigenous Sami population, small populations of Roma, Tornedal, and Jewish minorities have lived in Sweden for centuries. From time to time there have also been substantial influxes of entrepreneurial immigrants from Germany, Scotland, Belgium, and other countries. After World War II, multiple waves of refugees, as well as labour migrants from Greece, the Baltic countries, Turkey, and former Yugoslavia, made substantial contributions to the Sweden's flourishing industry and expanding public welfare apparatus.

Since the 1990s Sweden has received more refugees and asylum seekers than any other European country relative to the size of its

own population (Migrationsverket 2010). Moreover, the number
of second- and third-generation immigrants is steadily increasing,
thus making 'Swedish Muslims', or 'Muslims in Sweden', the most
adequate terms for the purpose of this chapter. More than 300,000
first-generation immigrants come from Muslim dominated countries, most originating from Iraq (100,000), Turkey (70,000),
and Bosnia (70,000) (Utbildningsradion 2011). During 2013 the
largest immigrant groups came from Syria and Somalia (Statistiska
Centralbyrån 2014). How many of the immigrants are practicing
Muslims we do not know, as Swedish law does not allow registra-
tion of people by religion and language. Estimates vary between
110,000 and 150,000 practising Muslims in Sweden, although the
number of immigrants originating from countries with a dominating Muslim country is larger (Larsson & Sander 2008; Larsson
2014).

In contrast to Christian churches and congregations Muslim
communities are not formalized in terms of administrative structures and established leadership, there is no outstanding 'pope',
'vicar' or 'patriarch' to ask for the correct interpretation of the
gospel. There are six different Islamic umbrella organisations
eligible for support by the Swedish Commission for Government
Support to Faith Communities [Nämnden för Statligt Stöd till
Trossamfund, SST] (SST 2014). Apart from these organisations
there are also a number of non-registered congregations for
Muslims (Larsson 2014:58–69). A rough estimation based on
reports to SST says that the number of imams in Swedish Muslim
organisations amounts to more than 250 (Larsson 2014: 117–120),
and a survey carried out in spring 2013 found 140 Swedish based
Muslim internet sites (Andersson 2013:64–172). The Muslim
adult education association Ibn Rushd was explicitly modelled
on the Swedish tradition of adult education (*folkbildning*), and is
recognised as one of ten adult education associations receiving
public funding (more about Ibn Rushd below). Having the above
figures and facts in mind Islam in Sweden obviously includes a
great diversity of orientations, interpretations and conflicts, so far
largely neglected in research (Larsson 2014: 116).

Faith and Three Dimensions of Space

Beaumont (2010: 3) writes: 'it is in the urban that the shift from secular to post-secular in terms of public space, building use, governance and civil society is most intensively observed and experienced'. Referring to Goh (2003) he also states that cities 'become 'hot spots' or sites for split loyalties and demands, and the negotiation of multiple identities which need to include both religious and secular dimensions' (Beaumont 2010: 9). In a broader perspective there are 'sacred cities' which are religious centres for believers all over the world, like Mecca for Muslims, Bodhgaya for Buddhists, Varanasi for Hindus, and the Vatican for Catholics, as well as Jerusalem, the right to which three monotheistic religions, Christianity, Islam, and Judaism, all claim to find support in their respective holy books (Andersson 2011; Sheldrake 2001: 5). Apart from these particular cities, most towns and cities contain buildings and other sacred places with which at least believers in the official or majority religion can identify and where they can find a haven for worship and celebration. As stated by Yi-Fu Tuan in his classic work *Space and Place* (Tuan 1977: 150):

> Evidence from different cultures suggests that place is specific – tied to a particular cluster of buildings at one location – wherever the people believe it to be not only their home but also the home of their guarding spirits and gods.

However, even in highly secular cities, where few officially religious buildings may be available, the faithful may find places and even 'build their own 'church' out of parks, gyms and auditoriums', as described by Gemma Cruz in the case of female domestic workers, most of them from the Philippines, living and working in Hong Kong (Cruz 2006: 89). The religious, or rather spiritual dimension of place may even appear in somewhat unexpected contexts such as soccer, as illustrated by the text on T-shirts worn by football team supporters: 'Liverpool is my religion/ Anfield is my church/ True believers never walk alone.'[2]

Some theologians inspired by 'the spatial turn' in geography,

2   Attending a game at Anfield Road one is struck by the collectively orchestrated rituals framing the whole event, including the 'exit gospel', 'You'll never walk alone' sung by 30,000–40,000 Liverpool supporters.

anthropology, literary theory, history, and other fields of social science argue that cities themselves are, or at least have the potential
to be sacred spaces/places (de Haardt 2010: 170). This debate more
or less relates to and reflects Lefebvre's distinction between 'perceived, conceived and lived moments', which are 'three aspects of
a conceptual triad' equated with 'spatial practice, representations
of space, and spaces of representation' (Knott 2010: 24). Knott
applies this conceptual triad to a discussion of the city, whereas we
here draw a parallel to the mosque. Reference may also be made
to Edward Soja's triad of first space, second space, and third space
(Soja 1996; de Haardt 2010: 170–176). In the context of this chapter these triads are important in the sense that a mosque, whether
a real mosque or a cellar mosque, can also be read through any one
of these three conceptual lenses. As 'spatial practice', a mosque is a
place where Muslim believers more or less regularly go for worship,
ceremonies, and social intercourse. As a 'representation of space' it
is the conceived aspect, the meaning given to the mosque by imams
and other religious and secular elites. Finally, as 'spaces of representation' ('lived space') it signals how mosques 'are experienced
by citizens and migrants, and may be imaginatively constructed or
produced' (*cf.* Knott: 30–31).

Notably, the three dimensions of space identified by Lefebvre
and Soja, can be distinguished from one another only in theory; in
real life they 'exist at the same time and are intertwined in a tria-
lectic relation' (de Haardt 2010: 174). A simplified way of saying
this is that 'physical, social and mental spaces intersect and overlap'
(Knott 2010: 35; *cf.* Lefebvre 2009: 224–25). Applied to the topic
of this chapter this means that a mosque is a physical building, a
mental construct, and a place for social intercourse (a social hub)
all at the same time.

The location of mosques: proximity and visibility

Most villages, towns, and cities have buildings and places with
which many religious believers can identify and where they can
meet to express and share their faith. However, in a country like
Sweden, where Christianity has been the dominating religion for
centuries, Muslim and other non-Christian immigrants have no
such places with which to identify. This is in striking contrast to the

experience of Christian immigrants, for example Syrian-Orthodox immigrants escaping Turkey and coming to Sweden in the late 20th century (Deniz 2001). Although they did not find churches especially designed for their interpretation of the Christian gospel, Syrian-Orthodox immigrants are at least familiar with the general appearance and function of the old church buildings in Sweden. Moreover, when they wished to build their own church premises, while they may have met with some opposition, they nevertheless could find enough local support to succeed. One illustrative example is the case of the Syrian-Orthodox Church near the district of Varberga in Örebro. Despite some local protests, in 1990 the local government approved the proposal, including the proposed site, with little delay (Johansson & Uddin 1994).

A few years later, the Islamic Cultural Centre in Örebro faced tougher resistance, also from some local Christian free-church leaders, when it wanted to build a provisional mosque in the form of a community hall (*i.e.* not a 'real' mosque with a minaret) close to the district of Vivalla in Örebro (Johansson & Uddin 1994). It was not until 2010, after a period of being housed in cramped quarters in the city centre, that the Islamic Centre took over a building constructed by the Jehovah's Witnesses. It is located adjacent to the district of Vivalla, which is inhabited by people with a wide variety of national, ethnic, cultural, and religious backgrounds. In both cases, the adherents of the two religions found a physical space for themselves (though in the Muslim case not a full-fledged mosque) that gave them room for worship and ceremonies, as well as for social activities like language courses and choirs; or that could serve as a social meeting place for children, housewives, the unemployed, etc., to which we shall return below.

Most Swedish mosques are located in basements of residential buildings in multi-family housing areas or former industrial locations ('cellar mosques' or 'basement mosques'). This is an important difference in relation to the Christian locations, as stated by Abd al Haqq Kielan, imam and secretary of the Swedish Islamic Academy:

It is important to be able to move up from the lower level and into a real mosque. As long as we are in a basement, we do not really exist. It is important to leave the basement, partly

for practical reasons, because down there it is crowded, poorly
ventilated and has bad lighting, but also for status reasons. A
visible mosque wins prestige and means a lot for integration.
Muslims would then feel that we are also part of society and
it would be easier to socialise on equal terms. (as quoted in
Larsson and Sander 2010: 124–125)

Another imam says: 'Even if there is a local premises, one wants to
visit a real mosque' (Karahaki 2009).

The difference between a provisional and a real mosque could
be illustrated by the case of Skärholmen, a multicultural suburb of
Stockholm. The present mosque is located in an office building in
the commercial centre of the district. With an area of 300 square
metres, it is far from adequate to welcome the many Muslim believers in the area, as compared to the 3000 square metres of the new
mosque that is planned to be finished in 2014: 'This is something
I have longed for for 20 years [...] there should be no doubt what
kind of building it is' says Fikret Tümtürk, chairman of Skärholmen
Islamic Association. Plans to decorate the mosque in the traditional
Swedish Falun-red colour in an attempt to emphasise the Swedish-
Muslim brand were dismissed, however, as going too far (*Dagens
Nyheter* 2011b). The local parish of the Church of Sweden publicly
supports the building of a mosque in the commercial centre, and
one of the priests says:

> Our congregation thinks that it would be good to have a cen-
> trally located mosque here. We are positive to the idea of a
> mosque that looks like a mosque. I think that the politicians
> have listened a little bit extra to the Christian Churches when
> it comes to this. (Billinger 2009)

Inter-religious co-operation is becoming more institutionalised,
and hence is also a factor determining the physical location of Islam
in Sweden. One example is the Christian-Muslim Social Service
Centre in Nacka, Stockholm. The Well [Källan], as it is named,
a collaboration between Stockholm City Mission, the Church of
Sweden parish, The Muslim Association, and St Conrad's Catholic
Church, offers counselling and advice on practical matters related
to public authorities and other organisations. A social worker and a

deacon work at the support centre, and consultations are also available with a priest from Church of Sweden or the Catholic Church, or with an imam. There is also a room for prayer that is open to anyone. The Well is not a public authority, so visitors may remain anonymous (Markovits 2009). In a similar vein, joint activities have been organised between the Christian and Muslim faith communities in Rosengård (Malmö), for example joint celebration of Midsummer Eve and the Swedish National Day (*Dagen* 24 June 2010). The invitation illustrated by a painting of the Malmö Mosque, was published in the Church of Sweden parish newsletter (Västra Skrävlinge Församling 2010).

One spectacular exception to the many basement mosques is the conspicuous Stockholm Mosque in the very centre of the Stockholm neighbourhood of Södermalm. Zayed bin Sultan Al Nahyan's Mosque (Swedish: *Zaid Ben Sultan Al Nahayans moské*, Arabic: جامع زايد بن سلطان آل [نهيان], commonly known as the Stockholm Mosque (*Stockholms moské*) or the Stockholm Grand Mosque (*Stockholms stora moské*), is the largest mosque in Sweden. Inaugurated in 2000, the Stockholm Mosque is administered by the Islamic Association in Stockholm. In March 1995, after consulting Islamic leaders, the city council of Stockholm decided to convert the old electric power station Katarinastationen (*Katarina Station*) into a mosque.

ISLAMIC CENTER
INBJUDAN

Välkomna att fira
Sverige nationaldag
hos oss på Islamic Center
söndagen den 6 juni , kl 11.00

Figure 1. Invitation of the Islamic centre to the church of Sweden parish in Västra Skrävlinge, Skåne (Scania).

The building, designed by Art Nouveau architect Ferdinand Boberg and completed in 1903, was influenced by 'Moorish' Islamic architecture. Boberg was inspired after a visit to Morocco and designed the building to be turned toward Mecca and to have high, arched windows (Stockholms Moské 2010). Easily reached by a well-connected subway system, the mosque is first and foremost a house of prayer for the Muslims living in the Stockholm area, but is also important to other Muslims in Sweden, as it hosts annual elections and meetings of the national umbrella organisation, Muslim Council of Sweden, at which 3,000 members participate.

Apart from being an important node for Muslims not only in Stockholm but all over Sweden, the Stockholm Mosque also functions as a community centre and is increasingly becoming a centre not only for worship and social intercourse, but also for developing contacts with non-Muslims:

> This is a very special mosque, because it is so centrally located. There are many advantages of a central location [...] This environment is different. [...] We have changed some things, but the walls and ceilings are the same. It was built in 1905, a hundred years ago. This particular mosque is special. Tourists come here to look at it from France and Italy. It has become popular in Stockholm. Some people thought there might be problems, but instead it has enriched the area. (Kharraki, 2009)

The other two major cities in Sweden, Malmö and Göteborg, also have big mosques with similar functions as the one in Stockholm, though they are not as centrally located, and the buildings are not as traditional. The Islamic Centre Mosque in Malmö is located close to the large, multi-ethnic neighbourhood of Rosengård, and the major mosque in Göteborg is located in Hisingen, an area with a number of large multi-ethnic housing estates. In addition, basement mosques, and other provisional mosques are also quite frequent in these kinds of neighbourhoods. There are also physically visible, 'real' mosques in Uppsala, Umeå, and other cities.

Thus, the availability, proximity, and visibility of sacred places for prayer and other faith ceremonies among Islamic believers in Sweden is gradually improving. Even in smaller towns, mosques are becoming more common. For example, in the municipality of Flen, an old Pentecostal church building was recently sold to the Alhouda Muslim Centre.[3] Although there are different opinions on the mat-

---

3   Protests from congregation members were countered by the pastor of the local Christian congregation: 'What would Jesus have done? I can't believe that he would have closed the door; obviously the message of love must also pertain to

Figure 2. The Stockholm mosque. Photo: Gabriel Ehrnst Grundin, 7 January 2006.

ter among Christian believers, several Christian church officials openly welcome the building of mosques, and few seem to oppose it.

Imaging Swedish Muslim identity

There is no single Swedish Muslim identity that encompasses all currents of Muslim faith in Sweden. Neither is it solely a product of discourses produced by the Muslim community, as it is embedded in a hegemonic non-Muslim discourse about Muslims in Sweden, which in turn has a strong influence upon Swedish Muslim identity.[4] A Muslim adult education association, Ibn Rushd, was founded in 2007, and is one of ten adult education associations recognised by the Council of Adult Education in Sweden.[5] A Muslim adult

---

Muslims. We try to build good relations with everyone, and in the long run I believe this will lead to something better than if we had said no' (*Dagen* 10 May 2011).

4   It is hegemonic precisely because of the obligatory reference to it (Fridolfsson 2010).

5   Named after the Muslim scientist/philosopher based in Cordoba, Spain, during the 12th Century. The name is derived from the words 'Ibn' meaning son and 'Rushd' meaning reason (Ibn Rushd 2011).

education association, Ibn Rushd, was founded in 2007, and is one of ten adult education associations recognised by the Council of Adult Education. This association institutionally links the Swedish Muslim community to the Swedish corporatist tradition with strong ties between civil society and popular movements, on the one hand, and the State, on the other. A current project at Ibn Rushd, 'The promotion of Islamic Peace Culture', targets Muslim youth across the country, training them to become peace activists:

> The long-term aim is to combat islamophobia (fear and ani- mosity towards Islam, mainly among people in the West) and westphobia (fear and animosity towards the West, mainly among Muslims). Within the framework of the project a foundation has been laid for a Muslim peace movement. (Ibn Rushd 2011)

The very existence of the programme articulates an intention to eradicate prejudice and it is arguably a means for constructing a Swedish Muslim identity by emphasising the emergence of a new Muslim peace movement. However, in doing so, the idea of an existing non-peaceful Muslim movement is hereby also implied and recognised as valid. In Althusserian terms (Althusser 1970), this self-reference is an example of how ideology produces the subject through interpellation.

Mosques and other Islamic centres can also offer advice and assistance on matters of great diplomatic concern. In connection with republication of the Mohammed caricatures in a local Swedish daily newspaper, representatives of the Stockholm Mosque met with the Prime Minister and other government officials. According to Abdallah Salah, 'we contributed to limiting the problem, so that it would not become the same as in Denmark', referring to racist, islamophobic, anti-immigrant flavoured social unrest that arose in the wake of a similar publication there.[6]

6   The so-called Cartoon Crisis in Denmark began on 30 September 2005 when the newspaper *Jyllands Posten* published a blasphemous picture of Mohammed. For the following debates and conflicts, which are intimately related to the cul- ture and ideology of 'Danishness' (*danskhet*) see Bachora, Elander & Fridolfsson (2011: 8–9 and passim), Kahn (2009), and Kinnvall & Larking 2010).

Fredrik Reinfeldt [the Prime Minister] asked us: "What can we do to avoid things becoming the same as in Denmark?" We told him: "You don't need to do anything; we have already sent press releases to all the international news media." International media contacted the Mosque to get statements on the developments, but the Mosque did not want to inflate the issue. "This is Sweden, this is a local problem, we can handle it here and we are capable of solving this", was our message to the journalists. (Salah 2009a)

Abdul Rashid Mohamed, imam, teacher of the subject of Islam, and a representative of the Islamic Association in Göteborg, explains how Islamic organisations viewed their role in trying to develop an Islamic identity in a new social and religious context (Mohamed 2009):[7]

It is difficult to separate what is secular and what is religious within Islamic organisations. Everything is everything. Belief is not separate from everyday life. We are kind of "secular-religious" ['sekulärreligiösa']. We are doing everything; we are active in Islamic rituals, Ramadan, solemn celebrations [...] We are pursuing a lot of activities, the Islamic Information Association, the Islamic school.

The mosque as a community centre

Apart from being important spots for worship and celebration, mosques also function as community centres, including outreach activities for non-Muslims:

There is essentially no limit to what kinds of activities that can be carried out at the mosque. The problem is that a mosque is automatically associated with religion. But a mosque is more like a community centre (*Folkets Hus*). Out of the 50–60 activities organised at the mosque each week, a maximum of 10

7   Quoted from an interview with Abdul Rashid Mohamed at Römosseskolan 8 [Römosse School], Gårdsten (Angered), 12 May 2010.

percent have religious content. People want to spend time in the mosque doing other things too; it is a good environment where people feel comfortable. (Salah 2009a)

For example, although the Stockholm Mosque is basically a house of prayer, a number of other cultural and welfare activities have emerged, and now predominate. These activities include marital support sessions, youth activities, female gym classes, and swimming lessons. 'We are part of society. Saving souls is not enough', president of the Islamic Association in Stockholm at that time Abdallah Salah told us in an interview (Salah 2009b). Every day up to eight groups of around 30 people each, predominately teachers with their classes, visit the mosque. It is also frequently visited by politicians and public servants. They have quite friendly relations with the homeless people and/or people with drug problems who hang around the adjacent Medborgarplatsen (literally 'Citizens' Square') and its subway station. During Ramadan people can also stay overnight in the mosque. Its close proximity to the subway also means that Muslim people from other parts of the city, as well as visitors from other parts of Sweden and abroad, can easily reach the Stockholm Mosque. 'Just the location of the mosque in central Stockholm is itself the greatest integration project' (Salah 2009a)' In line with this, the goals for the United Islamic Congregations in Sweden are: 'integrating Muslim people in society', 'helping Muslims to preserve their cultural, social and religious identity', and 'working as a bridge builder between the Swedish authorities and majority population and Muslims' (Kharraki 2009).

The imams and other representatives of mosques whom we have interviewed stress the mosques' preventive measures against social exclusion and poverty in a broader sense. This includes their function as an arena where people can find friendship, connection with others, and a sense of belonging. The Islamic congregations that have been extensively studied use non-religious activities such as sports, adult education, study circles, and other social activities as means to indirectly prevent social exclusion and promote integration (Elander & Fridolfsson 2011: 46–53).

In terms of producing social capital, these policies and actions can be defined as both bonding and bridging (*cf.* Ley 2008). The bonding dimension includes the creation of positive role models and a sense of community. The bridging capital, on the other hand, concerns matters such as language workshops, integration, and networking with the surrounding community. Often activities are both bonding and bridging, such as teaching computer skills, which may help someone keep in touch with people back home, as well as help the same person find a new job in Sweden. Other activities include providing assistance and advocacy for people who for one reason or another have experienced problems in their relations with the public authorities. The Stockholm Mosque provides support on an individual basis and refers people to local government institutions or other statutory, FBO, and NGO organisations when necessary (Salah 2009b).

Conclusion: The Shaping of a Swedish Muslim Identity

Most Muslims in Sweden are first- or second-generation immigrants, though the number of converts with Swedish ethnic background is increasing[8]. This means that the people who gather in the mosques come from very different backgrounds, speak different languages, and bring with them different Islamic customs. For this reason many Swedish Muslim congregations, leaders, and committed individuals are working hard to build a Swedish Muslim identity. To achieve this aim, having a real mosque is of great material and symbolic importance. As illustrated by interviews quoted in this chapter, basement mosques and other provisional mosques are important places where Muslims can meet and practise their faith together. However, 'As long as we are in a basement, we do not really exist' (Abd al Haqq Kielan, imam and secretary of the Swedish Islamic Academy, as quoted in Larsson and Sander 2010: 124–125).

Mosques are important not only as sacred places in a strictly religious sense, they are also social hubs for Muslims, *i.e.* places

8   Due to immigration contacts between people with different beliefs are increasing, implying conversions from Christianity to Islam and vice versa (Interviews with researchers and representatives of Church of Sweden and Muslim Association of Sweden as reported in Swedish daily newspaper *Svenska Dagbladet* (2007).

for creating social capital both in a bonding and a bridging sense.[9] In other words, they are places where a Swedish Muslim identity may be sown and cultivated, as vividly expressed by a leading representative of the Islamic community, who mentions three crucial functions of the Islamic organisations in Sweden (Kharraki 2009):

> The most important goal is integration, to integrate Muslims into Swedish society. The organisation also works to help Muslims keep their identity as Muslims in cultural, religious, and social terms. Third is that the organisation functions as a bridge between the Swedish majority and Muslims [...] One should co-operate, be on speaking terms, and have acceptance. Then there will be understanding, understanding creates dialogue, and dialogue means that we feel like a group. I think Sweden is like a boat on which we are all on board. We should unite to foster peace so that there will be a good livelihood for all of us.

Notably, what is expressed in this quotation is not an unconditional will to integrate Muslims or make them submit to Swedish society; *i.e.* it is not a question of assimilation. Nor is it a will to unconditionally preserve or protect a 'pure' or 'real' Muslim identity, whatever this might be. It is rather a question of mutual accommodation, *i.e.* not merging one's identity as a Muslim with a Swedish national identity, but rather, as one of our spokesmen said, seeking understanding:

> We want to get more understanding from society. For Islam not to be considered an alien religion. That's what complicates the situation for us Muslims. [...] Islam should have a self-evident place here as a religion. If someone wants to become a Muslim then it should be the same as for Christianity or Buddhism; why look at it differently? [...] Freedom of speech is

---

9   As illustrated by Katarina Nylund in a study of local Muslim and Christian congregations, first-generation immigrants commonly find these to be a basis for strengthening their sense of belonging (bonding capital), whereas second-generation immigrants may rather (or also) use their membership in these as a platform for linking themselves to, and participating as citizens in society at large (Nylund 2007, *cf.* Ley 2008).

parallel to religious freedom. One should not oppress religion in the name of freedom of speech. Sweden has become very good at this, but it is still difficult. There is this wall saying 'alien religion'; that is what we find problematic'. (Mohamed 2009)

Here the interviewee refers to a hegemonic discourse in which Islam represents the exception from the Swedish Lutheran norm, where individuals with Muslim faith are accepted, but not Muslims as a collective.

In this emerging interreligious dialogue concerning basic values and identities, mosques, including their provisional forms, are a crucial arena not only for preserving Muslim identity and developing internal religious, ethnic, and cultural bonds, but also for creating bridges to the secular Lutheran society in Sweden, and perhaps also for developing a Swedish Muslim identity. As argued by Kinnvall and Nesbitt-Larking (2010), this may be understood as a process of desecuritisation, *i.e.* removing a previously conflict-ridden issue 'from the realm of existential survival, thus making it easier to resolve through cooperative and/or routine means of problem solving in civil society'. In line with this argument, Hetty Zock (2010:132) reminds us that 'cultural misunderstandings abound, and [...] this goes especially for the conflicts in which religious and identity elements are involved. Therefore, individuals are required to develop strong communicative skills and imaginative, creative capacities in order to be able to deal with diversity'. As illustrated in this chapter, mosques not only function as inward-looking markers of religious faith, but can also be arenas for developing links to both Christian and secular parts of Swedish society.

References

Althusser Louis (1984) *Essays on Ideology*. London: Verso.

Andersson, Ann-Cathrine (2013) *Islam på nätet – ett svenskt cybermuslimskt landskap i förändring* [Islam on the internet – a Swedish cyber-muslim landscape in change] Göteborg: University of Göteborg. http://gupea.ub.gu.se/handle/2077/33616 [Accessed 30 October 2014]

Andersson, Ann-Catrin (2011) *Identity Politics and City Planning: The Case of Jerusalem*. Örebro: Örebro University. [PhD thesis]

Bachora, Larissa, Elander, Ingemar & Fridolfsson, Charlotte (2011) *Faith-based Organisations and Social Exclusion in Denmark*. Leuven/Den Haag: Acco.

Bäckström, Anders & Davie, Grace (2011) 'Welfare and religion in Europe: themes, theories and tensions', in Anders Bäckström, Grace Davie, Ninna Edgardh & Per Pettersson (eds), *Welfare and Religion in 21st Century Europe*, Vol. 2. Farnham: Ashgate.

Beaumont, Justin (2010) 'Transcending the particular in postsecular cities'. pp. 3–18 in Arie L. Molendijk, Justin Beaumont & Christof Jedan (eds) *Exploring the Postsecular. The Religious, the Political and the Urban*. Leiden & Boston: Brill.

Billinger, Kerstin (2009) Interview by Charlotte Fridolfsson. Church of Sweden Parish Skärholmen. [Svenska kyrkan Skärholmens församling] 1 April 2009.

Cruz, Gemma T. (2006) *Into the Deep: A Theological Exploration of the Struggle of Filippina Domestic Workers in Hong Kong*. Nijmegen: Radboud University. [PhD thesis]

Dagen [The Day – Swedish daily on Christian foundation; 17,000 subscribers] (2011) 'Gammal pingstkyrka blir moské' [Old Pentecostal church becomes a mosque] 10 May 2011.

Dagens Nyheter [Swedish daily newspaper] (2011a) Svenska kyrkan krymper snabbare [Church of Sweden shrinks faster] http://www.dn.se/nyheter/sverige/svenska-kyrkan-krymper-snabbare [Accessed 25 February 2011]

Dagens Nyheter [Swedish daily newspaper] (2011b) 'Ny moské i Skärholmen snart verklighet' [New Mosque in Skärholmen Soon a Reality] [Accessed 15 April 2011]

Deniz, Fuat (2001) *En minoritets odyssé. Det assyriska exemplet* [The odyssey of a minority. The Assyrian example] Örebro Studies in Sociology. Örebro: Örebro universitet.

Dierckx, Danielle, Vranken, Jan & Kerstens, Wendy (2009) *Faith-based Organisations and Social Exclusion in European Cities*. Leuven/Den Haag: Acco.

Elander, Ingemar & Fridolfsson, Charlotte (2011) *Faith-based Organisations and Social Exclusion in Sweden*. Leuven/Den Haag: Acco.

Fridolfsson, Charlotte (2010) 'Ett antimanifest för den goda statsvetenskapen' [An anti-manifesto for good political science] *Statsvetenskaplig tidskrift* 112 (4): 399–401.

Fridolfsson, Charlotte & Elander, Ingemar (2012) 'Faith and place: constructing Muslim identity in a secular Lutheran society'. *Cultural Geographies* 20 (3): 319-337. DOI: 10.1177/1474474012464024.

Gallup (2009) What Alabamians and Iranians have in common. [Online] Source. Available from: http://www.gallup.com [Accessed 25 August 2010]

Gardell, Mattias (2010) *Islam och muslimer i Sverige* [Islam and Muslims in Sweden] Stockholm: Arvsfonden.

Haardt, Marike de (2010) 'Making sense of sacred space in the city?' pp. 163-182 in Arie L. Molendijk, Justin Beaumont & Christof Jedan (eds) *Exploring the Postsecular. The Religious, the Political and the Urban*. Leiden & Boston: Brill.

Ibn Rushd (2011) Ibn Rushd Educational Association. [online] Source. Available from: http://www.ibnrushd.se/filer/ibn-rushd_engelska.pdf [Accessed 30 November 2011]

Islamic Centre Center i Malmö (2010) Startpage [Online] Available from: http://www.mosken.se/ [Accessed 5 September 2010]

Johansson, Marcus & Uddin, Thomas (1994) *Frihet och tol-erans. Debatt och konflikt kring lokaliseringen av en syriansk-ortodox kyrka och ett islamiskt kul-turcentrum i Örebro* [Freedom and tolerance. Debate and conflict on the localisation of a Syrian-Orthodox Church and an Islamic Cultural Centre in Örebro]

Report No. 31. Örebro: Örebro University, Centre for Housing and Urban Research.

Kahn, Robert A. (2009) *Flemming Rose, the Danish Cartoon Controversy, and the New European Freedom of Speech*. Legal Studies Research Paper Series No. 09-24. Minnesota: University of St. Thomas, School of Law.

Kharraki, Mostafa (2009) Interview by Charlotte Fridolfsson. The United Islamic Congregations in Sweden, Stockholm, 29 January 2009.

Kinnvall, Catarina & Nesbitt-Larking, Paul (2010) 'The political psychology of (de) securitization: place-making strategies in Denmark, Sweden, and Canada'. *Environment and Planning D: Society and Space* 28 (6): 1051-1070.

Knott, Kim (2010) 'Cutting through the postsecular city: A spatial interrogation'. pp. 19-40 in Arie L. Molendijk, Justin Beaumont & Christof Jedan (eds) *Exploring the Postsecular. The Religious, the Political and the Urban*. Leiden & Boston: Brill.

Larsson, Göran (2014) *Islam och muslimer i Sverige - en kunskapsö-versikt* [Islam and Muslims in Sweden - a survey of knowledge] SST:s skriftserie 4 [The Swedish Commission for Government Support to Faith Communities Report 4]

Larsson, Göran & Åke Sander (2008) *Islam and Muslims in Sweden: Integration or Fragmentation?: A Contextual Study*. Berlin and Münster: Lit-Verlag.

Larsson, Göran & Sander, Åke (2010) 'From cellar to dome and minaret', pp. 123–128 in Helena Holgersson, Catharina Thörn, Håkan Thörn & Mattias Wahlström (eds) *(Re)searching Gothenburg*. Göteborg: Glänta Produktion.

Lefebvre, Henri (2009) 'Space and the state' (1978). pp. 223–253 in Neil Brenner and Stuart Elden (eds): *State, Space, World: Selected Essays. Henri Lefebvre, Selected Essays*. Minneapolis and London: University of Minnesota Press.

Ley, David (2008) 'The immigrant church as an urban service hub'. *Urban Studies* 45 (10): 2057–2074.

Markovits, Marika (2009) Interview by Charlotte Fridolfsson, Stockholms stadsmission [Stockholm City Mission], 15 April 2009.

McLennan, Gregor (2010) 'Spaces of postsecularism'. pp. 41–62 in Arie L. Molendijk, Justin Beaumont & Christof Jedan (eds) *Exploring the Postsecular. The Religious, the Political and the Urban*. Leiden & Boston: Brill.

Mella, Orlando (1996) *Searching for the Sacred. A Comparative Study of Popular Religiosity among Refugees in Sweden*. Stockholm: CEIFO Publications.

Migrationsverket [The Migration Board] (2010) *Migration 2000–2010*. Rapport 2010: 2. [Online] Available from:http:// www.migrationsverket.se/info/ start_en.html [Accessed 28 September 2010]

Mohamed, Abdul Rashid (2009) Interview. Islamiska förbundet i Göteborg [The Islamic Association in Göteborg], Angered, 12 May 2009.

Nerikes Allehanda [Swedish daily newspaper] (2011) 'Gamla samfund bildar ny kyrka' [Old congregations make a new church] 4 June 2011, section 1, page 10.

Nordin, Magdalena (2004) *Religiositet bland migranter: Sverige-chilenares förhållande till religion och samfund* [Religiosity among migrants: Sweden-Chileans' relationship to religion and congregations] Lund: Lunds universitet.

Norris, Pippa & Inglehart, Ronald (2004) *Sacred and Secular: Politics and Religion Worldwide*. New York: Cambridge University Press.

Nylund, Katarina (2007) 'De religiösa samfundens betydelse som offentliga mötesplatser för människor i förskingringen' [The importance of religious congregations as public meeting places for people in the Diaspora] pp. 333–383 in Katarina Nylund (Ed.) *Periferin i centrum. Gränsöverskridande praktiker i Stockholms offentliga rum* [The periphery at the centre. Border-crossing practices in the public spaces of Stockholm] Göteborg: Daidalos.

Pickel, Gert & Müller, Olaf (2009) 'Introduction – the comparative empirical view on religion and religiosity', pp. 7–12 in

Gert Pickel & Olaf Müller (Hrsg) *Church and Religion in Contemporary Europe. Results from Empirical and Comparative Research*. Wiesbaden: VS Verlag für Sozialwissenschaften.

Salah, Abdallah (2009a) Interview by Charlotte Fridolfsson. The Islamic Association in Stockholm, Stockholm Mosque, 12 March, 2009.

Salah, Abdallah (2009b) FACIT Cross evaluation interview. The Islamic Association in Stockholm, Stockholm Mosque, 14 September, 2009.

Sheldrake, Philip (2001) *Spaces for the Sacred Place, Memory and Identity*. Baltimore, Md: Johns Hopkins University Press.

Sjödin, Daniel (2011) *Tryggare kan ingen vara. Migration, religion och integration i en segregerad omgivning* [You Cannot Be More Confident. Migration, Religion and Integration in a Segregated Surrounding] Lund: Lund University. [PhD thesis]

Soja, Edward (1996) *Thirdspace: Journeys to Los Angeles and Other Real-and-Imagined Places*. Oxford: Blackwell.

SST (2013) Nämnden för statligt stöd till trossamfund. Årsbok 2013 [The Swedish Commission for Government Support to Faith Communities: Yearbook 2013] http://www.sst.a.se/ [Accessed 12 June 2013]

SST (2014) Nämnden för statligt stöd till trossamfund. Årsbok 2014 [The Swedish Commission for Government Support to Faith Communities] http://www.sst.a.se/ [Accessed 2 November 2014]

Statistiska Centralbyrån [Statistics Sweden] (2014) Invandring 2013. Invandringen på rekordhög nivå [Immigration 2013 all time high]. http://www.scb.se/sv_/Hitta-statistik/Artiklar/Invandringen-pa-rekordhog-niva/ [Accessed 2 November 2014]

Stockholms Moské [Stockholm Mosque] startpage, http://hem.spray.se/kifah.f [Accessed 29 June 2010)].

Svenska Dagbladet [Swedish daily newspaper] (2007) 'Fler kristna väljer att bli muslimer' [More Christians are becoming Muslims] 19 November 2007

Svenska Kyrkan (2011) *Inträden i och utträden ur Svenska kyrkan år 1970–2010* [Enrolment in and exit from the Church of Sweden 1970–2010] . [Online] Available from: http://www.svenskakyrkan.se/default.aspx?id=645562 [Accessed 7 August 2011]

Svenska Kyrkan (2012) *Church History* [Online] Available from: http://www.svenskakyrkan.se/default.aspx?id=657802 [Accessed 24 January 2012]

Tuan, Yi-Fu (1977) *Space and Place. The Perspective of Experience*. Minneapolis and London: University of Minnesota Press.

Utbildningsradion [Swedish Educational Broadcasting Company] (2011) *Muslimer i Sverige* [Muslims in Sweden] .

[Online] Available from: www. ur.se/Ung/Amnen/SO/Religion/ Islam/Islam-i-Sverige [Accessed: 7 August 2011]

Västra Skrävlinge Församling (2010) Församlingsblad. Nummer 2 Malmö [Newsletter Number 2 from the Västra Skrävlinge Parish, Malmö].

Zock, Hetty (2010) 'Voicing the self in postsecular society: A psychological perspective on meaning-making and collective identities, pp. 131–146 in Arie L. Molendijk, Justin Beaumont & Christof Jedan (eds) *Exploring the Postsecular. The Religious, the Political and the Urban*. Leiden & Boston: Brill.

The place of music
– the place of becoming
Heavy metal identity formation in Gothenburg city

Susanna Nordström

Introduction

Music, place, and identity are so intrinsically bound up with each other that their relation to each other is often taken for granted. Music is history; it is culture. It says something about where people are from and their national pride (Whiteley, Bennett & Hawkins, 2004). It speaks of physical points of origin and specific spots in the world where music has been used as a means of expressing joy, sadness, hate, and rebellion, of expressing one's identity. It has also been used to transport people into places of fantasy, to places where they are allowed to express their own being without being challenged. Leyshon *et al.* (1998:2) claim that it is crucial to give focus to 'spatial processes by which sounds are differentiated and through which the economic, social and aesthetic geographies forged through musical practices are intimately bound up with the production of space and place'.

Music, identity, and place are entwined by various factors. In many cases, the anchoring of music to a certain location is used to come to grips with the effects of diaspora, with the music being a means by which people can symbolically travel back to a home country or to a believed place of birth or upbringing (Sernhede, 2002; Daynes, 2004; Cohen, 1995). Music can also be historically linked to a place to such an extent that it stimulates both national identity and tourism, as in the case of Jamaica and the reggae culture (Nurse, 2002) or be transformed into a lucrative music industry resting on a regional identity, such as in Nashville (Florida & Scott, 2010). Last but not least, youth, subculture, and place make up a frequently occurring theme (*e.g.* Toth, 2008; Williams, 2006).

The heavy metal[1] subculture, with its forty-year history, emerged as a white, male culture reflecting its time from a class perspective in the grim, worn-down industrial areas of Birmingham, England (Weinstein, 2000). 'I was a kid who always wanted to have fun and there wasn't much fun in Aston. There was only grey sky, corner bars and gloomy people who worked like animals along the conveyor belt', writes heavy metal musician Ozzy Osbourne (2009:26. Author's translation), giving witness to the poverty, desperation, and lack of inspiration in the birthplace of heavy metal. Though Birmingham was by no means a place of opportunities and success, its grimness has undoubtedly provided a reason for people to engage in music creation, and is echoed in the harsh and unforgiving thematics and aesthetics of the heavy metal culture. As such, the city has played a definite role in awakening the heavy metal culture and forming its distinctive character.

Like Birmingham, Gothenburg, a city of some 550,000 inhabitants in Sweden, is a centre of heavy metal musicianship (Dunn, 2004; Sweden Abroad, 2014). While Birmingham is regarded as the birthplace and a long-time catalyst of heavy metal bands and music, it is not today commonly known for having a particularly metal scene. Cities such as Gothenburg, with considerable amounts of music, and heavy metal music in particular, can to some extent be considered Birmingham's heirs, places where people are actively negotiating its world-renowned heavy metal musical existence in relation to other cities. The city of Gothenburg has been chosen as the backdrop of this study of urban influence on subcultural identity for two main reasons. Research on heavy metal from a place- and -identity perspective is practically non-existent. Furthermore, the heavy metal subculture and its music have lived in a medial vacuum for the greater part of their existence (Weinstein, 2001), which is why it is important to research the mechanisms that makes such an obscure business blossom in one particular place, specifically

---

1   'Heavy metal' as used in this chapter does not primarily refer to any specific genre of heavy metal but functions as an umbrella term. It is freely translated from the Swedish term 'hårdrock', colloquially used to describe all forms of hard rock, heavy metal and metal and the genres they include.

through 'the narrativization of place', that is, 'the way in which people define their relationship to local, everyday surroundings' (Whiteley, Bennett & Hawkins, 2004:2). The main purpose of this study is to explore how identity and heavy metal can be tied to place and the social mechanisms by which this is done. First, though, some theoretical considerations will be addressed.

Theoretical considerations

Even the most basic theory of identity contains a number of variables, which underlines the complexity of the concept. A few of Antaki and Widdicombe's (1998:3) variables can be presented here. The individual is commonly a member of a category of people who share certain characteristics, and from this category he/she constructs identities. Having a particular identity is also reinforced by the 'consequentiality' of interaction in reference to a specific role (*ibid*, 13). This makes room for an intricate interplay between the roles and identities of a human being. Last, identity becomes readily visible only in the structures of conversation and action. It is hence in the meeting with others that characteristics can be negotiated and imprinted.

Moving on to place, a definition of the concept should not only take into account specific physical surroundings or GPS coordinates. Hudson (2006:627) rather claims that 'Places are contested and continually in the process of becoming, rather than essentialized and fixed, open and porous to a variety of flows in and out rather than closed and hermetically sealed'. Not only is the place open and malleable, it is also negotiated in different ways by different people. A place is created and reproduced in relation to people ascribing it meaning, *i.e.* creating 'a sense of place' (Tuan, 1977:8). This does not exclude the possibility to view place both in terms of something physical, *e.g.* wall, land, and as something symbolic, charged with a meaning that goes beyond its physical connotations. Interestingly, the openness and malleability of a place is in many ways similar to the negotiation around and interchangeability of human nature, and thus of identity (compare 'a sense of place' with 'a sense of self' accumulated over time and in relation to other people). Different people will, however, attach different sentiments and characteristics to the same place, even though one particular group, when scrutinized, can be highly consistent in its portrayal of the place to others, as well as in its actions in relation to this place. It is thus important to underline that individual groups can be quite strict in their view of a place. On a macro level, though, the city, being physically 'intact' as a place, holds an endless number of meanings which can shift rapidly. One distinct conclusion can consequently be drawn from the similarities of human identity and that given to a place and the interchangeability of them: the importance of place to human being can change with identity construction as much as identity construction can change with the importance of the place. A place, for human beings, can be consistent with identity just as much as identity can be consistent with place. They are inextricably intertwined, no matter at which level. Having now stated the relationship between place and identity, we should move on to the concrete city as a place and the identities formed here in the name of music.

As a place, the city is a melting pot of cultures. It can draw people into it with its possibilities but it can also create tension and conflict, all of which are important aspects of positioning and, consequently, identity creation. People who live in the city may feel a need to use music either as a means of passing time or a stepping stone to break out of a state of desperation or even depression caused by poverty and urban segregation, for example (*e.g.* Arnett, 1996). The music then amplifies and communicates the identity of the individual, an identity which otherwise would not be heard. Ozzy Osbourne gives witness to this kind of a relationship to music.

People who are not already residents of the city may move there in search of an arena for style in general, what Polhemus (1994:149–150) calls the 'supermarket of style'. The population density and cultural diversity of the city make it possible to start over, to create new identities in the vast number of contexts and the relative anonymity that are available. On the other hand, the 'supermarket of style' also offers the possibility to find people with an identity that individuals see themselves as already having, and hence it is a melting pot of belongingness. An important aspect of this magnetic characteristic of the city is the 'urban ethos' associated with it, that is, an idea of how cities are generally disposed in relation to rural areas and the possibilities that emerge from it

(Krims, 2007:7). This disposition of the city, in general or more specific senses, is often used as a representation of the city. One type of representation, specifically related to a particular music scene, is the 'mythscape', explained as 'picturing, discussing and debating a city, its people and a musical style which is deemed to have emerged from a particular set of local circumstances' (Bennett, 2007:88). Thus the city, by virtue of this representation, seemingly takes on a life of its own through the spreading of myths.

Possibilities and representations aside, however, people also adopt positions within the city in the light of less positive actions, such as conflicts between groups and 'difference producing' (Stokes, 2004:175). People pushed together in a limited living space are bound to create friction by organizing into groups reflecting special interests, for example music lifestyles (Brake, 1985). By using their subcultural identity, emphasising music and symbols to portray this belongingness, they effectively enhance their in-group identity in relation to the out-group, creating an 'us- and- them-mentality'. While there is research to suggest that music also can have a unifying function in relation to groups in conflict (Lipsitz, 1994), one of the main creators of collective identity is precisely that identification with what one is *not*. As Bauman argues: the 'we' needs 'them' in order to build a strong ingroup definition. It is common to actively malign the 'them' while praising one's own group in order to strengthen the external barriers of the group as well as its internal morale (Bauman, 1991). Thus, following Krims (2007), the emotional investment made through the process of a constant contestation of other people's right to be in the city territory, or in relation to other cities of rivalry is a romanticization. The city is not only a place where one lives, but also a place one lives *through* (Krims, 2007), and it thus creates a basis for a strong local identity.

Method

The empirical material used in this article was gathered on two occasions. The first and main group of interviews was performed with young heavy metal fans between the ages of 18 and 27 in Gothenburg. In total, 26 fans have been interviewed, and the interviews consist of six focus-group interviews and four single interviews. A letter explaining the purpose of the study was distributed via the Swedish alternative community 'Helgon' ('Saints'). This community serves as a forum for people involved in alternative music lifestyles. Though not specifically directed towards heavy metal fans, the Helgon community serves as an important forum for them, involving around 10,000 heavy metal fans of all kinds throughout Sweden. A total of 218 persons identified as heavy metal fans, aged 18–27 years and living in or around Gothenburg were invited to participate in an interview. During the interviews, questions about the heavy metal lifestyle and Gothenburg as centre of heavy metal were discussed, following a semi-structured interview guide.

Further empirical material was later gathered at the Helgon forum from four of the previous interviewees, though at this time via personal messages on the forum. The questions on this occasion were specifically constructed in relation to the theme of the city and heavy metal.

Empirical findings

The city of Gothenburg and the identity which people attach to it can be viewed from different perspectives. There is a highly concrete aspect to the city, where the physical arena of music and style is brought to the fore. Contrary to the physical aspect of the arena, there is an abstract aspect of mythscaping to the city. Here the city's reputation has taken on a life of its own, in a sense continually creating its identity, though not necessarily fulfilling it. Finally, and in a sense filtered through the above-mentioned aspects, there is an underlying relativity, which is connected to how the city is compared to other arenas for music making and identity creation. These aspects will now be dealt with in depth.

The city as a forum

Identity, as explicated by Antaki and Widdicombe (1998:3), presupposes the sharing of characteristics with other people. This may take the form of similar ethnic appearance, attributes, jargon, and manners. It may also take the form of a shared way of behaving or shared opinions on a specific matter. For the heavy metal people of Gothenburg, the prime issues are a) to be among equals and b) to be seen as a heavy metal persona by equals, two things that are not always easy to achieve. Emil tells us:

> You know … where I come from, we had to go to the Red Cross store and buy tight fitting women's trousers if we wanted to look anything like our idols (laughs). I remember the clerk would look suspiciously at me for shopping from the women's department so I used to quickly explain that I was buying them for my girlfriend and asked to have them gift wrapped. I felt like a pervert. There were no stores for us heavy metal fans, we just did the best we could with what we had … homemade studded jackets and bracelets … In Gothenburg there are stores just for heavy metal fans and you can find a pair of tight-fitting men's jeans anywhere. It's so much easier nowadays.

Emil establishes the importance of looks by describing his own struggle to look the part of a heavy metal fan. Either the clothes are homemade, or he has to hide his heavy metal identity and look like a fool when buying them. In narrating this small struggle of his, he tells us that the place from which he comes is not at all used to the style of heavy metal. Having to resort to wearing women's trousers and feeling like a pervert is the price you have to pay in order to live in accordance with your heavy metal persona. Hence what also becomes clear here is that there is a relative notion of place in identity formation. While Emil's hometown is considered 'outdated', a place where he meets with what he experiences as narrow-mindedness, Gothenburg is a place where he can flourish in the identity he sees himself as having. He thus effectively compares his previous life with his life in Gothenburg by showing that looking like a heavy metal fan is no struggle in Gothenburg. This invokes the 'urban ethos' (Krims, 2007:7) and to some extent, the endless possibilities and grandiosity of the city. By saying that it is so much easier nowadays, he also conveys that in Gothenburg the heavy metal way of life is natural. This is evidence of the form of authenticity that is struggled for in his hometown, but easy to come by and true in Gothenburg. In comparison to Ozzy Osbourne and the gloomy life of the Birmingham area, Emil's desperation rather seems to lie in the difficulty of growing up in a more rural setting and the outsidership that this entails. However, and this needs to be taken into consideration, although the interviewee' economic and social situations and backgrounds range over the entire spectrum, and several of the interviewees have other ethnic backgrounds than Swedish, the desperation and the political, social, and economic oppression of the youngster in Brake's study (1985) is not underscored by the interviewees in this study. This may be due to factors related to the nature of the interviews or the interviewees themselves, but is still worth emphasising.

Returning to identity, being a heavy metal fan thus presupposes that people recognize one as such. There is, however, an extra dimension to being recognized as a heavy metal fan, no matter what the context. Just as the heavy metal genealogy stretches far back in time, it has also grown in different directions causing the subculture to exhibit great internal diversity in terms of subgenres and the styles associated with them. Linus illustrates this as follows:

> The most important thing is that they get what KIND of heavy metal fan you are … of course they understand you're a heavy metal fan (…) you just hope they recognize certain bands and attributes. I have to admit, I'm worried about being misinterpreted. In Norrland (northern parts of Sweden) for example, they'd never know'.

The importance of being recognized by virtue of one's position on the heavy metal map is indicative of the nuances which obviously only would have a chance to be addressed in a city where enough people adhere to the heavy metal subculture. Who 'they' are is not conveyed in Linus's statement, but on account of 'their' knowing that he is a heavy metal fan at all, 'they' are implicitly other heavy metal fans. This further emphasises the 'supermarket of style' (Polhemus, 1994:149–150) and sheds light on the fact that the climate of the Gothenburg heavy metal scene and culture has given rise to a number of sub-styles that not only exist as identity markers of heavy metal as such, but also serve as divisions between different kinds of heavy metal fans as well. The heavy metal identity has thus, over time and in this specific climate, been finely tuned in accordance with specific forms of attributes that can only be related to one style. This style can only be pinpointed by people with knowledge of heavy metal and in relation to all the other styles. In Norrland, however, Linus's place of birth, people would never know the difference, he says, in effect ascribing greater value to Gothenburg as a place of relative knowledge where the nuances of his subcultural identity can be read. He is thus making room for more identity elaboration as well as seriousness. Note that the friction between groups described by Brake (1985) is absent. This is partly due to the fact that none of the interviewees manifest their identity in relation to other subcultures of the city, and in the case of the subgenres above, a certain amount of respect seem to characterise their mutual relations due to the fans' common musical and stylistic origins.

Apart from the attributes and appearance of the heavy metal fans in Gothenburg, there is also another aspect to the concrete identity-creating aspects of Gothenburg: a thriving live scene. Nils enlightens us about this as follows:

> In any given week there are at least two major heavy metal bands playing in Gothenburg. And if you're into the underground stuff, you can see two bands a day if you want to. There is ALWAYS something happening. And if nothing's happening at all, you can get out of town really quickly. To festivals and stuff, I mean.

Not only does he underscore that heavy metal is close at hand, at least in live form, he also brings up a purely geographical and infrastructural aspect that affects him and his subculture. Gothenburg is not only a hot spot for heavy metal fans internally, it is also a hub when it comes to getting to places. As such the city is an infrastructural stepping stone for any other heavy metal related activity, though the interviewee is keen on delivering the image of a rather self-sufficient music scene.

There are two perspectives on why Gothenburg is filled to the brim with different heavy metal styles, and thus also has a good supply of heavy metal related venues and shops. Regarding the

bottom-up perspective, Sandra fills us in on the first: 'There are A
LOT of heavy metal fans here, a lot of clubs and ... it is POSSIBLE
to be a heavy metal fan here', yet again evoking the view of the
'urban ethos' (Krims, 2007:7). The reason is simple: there are
enough heavy metal fans in Gothenburg for heavy metal shops
to stay in business, for clubs to stay open, for live concerts to
take place, and for people to meet. People move to the city to be
a part of this thriving identity forum, the 'supermarket of style'
(Polhemus: 1994:149–150, and hence further contribute to the
climate. Secondly, and in a more top-down manner, both private
investors and the city culture council have taken decisions favourable for heavy metal fans, thus creating an arena for them. As an
example, two long-term musical figures started the annual heavy
metal festival 'Metaltown', which used to be held in the very
centre of Gothenburg during some of the busiest tourist weeks
of summer. The festival draws some 30,000 visitors. Rugged and
loud, the music could indeed be deemed a nuisance to people in its
vicinity, but permission to hold it in the city centre was renewed
every year until only recently, when the festival outgrew its arena.
In recent years during headline acts the heavy metal fans jumped
to such an extent that the nearby Göta Älv bridge, one of the main
transportation links of Gothenburg, started shaking (Strage, 2011).
Furthermore, at the annual Gothenburg Culture Festival, a free
event sponsored by the City, heavy metal acts are frequent participants, regularly playing the biggest stages.

Returning to Antaki and Widdicombe (1998), identity is indeed
reinforced by the consequentiality of interaction as well as the
visibility of structures of conversations and action. The reason for
this consequentiality, interaction, and negotiation is thus the very
density of heavy metal fans in a relatively small spatial area and
the fact that the forum for heavy metal fans is continuously being
encouraged by the city's cultural planners and by enthusiasts in the
form of individual heavy metal fans or groups. When heavy metal
fans have many opportunities to meet other fans, the resulting
basic validation of the heavy metal style can lead to an elaboration
of the style, perhaps by causing fans to identify to a greater extent
with smaller fractions of the heavy metal community. The subcultural identity thus becomes more firmly established with every
chance to reflect oneself in equals.

While this portrayal of identity appears firm and exponentially firmer due to this specific geographical location and its possibilities, the interviewees' view of identity also becomes evident in relation to other places of identity manifestation.

The fixed and the flexible identity/place constellation

Collective identity in this sense is always relative to others, just as individual identity is relative to the context and the role enacted in it. This feeling of 'we' is frequently expressed in geographical terms, whether it manifests itself through celebrations on national days (Blehr, 1999), in relation to the local football team (King, 1998, or perhaps via long-term territorial conflicts (Andersson, 2011). Jimmy claims:

> 'Oh come on ... heavy metal fans in Stockholm ... what the hell are they? They are ONLY posers! There's a lot of that over there, while here ... how many groups have an image at all? It feels more genuine here ... we have a lot of bands, we've got Metaltown, and I don't think that that concept would've worked in many other cities.

Stockholm, the capital of Sweden, is belittled here for being fake by the Gothenburg heavy metal fan. Not only is it important to Jimmy to compare and contrast Gothenburg with the largest city in Sweden (by which everywhere else is always judged), it is also important to prove that there is a special climate in Gothenburg when it comes to looks and venues. To him, this climate is specific to Gothenburg, and has given the city its reputation and authenticity, which is here evidently important in relation to the music and its place (Connell & Gibson, 2003). By doing this, he builds up the Gothenburg heavy metal community while deliberately blackening the rival's reputation, as theorized by Bauman (1991). He is also romanticising the city by bringing forward a generalized picture of a stylistic faux pas that the Gothenburg crowd would never commit. This categorization is important as an overall form of geographical confirmation. It effectively distinguishes the heavy metal fans in Gothenburg from those in Stockholm, Malmö, or other big cities in Sweden. Note, though, that Jimmy primarily expresses his identity through the heavy metal city, not by speaking favourably about his own persona or way of dressing.

However fixed the heavy metal identity may be within the Gothenburg communities, as the above positioning gives witness to, place is also flexible and mobile in reference to the heavy metal theme and identity. The city is seen as something to be compared and contrasted with Stockholm, for example, but relativity can also be observed in relation to identity when travelling outside the city. While the city is a haven for heavy metal fans, heavy metal attributes are easily spotted and are used as markers of recognition between people when they are elsewhere. Lisa gives us an example:

> I was travelling by bus to Malmö a while ago, and there were only ... well, normal people, except for me and this other guy who was also a heavy metal fan. At that point I felt that there was a connection. Not just because he was a guy and I am a girl. You look at the other person and feel that we belong to the same group.

What is evident here is that the city of Gothenburg acts as a protective shield against other cities, scenes, and heavy metal fans, to which one has to make comparisons. When the fans leave the city, however, their main form of belonging is via their heavy metal persona, which is why the 'normal people' become the outsiders instead of the heavy metal fans in Stockholm. Interestingly, place is of importance to identity when in the city, and identity is of importance to place when outside the city, which even further underscores the flexibility of place and the importance of identity to place research, as described by Hudson (2006) and Leyshon *et al.* (1998).

To sum up, as a forum for heavy metal identity creation, Gothenburg has proven to be both internally constructive, for instance with its many venues and the possibility to follow a heavy metal dress code, and externally constructive, helping people to find heavy metal venues and connect with other heavy metal fans outside the city. For the inhabitants of Gothenburg, however, the city is not merely a place to live out a heavy metal identity, it is also a mythscape reaching far beyond the borders of the city.

Gothenburg as a mythscape

One of the ways by which the heavy metal collective has created a place-bound identity is the establishment of a 'mythscape' (Bennett, 2002). Ascribing the city a specific role in the creation of heavy metal music and culture is highly frequent in the empirical material. Certainly, when it comes to Gothenburg these myths have a basis in fact. During the late 1980s and early 1990s, a specific form of metal arose among bands in Gothenburg. This later gave rise to the genre widely referred to as 'Swedish Melodic Death Metal', which was characterized by the typical 'Gothenburg sound' (Dunn, 2004:101). As a consequence, Gothenburg soon earned the title of the Heavy Metal Capital of Sweden. Though long gone as a coherent music scene, the interviewees consistently return to the topic of Gothenburg as being a haven for heavy metal. Michael describes how he was met with awe and admiration when telling a heavy metal fan abroad that he was from Gothenburg:

> We were on tour in Hungary and we went into this really big heavy metal bar ... three floors! I saw a girl working the bar with the colours of the Swedish flag painted on her nails and I asked her if she was Swedish. She wasn't, and I thought in that case it was kind of odd to have the Swedish colours painted on her nails. When she realized I was from Gothenburg I thought she'd fall to the floor and worship me. She was just awestruck and kept talking about Gothenburg as if it was heaven. All her friends wanted to go there, you know ... I don't know why. We were in the biggest heavy metal bar I've ever been to and the thing is we've got nothing like that in Gothenburg.

Peter fills in: 'I've met people around the world and they see the Swedish, and specifically Gothenburg scene as some kind of holy grail. They want to make pilgrimages to Sweden for that reason ... so strange'. Carolina Kolodziej, a German journalist and correspondent, moved to Gothenburg for the heavy metal climate. She says that 'sometimes it feels as if musicians around Gothenburg are born with heavy metal in their blood' (Hankins, 2009).

This view of the heavy metal city and the identity associated with it is not solely the result of specific bands bearing a trademark sound or individuals spreading the news about Gothenburg.

It seems, from the puzzled responses of the interviewees when encountering this awe among people abroad, that the word around the world concerning Gothenburg is by all means a mythscape, making it appear more grand than it actually is. The representation of the city has reached far beyond any publicity and advertisement that the fans and bands could produce. Michael continues:

> You know ... I told that bartender girl that in Gothenburg, we've got Rockbaren, a place no bigger than my cellar, and Sticky Fingers, a place no bigger than my living room. It didn't make any sense. They've got Whig Wham in Hungary; that place fits some 4000 people. They've got the Avalon Club, four floors and they only play metal. But it didn't seem to matter. I think it's something about the attitude and the naturalness of heavy metal in Gothenburg.

Contrary to the original meaning of the term 'mythscape' (Bennett, 2002), this view of Gothenburg as a heavy metal city goes beyond the mere Gothenburg sound, it is enhanced by people abroad to a further extent than by local heavy metal fans. While the interviewees see the city as a concrete scene of heavy metal, as well as a way of being, the people from abroad have an almost exotified image of the town, making it a sanctuary for heavy metal fans. This difference in the two views of the city, however, only serves as a justification of the Gothenburg heavy metal fans and their own identity. Though struck by the superlatives concerning the city, the Gothenburg heavy metal fans still manage to find explanations of why the city has such a reputation. The attitude, the freedom, the possibility to manifest one's subcultural identity together with many others are all natural things for them. As seen in the above excerpts, the city seems to have an identity of its own. Of course this identity is built from the practices of the city's heavy metal fans, but it underscores the give-and-take between place and people in their identity creation. Heavy metal fans built the Gothenburg sound, a sound which, though not currently as widely practised in Gothenburg, has gained momentum in the world. The reputation of Gothenburg took on a life of its own, attracting people to the city to live a heavy metal lifestyle. Living in the city, the fans continually negotiate and make evident the splendour of the city.

Conclusion

As a place, the city is undoubtedly a complex life form. It functions as a base on which the heavy metal fans stand to create a geographical identity. It functions as a wall behind which they shelter when comparing their heavy metal scene to those of other cities. The city is evidently nowhere near being only fixed and rooted in the soil. It is the pride that people take with them when travelling, it is the untouchable mythscape with a life and reputation of its own, and it functions as a loudspeaker blaring out the heavy metal fans' identity elaboration.

A few conclusions can be drawn about the city of Gothenburg as a place of identity creation for heavy metal fans. First, identity requires that there are people around who share certain characteristics. By the looks of the interviewees, Gothenburg is densely populated with heavy metal fans, and by virtue of meeting other heavy metal fans, going to concerts and clubs, and visiting shops, this identity is continuously being renegotiated and reproduced. The identity of the heavy metal fan can also be sharpened and niched in this 'supermarket of style' (Polhemus, 1994:149–150), taking the fan from being a heavy metal fan in general to having an identity with more specific requirements in terms of attributes and style. This development can only take place if there are others with the same subgenre orientation against whom one can reflect oneself. The places where this self-reflection occurs, such as concerts, clubs, and shops, are reproduced by virtue of the people visiting them. The social mechanism of belonging is thus largely responsible for heavy metal fans coming to or staying in Gothenburg. Secondly, for a heavy metal fan in the city, the city is a good part of his or her identity. It is in this city that the attributes can be worn, the comparisons made, the ideas expressed, and the actions taken that produce the continuity needed for identity creation. Sometimes, though, it is through the city, not in reference to oneself, that other cities are belittled. This strengthens the picture of the heavy metal city and its inhabitants. When the heavy metal fan leaves the city, a general heavy metal identity kicks in, tearing down the walls of Gothenburg city. The identity-based placeformation as such is strong in the city, but is inadvertently dismantled in favour of other bases of comparison when outside the city. The sense of place thus shifts somewhat. The social mechanism of comparison is a result of the identity-based placeformation. Thirdly, it is important to distinguish between the city's identity and the individual heavy metal fan's identity. While the heavy metal fans agree that there is a certain 'naturalness' to the city, this could be an effect of all the people living in the city creating a certain climate, not merely the heavy metal fans. The origin of the mythscape surrounding Gothenburg and giving it its celebrated heavy metal identity is difficult to pinpoint. The 'Gothenburg sound' has had an impact worldwide, but apart from that, none of the heavy metal fans can understand the myth's grandiosity. This could be the result of the city having an identity which in part is shaped by people outside the city. Many years of myths turning into truths among non-residents of Gothenburg have given it a life of its own. The heavy metal fans are nonetheless strengthened in their heavy metal identity by this mythscape because it is evidence that the heavy metal fans are geographically in the right place with regard to their subculture and it presents a possibility to compete with other places/cities and consequently with identities. Representation is thus a second social mechanism fostered by identity-based placeformation.

In conclusion, as a place, the city forms heavy metal identities by serving as an arena of the subculture, being used as a means of comparison, and hosting a mythscape continuously upheld and reproduced by people outside of the city. All actions are performed in an intricate interplay between place and identity, where the social mechanism of belonging is the starting point, the social mechanisms of comparison and representation are a continuation, and there is never a complete balance between place and identity.

References

Andersson, Ann-Catrin (2011) *Identity Politics and City Planning. The Case of Jerusalem* Örebro University: Örebro Studies in Political Science 30. (Ph.D thesis)

Antaki, Charles & Widdicombe, Sue (1998). *Identities in talk.* London: Sage, 1998.

Arnett, Jeffrey J. (1996). *Metalheads – Heavy Metal Music and Adolescent Alienation.* Westview Press: Boulder, Colorado.

Brake, Michael (1985). *Comparative Youth Culture – The sociology of youth culture and youth subcultures in America, Britain and Canada.* London: Routledge.

Hudson, Ray (2006). 'Regions and place: music, identity and place'. *Progress in Human Geography,* 30(5):626–634.

Baron, Stephen W. Bauman, Zygmunt (1999). *Thinking sociologically.* Oxford: Blackwell.

Bennett, Andy (2002.'Music, media and urban mythscapes: A study of the "Canterbury Sound"'. *Media Culture and Society,* 24(1):87–100.

Blehr, Barbro (1999). 'Sacred Unity, Scared Similarity: Norwegian Constitution Day Parades'. *Ethnology,* 38(2):175–189.

Cohen, Sara (1995). 'Sounding out the City: Music and the Sensuous Production of Place'. *Transactions of the Institute of British Geographers, New Series,* 20(4):434–446.

Connell, John and Gibson, Chris (2003). *Sound Tracks: Popular Music, Identity and Place.* New York: Routledge.

Daynes,Sarah (2004). 'The Musical Construction of the Diaspora: The Case of Reggae and Rastafari' p. 25–41 In: Sheila Whiteley, Andy Bennett & Stan Hawkins, (eds.), *Music, Space and Place: Popular Music and Cultural Identity* (Burlington, VA: Ashgate).

Dunn, Sam (2004) 'Lands of Fire and Ice: An Exploration of Death Metal Scenes'. *Public: New Localities,* 29:107–125.

Florida, Richard & Jackson, Scott (2010). 'Sonic City: The Evolving Economic Geography of the Music Industry.' *Journal of Planning Education and Research,* 29(3): 310–321.

Hankins, Markus (2009). 'Carolina lämnade Berlin för hårdrock I Göteborg'. *GT/Expressen,* January 19.

Hudson, Ray (2001). *Producing Places.* New York: Guilford.

King, Anthony (1997). 'The postmodernity of Football Hooliganism'. *The British Journal of Sociology,* 48(4):576–593.

Krims, Adam (2007). *Music and Urban Geography.* New York: Routledge.

Lipsitz, George (1997). *Dangerous Crossroads: Popular Music, Postmodernism and the Poetics of Place.* New York: Verso.

Leyshon, Andrew, Matless, David & Revill, George (1998). *The place of music.* Guilford Press: New York

Nurse, Keith (2002). 'Bringing Culture Into Tourism: Festival Tourism and Reggae Sunsplash in Jamaica'. *Social and Economic Studies,* 51(1):127–143.

Osbourne, Ozzy (2009). *Jag är Ozzy.* Stockholm: Norstedts.

Polhemus, Ted (1994). *Street Style.* London: Thames & Hudson.

Sernhede, Ove (2002). Alienation is My Nation – *Hiphop och unga mäns utanförskap i Det nya Sverige.* Stockholm: Ordfront.

Stokes, Martin (2004). '"Music, identity and the global city", orig. "Musique, identité et ville-monde"'. *Homme*, 171(2): 171–112, 371–388.

Strage, Fredrik (2011). 'Metaltown' Del 1. *Dagens Nyheter*, June 19.

Sweden Abroad: http://www.swedenabroad.com/en-GB/Embassies/Vienna/Current-affairs/News/Swedish-heavy-metal-for-beginners-sys/ (2014-04-14)

Toth, Csaba (2008). 'J-Pop and performances of young female identity – Music, gender and urban space in Tokyo'. *Young*, 16(2):111–129.

Tuan, Yi Fu (1977). *Space and Place: The Perspective of Experience.* Minneapolis: University of Minnesota Press.

Weinstein, Deena (2000). *Heavy metal: The music and its culture.* Boulder, Colorado: Da Capo Press.

Whiteley, Sheila; Bennett, Andy & Hawkins, Stan (2004) *Music, Space and Place – Popular Music and Cultural Identity.* Aldershot: Ashgate.

Williams, Patrick J (2006). 'Authentic Identities: Straightedge Subculture, Music, and the Internet'. *Journal of Contemporary Ethnography,* 35(2):173–200.

You and 'the other'

– *School as a meeting place*

Anders Trumberg

Introduction

One way or another, whether as pupil, parent, or teacher, almost everyone has been in contact with compulsory school. Therefore, almost everyone has an opinion about the school system based on personal experiences, and everyone has memories from the time they spent there. On an individual basis, school shapes us and our lives. During the course of our lives we spend a great deal of time in the place called school; it is there we meet friends and learn things about the world and, not least, about ourselves. If we take a moment to think back we will realise that the school system and the time we spent in it have had a great impact on our lives and have shaped our identities. But the school system has always changed over time, and the schools that our parents once attended are quite different from the ones you have experienced, and those your children are experiencing or will experience.

In Sweden, compulsory school has traditionally been highly centralised, and there has been little or no room for individual choice within the system. But during the 1970s a decentralisation process began that ultimately led to the responsibility for running schools being devolved from the state to the municipalities. This process reduced the long-standing opposition to the right for individuals to choose their school, and it also created a school system that is more focused on competition. In almost all political documents regarding the school system, schools are seen as a place for meeting 'the other', as a place where students with different backgrounds come together and participate in a common project (Swedish Board of

Education 2011, Sandberg 1998). What happens if the heterogene-
ity of the composition of the students is lost and school no longer
functions as a meeting place?

This chapter starts with some brief background on the Swedish
school system and the free-choice reform that was implemented
in the 1990s. Almost all research in this area has been conducted
in the major cities in Sweden (Bunar 2001, Skawonius 2005, Van
der Burgt 2006, Bunar & Kallstenius 2006, Kallstenius 2011).
This study looks instead at what effect the free school choice has
on the schools in a medium-sized city. The second part in this
chapter is a case study of two schools, with the aim to see who
chooses (measured by the pupils' socioeconomic background and
ethnicity) and how it effect the segregation among schools in the
city of Örebro.

This chapter is covering three main questions:
- How have pupils' choices of compulsory schools developed
  in Örebro in the 1990s and early 2000
- Who chooses their school? Are there any patterns regarding
  the pupils' ethnic and socioeconomic backgrounds?
- How has this development affected the school as a meeting
  place?

The Swedish school system – an overview

For a long time, the school system in Sweden was centralised
and under direct state control in order to make the educational
system homogeneous. The system was regulated by the central
government through different state agencies who were supposed to
guarantee equal opportunities for all pupils in compulsory school.
Between the 1940s and 1960s the system underwent a process
of centralisation and was regulated through laws and statutes
(Egidius 2001). A government inquiry in 1940 concluded that the
existing school system was not capable of providing an adequate
civic education. This civic education or upbringing was intended
to teach citizens their rights and responsibilities in a democratic
society. This mission was closely tied to the building of a strong
democratic society and welfare state in Sweden. The centralisation

of compulsory school was thus perceived as a means to achieve an equal and fair school system (Wahlström 2002).

The 1940 government inquiry suggested that the two parallel school systems[1] should be merged into one uniform system. However the thought was regarded as too bold; society was not ready to let pupils from two different social classes meet each other in school. It was not until the 1950s that this idea was realised. The changes that occurred in society around 1950, such as increased international contact and increased competition between companies, made it possible to implement the reform. The increased competition meant that industry needed a more educated labour force, making education a resource among other natural resources. At the same time, the government was trying to improve the general level of knowledge among pupils and handle growing concerns about stratification in the dual school system (Wahlström 2002).

During this period some criticism against centralisation and bureaucratisation was heard. For example a government inquiry objected to the perceived one-sidedness of the education. Their main objection was that:

> The pupils are not stimulated to engage in individual activity and the working method is too narrow too allow for cooperation between the pupils. (Egidius, 2001, p. 62)

The criticisms of (detailed) government control soon gained prominence in the public debate, as did the argument for a decentralised system in which responsibility for the schools would shift from the government to the municipalities. Around 1975 a process leading towards decentralisation was initiated. Piece by piece, the responsibility for running compulsory schools began to be shifted from the government to the municipalities. A necessary precondition for this school reform was to combine smaller municipalities into bigger ones, which was done in 1974. The 1974 reform resulted in larger and more financially solid municipalities, and aimed to enable better adaptation to local realities, a higher degree of civic involvement, and greater efficiency. The develop-

---

1   'Realskolan', which prepared students for higher education, and 'folkskolan', which mostly attracted pupils from the working class.

ment of the school system continued, and in the 1980s this mainly concerned increasing the role of goals and evaluations in controlling the system (Wahlström 2002, Egidius 2001). In practice, this meant that the municipalities bore the responsibility, but the government was still in control through goal formulation and evaluation. One reason for this development was that the public sector was perceived as too large, which raised questions about the future financing and political control of the state and the services it provides. Privatisation and outsourcing offered a way out of the growing problems, and even the school system was concerned with these questions.

In the late 1980s, the shifting of responsibility for compulsory schools from the government to the municipalities was completed in Sweden. The school system was, and still is, controlled though goals and evaluations administrated by the Swedish Board of Education (Skolverket), the public authority responsible for overseeing the municipalities regarding the schools.

Following the twists and turns in the development of the Swedish school system, you can see that different reports, investigations, and reforms can easily been traced and connected to changes in the rest of the society. One of the most important reforms was the reform of 1990–91, which allowed for freedom of choice and competition between schools. This clearly represented a break with previous school reforms; the government let the municipalities take over and was no longer the guardian of equality and equivalence (Sundberg 2005, Wahlström 2002, Lidström & Hudson 1995).

The reform stipulated that the municipalities should distribute their resources to all schools with compulsory attendance, *i.e.* both municipal and private schools (Richardsson 2004). At the same time the question about the freedom to choose one's school was the subject of lively debate in politics and media, and many municipalities introduced a voucher system[2] as a way to increase the freedom of choice (Montin 2004). The budget proposition of 1995 declared that:

---

2   In the voucher (or equalization-allowance) system every student is allocated a
     sum of money that is transferred to the school that he or she attends.

In the modern school system the public schools are independent units with a high degree of freedom and responsibility. They can be said to be competing with each other and with private schools. This competition, together with the freedom of choice available today, functions as a stimulus for development within the schools. (Swedish Board of Education, 1995, p. 11)

It was also declared that no school should be socially or economically segregated, and that schools should work against discrimination, racism, and xenophobia. All pupils in Swedish compulsory school should have the same chance to choose their school and it was important to have a mix of individuals with different experiences and from different backgrounds (Swedish Board of Education 1995). With this statement, the social democratic government expressed a similar view as the former centre-right government on decentralisation of the Swedish school system. With the 1990–91 reform and the following reforms that aimed to facilitate competition and freedom of choice, Sweden went from having one of the most publicly dominated and uniform school systems in the world to a system with a high degree of choice (Ahlin & Mörk 2005, Dovemark 2004, Blomqvist & Rothstein 2000).

This change also meant that school's role of fostering common democratic values was shifted towards a more individual perspective; *i.e.*, common values were replaced by individual values (Bunar & Kallstenius 2006, Dovemark 2005, Englund 2003). Education was now something that parents and their children had to choose as a way to manage their future (Quennerstedt 2006).

The free-choice reform means that if pupils do not want to attend the school that is recommended by their municipality (the school nearest their home), they can choose another school. If they do not make any choice, they are automatically placed in the school nearest their home.

Free choice and segregation

A number of studies have investigated the connection between free choice and segregation within the school system (Arnman

& Jönsson 1985, Blomquist & Rothstein 2000, Bunar 2001, Skawonius 2005, Van der Burgt 2006, Bunar & Kallstenius 2006, Kallstenius 2011). Most of them are confined to one of the three major cities in Sweden, and the smaller and medium-sized cities are somewhat neglected. The reason for this concentration of research on the three major cities is that both the school market and housing segregation are larger there, which leads to the effects of the students' choices having a greater impact on segregation within and across schools in these cities. The studies conducted before the free-choice reform was implemented discuss more of a socioeconomic segregation within the school system, regarding the choice of a theoretical or practical education dividing students into different tracks by socioeconomic class (Arnman & Jönsson 1985). But in studies conducted from the 1990s and onward, you can see that the schools have become both more socioeconomically and ethnically segregated from each other (Bunar 2001, Kallstenius 2011, Trumberg 2011). Even the different reports from the Swedish Board of Education are pointing out that the free-choice reform has led to a segregated school system (Swedish Board of Education 1996, 2003, 2004, 2009). As with the case of segregation in housing, you can see an 'ethnic turn' in the 1990s (Bråmå 2004, Trumberg 2011). In international studies you can see the same tendencies regarding the implementation of the free-choice reform and its effects on segregation (Gorard & Taylor 2002, Adnett & Bougheas & Davies 2000, Adnett & Davies 2003, Ladd 2003, Sikking & Emerson 2008, Bagley *et al.* 2001). Some conclusions are that the free-choice reform is not helping the schools that already are losing pupils, and it is high- and middle-income families of white or European background who are benefitting the most from the emerging situation (Ladd 2003).

> A closely related effect of choice schemes in many countries was increased polarization of the student body. Students within schools became more similar and across schools became more different in terms of income levels, and achievement. (Ladd 2003, p. 18)

The reason that pupils from high- and middle-income families are, to a higher degree, using the free-choice options is related to the families' educational background. Parents with higher education tend to be more involved in and concerned about their children's education (Bagley *et al.* 2001, Dustman 2004). Free choice can also serve as a way to get away from schools in areas with many inhabitants with foreign background (Sinkki & Emersson 2008, Lankford & Wyckoff 2001. Beargley *et al.* 2001). You could therefore say that international research is pointing out that in many countries the free-choice reform has led to segregation within the school system and the schools and their pupils becoming more ethnically and socioeconomically homogeneous.

Theoretical considerations

The school system is one of many different institutions in society that function as a meeting place for people with different socioeconomic and ethnic backgrounds (other places for this type of interaction are, for example, clubs and associations, workplaces, residential areas, etc.) These places or arenas are vital for individual network building. Such a network keeps you informed about certain things, for example job opportunities, which can help you make decisions. And in these places, you also acquire knowledge and understanding about other people, cultures, and habits, and feel that you are a part of society (Sandberg 1998, Vranken *et al.* 2003). The encounter with other individuals also functions as a network-building activity that influences one's chance to get, for example, higher education, a job, and an income. For a school to have mix of students from different socioeconomic and ethnic backgrounds creates opportunities for integration in society. One might at first think of this only in terms of students with foreign background mixing with students with Swedish background. But it is not only about ethnicity; in school you also have a meeting between different youth cultures, between youth and adults, and so on. If the school system is divided in the sense that students with the same ethnic and socioeconomic background, values, and culture are gathered in certain schools, then the function of schools as meeting places will be reduced, and the students will begin to create a picture of 'the other', others who live in other neighbourhoods, go to different schools, and speak and move differently, *i.e.* a picture of individuals who in all respects are different from 'us'. A mix of students could therefore hamper the creation of the stereotypical picture of the other. School could therefore help to create social contacts between students and function as a building ground for mutual understanding (Sandberg 1998, Vranken *et al.* 2003, Strömblad 2003). The mix of students also has an effect on the outcome; in other words if you have students from different backgrounds in the schools you also achieve better results in the school system overall (Swedish Board of Education 2009, 2010) School is therefore a space for promoting social integration, and it has an important task to fulfil as a meeting place. This is something of which politicians are aware, and the importance of having a mix of students is mentioned in various political documents (Trumberg 2011).

Method

Most studies of this topic are conducted in Sweden's three largest cities (Stockholm, Gothenburg, and Malmö) and studies looking at small or medium-sized cities are relatively few in number. With around 140,000 inhabitants, Örebro is a medium-sized city, and the sixth largest city in Sweden. It can also be characterized as a socioeconomically and ethnically divided city, with increasing segregation (Örebro Municipality 2009, Integrationsverket 2007). Örebro is an interesting city to study because the students' choices of school and the schools themselves are influenced by the neighbourhoods where the schools are situated (Skawonius 2005, Bunar 2001, Gustavsson 2006).

This chapter focuses on students in ninth grade, and how the ethnic and socioeconomic composition of students has changed over a twelve-year period. The data I use come from Statistics Sweden and are based on information compiled on all ninth-grade students for the years 1992, 1998, and 2004. The personal data contain different economic and social variables such as parents' educational background, employment status, and income or social allowance; students' grades; and so forth. The data material also includes the GPS coordinates of the students' home address and the GPS coordinates of the schools the students are attending. The other dataset with which I am working contains all of the inhabitants in the city of Örebro with similar socioeconomic and ethnic variables as for the students, though without the coordinates.

Segregation index

I begin by calculating some segregation indexes for the city and for the schools; these indexes are not comparable, but you can see the trend of segregation in housing and in schools, *i.e.* whether it is increasing or decreasing. The similarity index or segregation index that I am using was developed by Ducan and Ducan (1955), see appendix.

The index spans from o to 100, with o meaning that the areas have the same distribution as the city (*i.e.* that the population groups are evenly distributed and the city has no segregation), and 100 that the populations are living in entirely separate neighbourhoods (*i.e.* the city is completely segregated). I have used the sams (Small Area Market Statistics) areas, developed by Statistics Sweden, to calculate the indexes. Sweden is divided into about 5000 such small areas (at the block level in cities). These have not changed over the years studied, which indicates that they are robust, and they are commonly used in this sort of calculations.

GIS-analysis

Because the database contains GPS coordinates, I can perform a GIS analysis concerning the relationship between students' home addresses and the schools they attended. The problem is that the municipality officials do not have any records of the catchment areas for the schools. The basis of the catchment areas, however, is the 'nearest to home' principle, which means that students who do not specifically select a school are automatically assigned to the school nearest their home. So by creating an area around each school I could estimate the catchment areas. I have used the voronoi method to create different areas around the schools. The voronoi method is a GIS method that creates areas around different geographical points on a map, and each surrounding voronoi shows the area that is closest to the point.

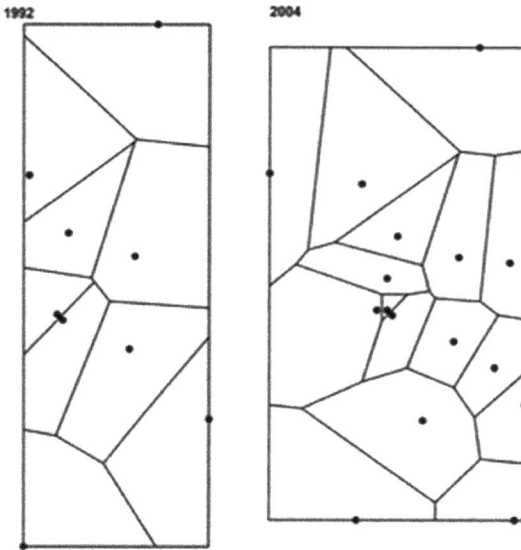

Figure 1. Voronoi diagram based on the ninth-grade schools in Örebro 1992 and 2004

Each point in Figure 1 shows a school with its estimated catchment area surrounding it. That means that if a student is living inside a voronoi, the nearest school is the point (school) connected to the voronoi. If you are attending a school but do not live inside that school's voronoi, the assumption is that you have actively chosen a different school.

The City of Örebro

As mentioned above, Örebro is a medium-sized city in central Sweden with roughly 140,000 inhabitants. It has 44 public compulsory schools and 12 independent compulsory schools which together host around 15,000 pupils. Örebro can be characterised as an ethnically divided city with a growing segregation index between the inhabitants with foreign background and those with Swedish background. The growing segregation in housing has an effect on the ethnic segregation between schools, and the segregation index based on ethnicity has increased regarding the schools.

The index shows that ethnic segregation has increased both in housing and in the schools situated in the city. The segregation in

Table 1. Segregation index 1992, 1998, and 2004.

Segregation index (%)	1992	1998	2004	Δ % between 1992 and 2004
Housing	30.3	37.6	37.7	7.4
Schools	25.9	34.7	35.3	9.4

housing has an effect on the segregation between schools because the neighbourhood that constitutes the immediate surroundings of the school affects the composition of pupils at the school. If the school is situated in a neighbourhood with a concentration of inhabitants of foreign background, this will be reflected in the composition of students. In Table 1 you can see that the segregation in schools is increasing faster than the segregation in housing. This could indicate that the number of students actively choosing their schools is increasing, and that this has an influence on the ethnic segregation between schools. The municipality does not have figures on how many students chose schools prior to 2004, and it is difficult to estimate how many did so in 1992 and 1998. But the numbers were probably much smaller than around 2000. When the free-choice reform was implemented in 1992 the total number of schools was more limited, because there were not yet any independent schools; this means that the school market was small. If you look at the number of students that made a choice in the years 2004–2009, you can see an increase between 2004 and 2009. The statistics are not robust because not all of the choices to attend independent schools have been counted for the years 2008 and 2009, so the number of students making active choices are most certainly much greater for these years. (Örebro municipality 2009).

But how are these choices affecting the schools as a meeting place? Are the choices making the schools more homogeneous with regard to their socioeconomic and ethnic composition, or are they leading to a greater mix of students? One aim of the free choice reform, when it was implemented in the early 1990s, was to decrease the segregation within and across the schools. Can one say that this aim has been fulfilled?

Table 2. Number of students that made a school choice in Örebro 2004–2009.

Year	Municipal schools	Independent schools	Total	Students that make a choice, of all students each year (%)
2004	112	168	280	2
2005	220	95	315	3
2006	330	249	579	5
2007	422	263	685	6
2008	415	7*	422	4
2009	471	122**	593	5

*only 3 of 9 independent schools counted ** only 2 of 11 independent schools counted*

The schools in Örebro municipality

We now turn to the percentages of students with foreign background[3] and whose parents have low levels of education[4]

Figure 2 shows all of the ninth-grade schools in Örebro in 2004 (E, P, M ...) and the percentages of students with foreign background at each school and students with parents that have less than 10 years of education. The differences are quite high between the schools, with school E having a large proportion of students with foreign background and from low educated families, and schools like H and N having a small proportion of students with foreign background and none from low-educated families.

The schools E, P, and M are situated in neighbourhoods that are highly segregated from other neighbourhoods (as are schools like H, N, and B); you can see a divide regarding students with foreign background and their parents' educational level across the schools in Örebro. The differences between the schools may be related to the segregation in housing, because the composition of the people living in the neighbourhood forms the composition of students in the school. But it can also be an outcome of the student choices; for example, some students that live near school E may choose other schools and therefore leave the school that they otherwise would attend. In the next part of the chapter, we take a closer look at

3   Foreign background= Born abroad or both parents born abroad.
4   Low educated = Compulsory school (up to 10 years of education).

**Students with foreign background in
ninth-grade schools in Örebro 2004**

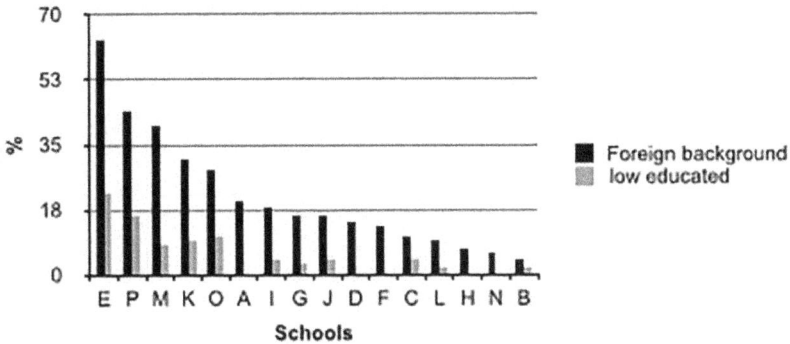

Figure 2. Schools in Örebro 2004

school E and how free choice of schools is affecting the socioeconomic and ethnic composition of the students at this school.

Neighbourhood E

School E is situated in a neighbourhood that has transformed. The
neighbourhood was built in the 1970s and is composed mainly of
blocks of flats. Relatively soon after it was built it became socioeconomically segregated due to the outflow of socioeconomically
strong individuals. Those who stayed mostly had a working class
background or a socioeconomically weaker position than those
who left the area.

In the mid 1990s you could see a change; the neighbourhood
experienced an inflow of ethnic minorities, and residents with
Swedish background started to move out. This was mainly due to
structural causes: the neighbourhood had a large number of vacant
flats and the immigrants who came to Örebro moved to neighbourhood E (or were placed there by the municipality). The result was
that Swedes started to move out which started a process leading
towards ethnic segregation. In 2004, 43 percent of the individuals
in the neighbourhood had foreign background. So neighbourhood
E came to have a different ethnic and socioeconomic composition
than the surrounding neighbourhoods. This is not an unusual

Table 3. Socioeconomic and ethnic measures for neighbourhood E: 1992, 1998, and 2004

Neighbourhood E	1992 (1523)	1998 (1709)	2004 (1797)
Median family income (SEK)	128 100	140 600	170 900
Higher education (%)	12	14	20
Unemployment (%)	25	29	22
Social allowance (%)	20	41	26
Foreign background (%)	19	39	43

process, and similar developments can be seen in other neighbour-hoods in Örebro and in other cities in Sweden (Bråmå 2004). The starting point for the study is accordingly a segregated neighbour-hood; the question is how this affects the school.

School E

Table 4 shows the socioeconomic and ethnic measures for the students in ninth grade in school E during three years. 1992 was the first year of the free-choice reform in Sweden. It was, in other words, the first year that students had the option to choose a school other than the one nearest to their homes. As the table shows, the number of students in ninth grade drops over the years (the figure in brackets) from 147 students in 1992, to 68 in 1998, and finally 46 in 2004. The median income for the students' families also drops from 269,700 SEK in 1992 to 264,200 SEK in 2004. Students from highly educated[5] families also decrease, while the unemployment[6] and social allowance rates increase. Students with foreign background also increased from 18 percent in 1992 to 63 percent in 2004. Finally, the mean cumulative grades[7] for

5   Highly educated: at least three years of tertiary education.
6   Unemployment: at least one of the parents is unemployed
7   The grade system was reformed between 1992 and 1998, so it is difficult to compare the figures for 1992 with those for 1998 and 2004. In the old system, a student received a final grade between 1 and 5, in the new system it was possible to achieve a maximum of 320 points. The mean for all students in ninth grade in Sweden in 2004 was 207 points, and in Örebro municipality 204.7 points.

Table 4. Socioeconomic and ethnic measures for school E: 1992, 1998, and 2004 (ninth grade)

School E	1992 (147)	1998 (68)	2004 (46)
Median family income (SEK)	269 700	273 900	264 200
Higher education (%)	35	48	8
Unemployment (%)	27	27	56
Social allowance (%)	13	13	41
Foreign background (%)	18	29	63
Grades (mean)	3.2	200	150

the school drop from 200 to 150 points between 1998 and 2004.

This means that the students and their families have become socioeconomically weaker, and that students with foreign background have increased rapidly during the period between 1998 and 2004, at the same time as the number of students in ninth grade has decreased. This can be interpreted in two ways. Either the schools are reflecting a development in the neighbourhood, with increasing ethnic and socioeconomic segregation, and therefore have more pupils from socioeconomically weaker families with a minority background, or students from socioeconomically stronger families with Swedish background remain in the neighbourhood, but are choosing other schools. The decreasing number of pupils can depend on natural demographic fluctuations (the ninth-grade cohorts are decreasing in size) or it can depend on school choice (students live near school E but are choosing other schools instead).

To clarify the mechanism underlying this development we carry out a GIS analysis of the students that live inside the area and attend school E, and those who live in the area but choose other schools.

In Figure 3, the school is represented as a square in the middle, and the small circles are students who live inside the voronoi. In 1992 there were only four students who lived near school E but chose other schools; in 2004 there were 37 such students. The greater part of the students who choose other schools live relatively close to the school. They choose schools all over the city, but 17 of them are attending an independent school just outside the catchment area. If you compare the ethnic and socioeconomic compo-

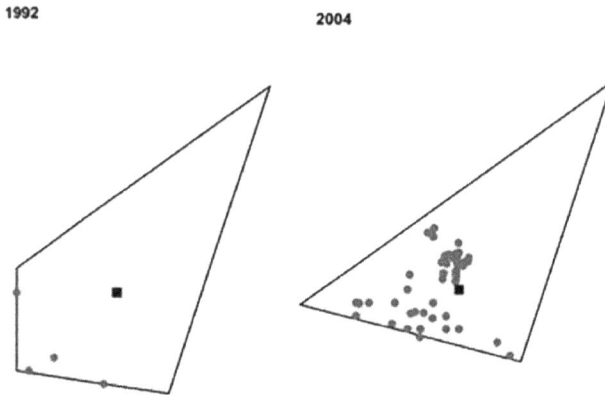

Figure 3. Voronoi for school E: students that live near school E but choose other schools.

sitions of the students who stay in school E and the students who leave the school you can notice some differences.

From Table 5 you can conclude that the students who live in the neighbourhood and attend school E have become both ethnically and socioeconomically homogeneous. The students in school E come from low income, low educated families, and most of them have foreign background and parents for whom unemployment and social allowance have increased over the years. The median income is lower in 2004 than in 1992, which indicates that it is low income families and families with foreign background who have moved into the neighbourhood over the years.

The number of students that live in the area but choose other schools has increased over the years, with 37 students living near the school but choosing other schools in 2004. You can see that these students come from families that have a different socioeconomic and ethnic background. Their parents have a higher income, are more educated, and have a lower unemployment rate and social allowance, and the students have better grades. You could say that these students are avoiding school E and are choosing other schools instead. The outflow of students is therefore high, and the school is losing students to other schools. The school is not functioning as a meeting place because the Swedish students are choosing other

Table 5. Ethnic and socioeconomic measures of students who attend and who leave school E respectively, in 1992 and 2004.

Students inside the voronio	1992 (42)	2004 (19)
Median income (SEK)	284 100	243 100
Higher education (%)	36	10
At least one parent unemployed (%)	19	63
Social allowance (%)	12	47
Foreign background (%)	12	74
Grade (mean)	3.2	166
Students inside the voronoi that choose another school	**1992 (4)**	**2004 (37)**
Median income (SEK)	148 600	289 800
Higher education (%)	-	43
At least one parent unemployed (%)	-	24
Social allowance (%)	0	13
Foreign background (%)	-	27
Grade (mean)	4	190

schools with the result that the school has become more socio-economically homogeneous. The school has a higher proportion of people with foreign background than the neighbourhood and the students come from families with more vulnerable social situation but a higher income than the neighbourhood as a whole. So you could say that the ethnic and social segregation is higher in the school than in the neighbourhood.

Conclusion

The number students that choose a school other than the one nearest their home has increased over the years. Because there are no statistics describing the overall choices that were made prior to 2004, it is difficult to see how many choices that were made before that year. But before the late 1990s there were a limited number of independent schools, and the municipal schools had not yet developed education profiles, so the 'education market' for the students was limited. They did not have as many schools to choose from because they were all alike. If you take this in account, as well as the fact that the reform was new (in other words that the students were not accustomed to making a choice), you can assume that the choices that were made before the late 1990s were limited in number. But in the early 2000s more students began to attend other schools than the one nearest their home (*i.e.* made an active choice). The trend is most certainly leading towards a more complex school situation, with students to a higher degree making use of their right to choose. If you look at school E, you can see that the students that are choosing other schools are those who come from a different socioeconomic and ethnic background. They have a stronger socioeconomic position and are primarily from a Swedish background. The school is being drained of students with Swedish background and is becoming more socioeconomically and ethnically homogeneous. Because the concentration of students with foreign background is higher in the school than in the neigh-bourhood, you could say that the school is not a reflection of the neighbourhood; in other words, the ethnic segregation is higher at the school level than the neighbourhood level.

The examples in this chapter show that in these cases the school has lost its ability to function as a meeting place for students with different ethnic and socioeconomic backgrounds. The free-choice reform therefore has an impact on the school as a place for students to meet other students with different ethnic and socioeconomic backgrounds.

References

Adnett N. & Bougheas S. & Davies P. (2000) 'Market-based reforms of public schooling: some unpleasant dynamics', *Economics of education review*, vol. 21, no. 4: 323–330, 2002.

Adnett N. & Davies P. (2003) 'Schooling reforms in England: from quasi-markets to co-operation?', *Journal of education policy*, vol. 18, no 4: 393–406.

Ahlin Å. & Mörk E. (2005) *Vad hände med resurserna när den svenska skolan decentraliserades?*, Rapport 2005:1, IFAU – Institutet för arbetsmarknadspolitisk utvärdering.

Arnman G. & Jönsson I. (1985), *Segregation och svensk skola – En studie av utbildning, klass och boende*, Studentlitteratur, Lund 1985.

Bagley C. & Woods P. & Glatter R. (2001), 'Rejecting schools: Towards a fuller understanding of the process of parental choice', *School leadership & management*, vol. 21, no 3: 309–325.

Blomquist P. & Rothstein B. (2000) *Välfärdsstatens nya ansikte – demokrati och marknadsreformer inom den offentliga sektorn*, Agora, Stockholm 2000.

Board of education (2011) *Lp 2011, Läroplan för grundskola, förskoleklassen och fritidshemmet 2011*, Board of education, Stockholm 2011.

Bråmå Å. (2004) *Utvecklingen av boendesegregationen i mellanstora städer under 1990-talet*, Bilaga till Rapport Integration 2003, Integrationsverket, 2004.

Bunar N. & Kallstenius J. (2006) *I min gamla skola lärde jag mig fel svenska' – En studie om skolvalfriheten i det polariserade urbana rummet*, Integrationsverket, Norrköping 2006.

Bunar N. (2001) *Skola mitt i förorten – fyra studier om skola, segregation, integration och multikulturalism*, Brutus Östlings bokförlag, Stockholm 2001.

Dovemark M. (2004) *Ansvar-flexibilitet-valfrihet En etnografisk studie om en skola i förändring*, Acta Universitatis gothoburgenesis, Göteborg 2004.

Duncan D. & Duncan B. (1955) 'A methodological analysis of segregation indexes', *American sociological review*, vol. 20, no. 2: 210–217.

Dustman C. (2004)'Parental background, secondary school track choice, and wages'. *Oxford economic papers*, vol. 56, no. 2: 209–230.

Egidius H. (2001) *Skola och utbildning – i historisk och internationellt perspektiv*, Natur och Kultur, Stockholm 2001.

Englund T. (2003)'Skolan och demokratin – på väg mot en skola mot deliberativa samtal?'i Jonsson B., Roth K.(red), *Demokrati och lärande – Om valfrihet, gemenskap och övervägande i skolan och samhälle*, Studentlitteratur, Lund 2003.

Gorard S. & Taylor C. & Fitz J. (2003) *Schools, Markets and Choice policies*, RoutledgeFalmer, London 2003

Gustavsson K. (2006) *Vi och dom i skola och stadsdel – barns identitets-*

178 Anders Trumberg

arbete och sociala geografier, Acta universitatis upsaliensis. Uppsala studies in education, No 11.

Integrationsverket (2007) *Statistikrapport 2007 – uppdatering av aktuella siffror, relevanta nyckeltal och indikatorer om integration*, Integrationsverket, Norrköping 2007.

Kallstenius J. (2011) *De mångkulturella innerstadsskolorna – om skolval, segregation och utbildningsstrategier i Stockholm*, Stockholm studies in sociology new series 49, Stockholms universitet 2011.

Ladd H.F. (2003) 'Introduction' i Plank D.N, Sykes G (eds.) *Choosing Choice – School choice in international perspective*', Teachers college press, New York, 2003.

Lankford H., Wyckoff J. (2001) 'Who would be left behind by Enhanced private school choice' *Journal of urban economics*, vol. 50, nr.2: 288–312.

Lidström A. & Hudson C. (1995) *Skola i förändring – Decentralisering och lokal variation*, Nerenius & Santérus förlag, Stockholm 1995.

Montin S. (2004) *Moderna kommuner*, 2 uppl. Liber AB, Malmö 2004.

Quennerstedt A. (2006) *Kommunen – en part i utbildningspolitiken?*, Örebro studies in education 14, Örebro universitet 2006.

Richardson G .(2004) *Svensk utbildningshistoria – skola och samhälle förr och nu*, Studentlitteratur, Lund 2004.

Sandberg A. (1998) *Integrationens arenor – En studie av flyktingmottagande, arbete, boende, förening*

-och församlingsliv i tre kommuner, Uppsala University, Department of Social and Economic Geography.

Sikkink D. & Emerson O. (2008) 'School choice and racial segregation in US schools: The role of parents education' *Ethnic and racial studies*, vol. 3, nr. 2: 267–293.

Skawonius C. (2005) *Välja eller hamna – Det praktiska sinnet, familjersval och elevers spridning på grundskolor*, Pedagogiska inst. Stockholms universitet, Stockholm 2005.

Strömblad P. (2003) *Politik på stadens skuggsida*, Acta universitatis upsaliensis, Statsvetenskapliga föreningen, Uppsala universitet 2003.

Sundberg D. (2005) *Skolreformens dilemma – en läroplansteoretisk studie av kampen om tid i den svenska obligatoriska skolan*, Acta Wexionensia Nr. 61/2005, Växjö University press 2005.

Swedish board of education (1995) *Att välja skola – effekter av valmöjligheten i skolan*, Skolverket 1996.

Swedish board of education (1996) *Likvärdighet – ett delat ansvar*, Skolverket, 1996.

Swedish board of education (2003) *Valfrihet och dess effekter inom skolområdet*, Skolverket 2003.

Swedish board of education (2004) *Elever med utländsk bakgrund*, Skolverket, 2004.

Swedish board of education (2009) *Vad påverkar resultatet i svensk grundskola? Kunskapsöversikt om betydelsen av olika faktorer*, Skolverket 2009.

Swedish board of education (2010)
Rustad att möta framtiden? PISA
2009 om 15-åringars läsförståelse
och kunskaper i matematik och
naturvetenskap, Rapport 352,
Skolverket 2010.

Swedish board of education (2011)
Läroplan för grundskolan, förskoleklassen och fritidshemmet
2011 (national curriculum for the
compulsory school), Skolverket
2011.

Trumberg A. (2011) Den delade
skolan – segregationsprocesser i
det svenska skolsystemet, Örebro
studies in Human Geography 6,
Örebro 2011.

Van der Burgt D. (2006) Där man
bor tycker man det är bra – Barns

geografier i en segregerad stadsmiljö,
Geografiska regionstudier nr 71,
Uppsala universitet 2006.

Vranken J. & De Decker P. & Van
Nieuwenhuyze I. (2003) Social
inclusion, urban governance and
sustainability – Towards a conceptual framework, UGIS collection
1, Garant, Antwerp 2003.

Wahlström N. (2002) Om det förän-
drade ansvaret för skolan – Vägen
till mål – och resultatstyrning och
några av dess konsekvenser, Örebro
studies in education 3, Örebro
universitet 2002.

Örebro kommun (2009)
Boendeplanering i Örebro kommun
till 2018 – med utblick mot 2035,
Örebro kommun, Örebro 2009.

Appendix

$$S_x = - \sum \left[\frac{N_{1i}}{N_1} - \frac{N_{2i}}{N_2} \right]$$

Figure 1: segregation index.
(White 1983)

(1) S_x = The share of population 1 (or 2) that would have to be
    redistributed for each area (i) to have the same distribution as
    the city as a whole.

(2) N_{1i} = Population 1 in area i.

(3) N_{2i} = Population 2 in area i.

(4) N_1 = Total population 1 in the city.

(5) N_2 = Total population 2 in the city.

Place and Unsafety

– How does place affect feelings of unsafety?

Monika Persson

The idea that place has a unique effect on feelings of unsafety, or fear of crime has been rejected. However, in most previous research only direct effects have been investigated. This chapter shows that we need to consider the alternative effects that place may have on our lives and perceptions. In the present study, place has a moderating effect on feelings of unsafety. In the Swedish city of Örebro, the variables with a direct effect on feelings of unsafety are what we could expect in light of previous research (for instance age, gender, and socioeconomic factors). In Vivalla, a segregated, multiethnic, and disadvantaged neighbourhood in the same town, trust in institutions, the police, and people in general are the variables with a unique effect on feelings of unsafety. Hence, place may not necessarily have a direct effect but can still alter the influence of other variables. This makes possible a more nuanced empirical understanding of the influence of place

Introduction[1]

In the last two or three decades community safety and local crime prevention policies have spread internationally and influenced national and local policy in numerous countries (Crawford, 2009). The social problem that these policies postulate and aim to address

---

1   A slightly different version of this chapter was published as Persson, Monika (2013). 'The relative importance of institutional trust in countering feelings of unsafety in disadvantaged neighbourhoods', *European Spatial Research and Policy*, 20(1): 73–95.

comprises not only crime, but also fear of crime or feelings of unsafety, viewed as a partly separate phenomenon assumed to have its own causes and effects (see *e.g.* Persson 2012; Lidskog & Persson 2012). Feelings of unsafety have become an urgent and prioritised policy issue. Fear, security, and feelings of unsafety are politicised issues (Robin 2004) and it has been argued that these feelings are fostered by the emphasis on risk in contemporary society (Bauman 2006). An ongoing conceptual consideration among researchers is whether fear of crime might better be understood as insecurity about certain aspects of modern living, such as quality of life, urban unease, fear of strangers, or perception of disorder (Hale, 1996, p. 84). The mainstream rationalistic paradigm is challenged by the symbolic paradigm (Elchardus *et al.*, 2008), which is becoming more influential (see, *e.g.*, Jackson, 2006; Lee & Farral, 2009; Cops, 2010; De Donder *et al.*, 2012). According to the symbolic paradigm, fear of crime has a symbolic nature. People's feelings of unsafety are connected to macro-sociological developments such as globalisation, urbanisation, emancipation, migration, and secularisation, and from attitudes of discomfort, threat, and helplessness in the face of the consequences of such developments (Cops, 2010). The increasingly influential fear-of-crime discourse that is linked to the risk society (Beck, 1992) is explained by the relative controllability of crime by the individual. Fear of crime, in this interpretation, may be a projection of more indefinable anxieties that derive from uncertainty and multiple life choices (*cf.* Giddens, 1991; Holloway & Jefferson, 1997).

As indicated in their name, these policies are directed towards the local level. The problems as well as their remedies are central factors of the dynamics of a local community (crime, fear of crime, feelings of unsafety, interpersonal trust, social capital). Emphasising the local also underlines the importance of the local context, or place, if you like. Different local contexts face different problems as well as possibilities and thus need to develop locally adapted solutions. However, despite this emphasis on locality the understanding of the effect of place on feelings of safety has its limitations. Aggregate level research has argued that place has no *direct* effect on people's feelings of unsafety; instead, geographically-clustered individual factors explain these feelings. However, few studies have investigated alternative effects of place.

Some researchers have argued that place has more explanatory power than is accounted for by its structural characteristics. They argue that place partially shapes our social identities (Castells, 1997; Forrester & Kearns, 2001). We cannot avoid the way we categorise the world (by ethnicity, gender, race, or place) or ignore the dominant connotations of those categories when we negotiate our identities (Putnam, 2007). The internal compositions of our neighbourhoods as well as others' perception of our neighbourhoods (*i.e.*, their reputations) are important for our socialisation (Forrester & Kearns, 2001; *cf.* Lilja, 2008, p. 173). Identities and perceptions are thus shaped by and embedded in the composition and relative categorisation of one's neighbourhood. According to this argument, the neighbourhood as a place, and not just its structural characteristics, should influence the individual's feelings of unsafety.

The aim of this study is to explore the effect of place on the neighbourhood inhabitants' general feelings of unsafety while controlling for the structural characteristics of place. Hence, place is measured as a physical area with certain characteristics, and the effect of place is examined as the residual explanation when other structural factors are accounted for. The study is based on case-study data from an urban neighbourhood (Vivalla in the city of Örebro, Sweden), using a random sample of the other neighbourhoods in the same city as a control group. Two alternative effects of place are examined: first, the effect that the perception of place has on feelings of unsafety above and beyond the structural explanations; and second, the importance of place for feelings of unsafety in relation to other variables (*e.g.*, gender, age, interpersonal trust, trust in the police, etc.). In summary, does place have a unique and direct effect on feelings of unsafety, or does it have a moderating effect? If the latter is true, how could we describe and understand that effect?

Theoretical models

This study is explorative in two respects. First, when examining the influence of place on feelings of safety, previous research (including the fear-of-crime research) does not proceed to investigate alternative models, such as interaction effects in the form of moderation after the identification of the direct effects. Second, operationalising the explanatory variable as feelings of unsafety, in accordance with the symbolic paradigm, means that the explanatory model is not established. The number of quantitative studies applying this concept is still limited. Therefore, like other studies that have used this concept (*e.g.*, Elchardus *et al.*, 2008; Cops, 2010; De Donder *et al.*, 2012), this study builds on the results and established variables of the rationalist paradigm. Feelings of unsafety, defined as fear of crime, are generally explained by individual characteristics such as gender, age, and descent, as well as socioeconomic status, including employment status and education level (Hale, 1996). These structurally based individual explanations are therefore included in the models together with exposure to crime, which is another key explanatory variable in the rationalist paradigm (Elchardus *et al.*, 2008).

However, the wider, symbolic definition of feelings of unsafety, as *general unsafety*, requires a broader set of explanations. Feelings of unsafety are related to concerns about the moral and social trajectory of society (including concerns in specific neighbourhoods) and are influenced by political actions (Lee, 2001; Jackson, 2006; Cops, 2010). Various forms of trust are said to be variables that may explain feelings of general unsafety (see *e.g.* Walklate, 1998). According to Goldsmith (2005, p. 444), 'Trust, through its presence or absence, is innately linked to feelings of existential safety'. Both concepts are connected to risk and the way we handle insecurity. The ability to cope with anxiety is, according to Giddens (1991), related to trust developed in childhood; this trust is then continuously shaped through social interaction. According to the literature on institutional trust, the way institutions function in a certain country affects not only the trust in those institutions but also the generalised trust and social capital among its inhabitants (Stolle, 2007; Rothstein & Stolle, 2008). By means of its type of welfare state, its degree of general subsidies, degree of predictability, and level of corruption, a country signals values and interacts with its inhabitants. By these means, a country can enhance trust (Rothstein & Stolle, 2008) and neutralise public insecurity. Institutions may thereby strengthen the ability of individuals to handle anxiety (Hummelsheim *et al.*, 2011, p. 337).

The forms of trust addressed in this study are generalised trust, institutional trust, and trust in the police. Our attitudes towards the police are assumed to influence our feelings of unsafety. If we are affected by or concerned about crime, the police is the institution to which we have to turn and in which we place our confidence and trust. Previous research has argued that excluded and marginalised groups generally tend to have less trust in institutions (Goldsmith, 2005), and of these, minority groups in particular tend to have less trust in the police (Tyler, 2005).

In this study two alternative models are tested. Model 1 tests if place has a unique effect on general unsafety (see Figure 1). Hence, Model 1 tests whether feelings of unsafety depend on a number of individual explanations, including individual characteristics, the level of social and institutional trust, and place (*i.e.* the neighbourhood of residence).

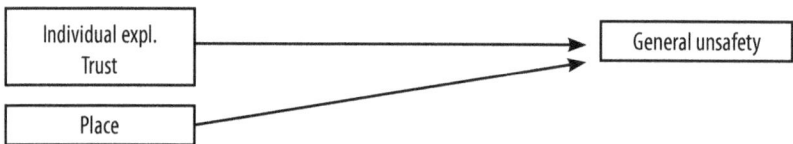

Figure 1. Persson, Theoretical model 1.

Model 2 assumes that place affects feelings of unsafety in a more complex way (see Figure 2). In this model, place does not necessarily have a direct effect on general unsafety; rather, place alters factors that are central to perceptions of the world as safe. Hence, Model 2 tests whether place has a moderating effect on the other explanatory variables of general unsafety.

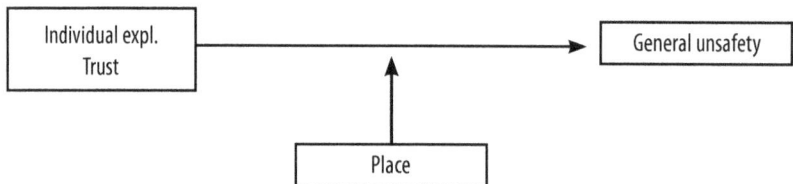

Figure 2. Persson, Theoretical model 2

The Place – A contextual description of Vivalla

Figure 1. Vivalla's geographical position in Sweden and in Örebro. (The map on the right shows the two samples. The map covers Örebro, with Vivalla marked.)

The two theoretical models were tested on quantitative data collected in Örebro, Sweden. Örebro is a medium-sized city in central Sweden with approximately 137,000 inhabitants. Like many Swedish cities of comparable size, it has ethnic segregation. The most segregated areas are the 'white' neighbourhoods, which are distanced from the socioeconomically disadvantaged and multi-ethnic neighbourhoods (Johansson, 2002, pp. 216–220). However, the neighbourhood (or place) investigated in this study is Vivalla, the Örebro neighbourhood considered the most problematic (Örebro Police, 2009). A sample population from the city of Örebro is used as the comparison reference point. The demographic composition of Örebro is comparable to other medium-sized Swedish cities.

In 2011 (the year following this study), the neighbourhood of Vivalla, had 6823 inhabitants. During the last decade the neighbourhood has had a steadily increasing population (Örebro Municipality, 2012). The neighbourhood was founded around 1967–1970. At that time, apartment housing was being built on a large scale in the suburban areas of Sweden, which in Vivalla's case resulted in the construction of a homogeneous neighbourhood dominated by small rental apartments. Before long, the neighbourhood began to be perceived and described as a 'problem area' and it has since been associated with negative connotations such as: criminality, unsafety, social problems, a high density of immigrants, and uniform apartments (Örebro Police, 2009), many of which are structural challenges that Vivalla faces. However, as Lilja (2008) notes, it is important to remember that the external images of a marginalised place may often be more negative than the image held by its inhabitants who have memories, life experiences, and a relationship to the place. See Table 1 for a listing of the demographic characteristics of the inhabitants of Vivalla and Örebro in general.

Table 1. Neighbourhood characteristics (Örebro Municipality, 2012)

	% with...	Higher education	Education <9 years	Open unemployment 18–24 years	Open unemployment 18–64 years	Foreign birth	Foreign background
Vivalla	Women	7.7	25.4	12.8	14.0	52.4	74.8
	Men	9.6	19.6	11.0	16.3	50.3	74.5
	Total	8.7	22.5	11.9	15.1	51.3	74.7
Örebro	Women	30.0	4.6	4.9	3.9	15.1	20.7
	Men	21.1	4.6	6.0	4.4	14.8	20.8
	Total	25.5	4.6	5.4	4.1	15.0	20.7

Unemployment (2011.10.31) = according to definition of the Swedish Employment Office

Table 1 shows that Vivalla has a higher unemployment rate than the city-wide average. Vivalla's inhabitants also have lower levels of education and more often have foreign backgrounds. In the last decade, the percentage of the inhabitants in Vivalla with foreign backgrounds has steadily risen (an average of 74.7 per cent in 2011 compared to 52.6 per cent in 2003) (Örebro Municipality, 2012). This increase is explained by the high turnover of inhabitants, with a relatively large number of 'native Swedes' moving away from the neighbourhood at the same time as more people with foreign backgrounds have moved into the neighbourhood.

Because Vivalla is the neighbourhood in Örebro with the most concerns about criminality, the Örebro police department has recently initiated neighbourhood policing (Örebro Police, 2009). The most alarming crime statistics pertain to violence against women in intimate relationships[2] and muggings. Both crimes are about three to five times more frequent in Vivalla than in Örebro in general. Other crimes, which are about twice as common in Vivalla as in Örebro, are physical assault outdoors, moped theft, and drug offences (Örebro Police, 2009). According to the police, there is also a serious problem with the recruitment of young men into criminal gangs as a consequence of the structural disadvantages of the neighbourhood (Örebro Police, 2009). Considering the conditions in Vivalla – its social composition and structural context – living there is likely to affect the inhabitants' identities as well as influence their feelings of unsafety.

Method

At the end of the millennium a major advance in research at the neighbourhood level occurred (Sampson et al., 2002). However, this research has been criticised. First, it is charged that many quantitative neighbourhood studies use neighbourhood boundaries that have been defined by administrative agencies. Therefore, these boundaries are not necessarily equivalent to social community boundaries (Sampson et al., 2002; Brunton-Smith & Jackson, working paper). Second, this research generally takes an aggregate-level approach in which the respondents describe the neighbourhood variables. It is questionable whether such an approach accounts for causalities, as proponents of this method tend to claim. Using a case study in which the neighbourhood boundaries and its characteristics are well-defined is appropriate because this permits a more nuanced analysis and avoids

---

2   The design of this study does not capture the particularities of this form of crime. This is arguably a limitation of the study because many researchers have shown that the home is the most dangerous location for women in terms of victimisation.

the trap of the respondents embodying all variables.[3]

For this research, a questionnaire was sent to 1000 potential respondents in the second half of 2010 (Örebro 400; Vivalla 600). The respondents were asked about their feelings of unsafety and trust, and about their views on the police, together with a number of control variables. The questions were in Swedish, but respondents could reply in English via the Internet. Four reminders were sent. The netto[4] response rate was 43.6 per cent (Örebro 61.8 per cent, Vivalla 30.8 per cent),[5] resulting in a sample size of N = 401 (Örebro 235, Vivalla 166). The lower response rate in Vivalla was arguably caused by the rapid turnover in its population as well as by language barriers.

In connection with the fourth and last reminder, we telephoned the potential respondents and encouraged them to answer the questionnaire. However, only about one-third of the potential respondents in Vivalla who had not yet answered had listed phone numbers (in the whole sample of non-respondents the number was 319 of 599). Of those who answered the phone call (just over half), together with those who returned the questionnaire without answering it, 15 explicitly said they could not answer the questionnaire because of language difficulties. In summary, this tells us that there may be a part of the population that is more mobile and less established, and for which this sample does not properly account. It is likely that the inability to answer the questionnaire due to language difficulties is even greater in this group. On the other hand, including transitory inhabitants would not necessarily be beneficial for the aim of this study.

To control for bias in the Vivalla sample due to non-responses, three variables of individual characteristics (gender, employment,

---

3   This is not to say that the inhabitants' understanding and experience are secondary (*cf.* Lilja, 2008). However, when studying mechanisms quantitatively, there can be methodological difficulties with taking them into account.

4   After subtracting those responses that were sent back blank.

5   As a consequence of the difficulty in obtaining high response rates, (which is typical in contemporary segregated areas), research has been conducted on the statistical effects and limitations that a limited sample imply. These studies show very limited differences due to nonresponses (Langer, 2003). Langer also emphasises that nonresponses have received disproportionate attention as far as reliability in relation to other methodological questions is concerned (such as constructs and choice of statistical method).

foreign birth) were compared with the municipal dataset. No significant differences were revealed.[6] The number of women and men are similar. The number of respondents born abroad in this data set is 49.1 per cent in Vivalla and 11.1 per cent in Örebro as a whole, compared to 50.1 per cent and 14.5 per cent, respectively, in the municipal dataset for 2010. Concerning employment the number of respondents in this sample describing themselves as unemployed were 9.1 per cent in Vivalla and 1.7 per cent in Örebro, compared to 9.3 per cent and 5.3 per cent, respectively, in the municipal dataset from the same year. Note that the Vivalla respondent percentages are closer to those in the municipal dataset than the Örebro respondent percentages as far as unemployment and foreign birth are concerned. This difference may partly be explained by the fact that the sample used in this study is from the city of Örebro, whereas the municipal statistics cover a wider area. To conclude, this test shows no considerable bias due to non-responses.

The statistical method used is regression analysis, with the moderating effect of place being evaluated by subgroup regression (Hartmann & Moers, 1999). Since the moderator is dichotomous, a subgroup regression approach to testing moderation equals a moderated regression analysis (MRA), which is the most common regression technique for evaluating moderation (Hartmann & Moers, 1999, p. 295). The significance of the differences between the subgroups is calculated using the z-score (Garson, 2011). Missing values on the index/variable level in the regression models are generally few, ranging from 0 to 7.5 per cent. Since listwise deletion is used in the regressions, the listwise number of missing values for some models is about 25 per cent. However, the comparison of listwise means and correlations with estimated means (EM) and correlations reveals no differences.

For an account of the questions posed and the variables used in the analysis, including the constructs, see appendix 1. For descriptive statistics, including skewness and kurtosis, see appendix 3.

---

6   It should also be noted that while the questions do not have strictly equal formulations, they do include comparable alternatives.

Characteristics of place – Vivalla compared to Örebro

Previous research gives us reason to believe that the level of perceived unsafety is higher and of trust is lower in segregated, disadvantaged areas because the inhabitants of such areas generally experience greater socioeconomic vulnerability and higher levels of victimisation. They also encounter more visible signs of disorder. These are all factors known to increase feelings of unsafety (measured as fear of crime). In addition, research from the US has shown that ethnic group differences account for the fact that some groups trust the police less than other groups (Tyler 2005; Stoutland, 2001). The initial consideration was therefore to learn whether there was a difference in trust and feelings of unsafety between Vivalla and Örebro as a whole. Related aspects were also investigated, one being civic engagement, which is often seen as a proxy for social capital and as fundamental for general safety (Stolle, 2007). Differences in the level of exposure to crime were also measured, however because it was already known from other data that these differences existed, these measures were included to control for the representativity of the respondents.

Table 2. Mean levels of central concepts: Vivalla in relation to Örebro as a whole

	Vivalla		Örebro			
	Mean	SD	Mean	SD	p<.05	Cohen's D
General unsafety	2.24	.85	2.44	.81	Sig.	0.24
Institutional trust	3.05	.88	3.17	.70	n.s.	
Trust in police	3.36	.93	3.29	.83	n.s.	
Generalised trust	3.13	1.13	3.70	1.00	Sig.	0.52
Civic engagement	2.66	1.37	2.73	1.28	n.s.	
Exposure to crime	1.47	.72	1.27	.54	Sig.	0.32

Table 2 shows that the inhabitants of Vivalla have higher general feelings of unsafety than the inhabitants of Örebro as a whole. The inhabitants of Vivalla also have lower generalised trust. These two variables show significant mean difference in an ANOVA test (p= 0.021, 0.000). The difference in exposure to crime was also tested and, as expected, a difference was found between Vivalla and Örebro. People living in Vivalla are more exposed to crime than people living in Örebro (p=0.002). The strength of the difference can be calculated using Cohen's D (Borg & Westerlund, 2006; Garson, 2011). According to Cohen's categorisation of effect strength (Borg & Westerlund, 2006), the difference in general unsafety and exposure to crime is small, whereas the difference in generalised trust is moderate.

Considering the socioeconomically disadvantaged situation of Vivalla's inhabitants, including the rapid turnover of population, these differences were expected. If anything, they could have been expected to be even larger. However, less expected was that no significant differences were found between Vivalla and Örebro as a whole with regard to institutional trust, trust in the police, and civic engagement. A complementary finding is that neighbourhoods with socially disadvantaged minority groups often give rise to socialisation processes and experiences that reduce trust in public institutions, including the police (Goldsmith, 2005; Tyler, 2005). It is often claimed that civic engagement has a buffering effect on such lack of trust (Ross & Joon, 2000). However, in the present study there is no support that this explains the lack of difference, since we found no significant difference in civic engagement between the two groups.

The moderating effect of place on feelings of unsafety

Having concluded that there is a difference in general unsafety, however small, we now turn to the central question of this study: Does place have a part in explaining the difference between the two groups regarding feelings of unsafety? Looking at the correlation matrix of the variables (see Appendix 2), we see that place has an individual effect on the dependent variable. Hence, Model 1 tests whether that effect remains when the other explanatory variables are controlled for (see Table 3).

In order to test Model 1, place was included in the same regression as the other independent variables which showed it has no unique effect on feelings of unsafety. The variables explaining variance in feelings of unsafety are gender, age, and education,

Table 3. Antecedents of general unsafety: The influence of place
(N total 306, N Örebro 199, N Vivalla 107)

	Total		Vivalla		Örebro	
	(Theoretical model 1)		(Theoretical model 2)			
	Regression model 1		Regression model 2		Regression model 3	
	Std. Beta	Sig	Std. Beta	Sig	Std. Beta	Sig
Individual variables						
Gender	.140	.006	.078	.365	.174	.007
Age	−.139	.011	−.035	.712	−.172	.011
Descent	−.091	.115	−.116	.217	−.056	.382
Education	−.152	.006	−.128	.147	−.180	.009
Employed/unemployed	−.031	.571	−.065	.468	−.017	.791
Exposure to crime	−.020	.703	−.118	.186	.023	.716
Trust variables						
Generalised trust	−.309	.000	−.209	.025	−.371	.000
Institutional trust	−.180	.007	−.323	.005	−.080	.331
Trust in police	−.117	.068	−.241	.028	−.036	.650
Place	.035	.553				
Adjusted R^2	.241		.267		.237	

plus the three trust variables: generalised trust, trust in institutions, and trust in the police. Women and the elderly feel more unsafe than men and younger people do. The more education an individual has, the more that individual trusts and the less unsafe he or she feels. This conclusion agrees with other research findings (see, *e.g.*, Hale, 1996; Sandstig, 2010). Employment status, descent and exposure to crime have no effect on feelings of unsafety. Victimisation increases fear of crime, but has less effect when measuring general unsafety (see also Elchardus, 2008, p. 464). In short, we can dismiss Model 1; place has no individual and direct effect on feelings of unsafety.

This is where many studies on the effect of place end. To investigate the matter further, however, we now turn to whether place has a moderating effect on feelings of unsafety. Subgroup regressions were made for the inhabitants of both Örebro as a whole and Vivalla. As regressions two and three show (Table 3), the explanatory effects of the other independent variables change. They are moderated by the effect of place. Different aspects influence feelings of unsafety depending on whether one lives in Vivalla or in the rest of Örebro. In Örebro, there are still unique effects for the individual explanations gender, age, and education, plus generalised trust, which is the dominant variable accounting for 14 per cent[7] of Regression Model 3's explanatory power. Institutional trust and trust in police lose significance.

In Vivalla, on the other hand, we find a new and somewhat reversed pattern. The traditional explanations disappear. Age, gender, education, descent, and employment status show no unique effect on general unsafety. The variables that are significant in the explanation of feelings of unsafety are generalised trust, the level of trust in institutions, and institutional trust in the police. Thus, trust is much more central than individual characteristics such as gender, age, employment, etc. Moreover, institutional trust and trust in the police are the strongest explanatory variables, accounting for 16 per cent of the variance in Regression Model 2. To conclude, trust in institutions, and the police in particular, seems to be more important for countering feelings of unsafety in neighbourhoods such as Vivalla than the city-wide average. It seems to be particularly important (or beneficial) to have a trustworthy police force and trustworthy institutions in disadvantaged neighbourhoods. Exposure to crime does not have a unique effect on feelings of unsafety in either of our models. Although such exposure may affect fear of crime, it does not seem to affect general feelings of unsafety (*cf.* Elchardus, 2008, p. 464).

The moderating effect of place causes two different explanatory patterns of unsafety in Vivalla and in Örebro as a whole. Up to this point, we have not accounted for the statistical significance of the differences between the subgroups. To account for these differences concerning specific variables, the significance of the difference between the standardised betas of Örebro and Vivalla (Table 3 regression models two and three) was calculated.[8] A one-tailed

---

7   Calculated by taking the squared Std. Beta.
8   Calculated by converting into z-scores and computing the standard error of difference (Garson, 2011).

significance test was used to identify significant differences in institutional trust and trust in the police. These are the central aspects
moderated by place. The conclusion that place moderates the effect
of traditional explanations such as gender, age, and socioeconomic
status needs to be confirmed by studies with larger respondent
samples. The limited sample of this study may lack the power to
confirm those relationships. However, the indication that strong
identity-forming factors (*e.g.* gender and age) have no effect on
how the inhabitants of Vivalla perceive their environment in terms
of general unsafety is an original finding that merits further study.

Discussion

A plausible reason for the relative influence of trust in institutions
and trust in the police on feelings of unsafety in Vivalla may be the
greater presence of and dependence on the police in such neighbourhoods. Trust in the police (as well as in other institutions)
may therefore be more essential in such neighbourhoods through
its having the ability to prevent feelings of unsafety. This could be
explained in terms of vulnerability, though in a different sense than
is portrayed in the literature on fear of crime. The inhabitants are
vulnerable because of their relatively greater dependence on public
institutions. This situation may explain why their level of trust in
such institutions is inversely related to their feelings of unsafety.

The crucial role of public institutions in preventing feelings of
unsafety is supported by a study by Hummelsheim *et al.* (2011)
showing that a high level of social expenditures and a higher degree
of decommodification of social welfare policy are correlated with
lower crime-related insecurity. The authors suggest that these
policy measures neutralise public insecurity and social anxiety
(*ibid.* p. 337). These results explain Sweden's relatively low levels of
unsafety as being a consequence of the country's social democratic
welfare state with its high level of decommodification (Esping-
Andersen, 1990). Hence, the differences in trust and feelings of
unsafety between disadvantaged, segregated neighbourhoods and
the city-wide averages may be greater in countries with other
welfare state models. The somewhat surprising fact that feelings of
unsafety were only moderately higher in Vivalla than in Örebro as a

whole suggests that the public institutions have somewhat neutral-ised the social insecurity that is a result of structural disadvantages.

A recent empirical study from the same local context pointed to the critical function of schools in disadvantaged neighbourhoods: schools can be safe havens for children (Svensson *et al.*, 2012). Young people in these neighbourhoods, in particular young immi-grants, perceive their schools as safe places where they have a meas-ure of influence that they typically lack in their neighbourhoods. In Svensson *et al.*'s study, as well as in this study, respondents in the disadvantaged neighbourhoods did not have higher levels of trust in institutions or greater perceptions of their own influ-ence, in comparison with control groups,. However, their trust in institutions and their perceptions of influence have a more critical function, as they seem to prevent feelings of unsafety and generate feelings of safety. Hence, to understand the full scope of the cen-tral factors influencing feelings of unsafety, one needs to consider moderating effects. In this case we have identified trust as a critical factor for feelings of unsafety in disadvantaged neighbourhoods, whereas other research designs would not have revealed its promi-nent function in these contexts. At the same time this means that the same variables have less impact in other areas than a purely random sample would suggest.

Conclusions

Feelings of unsafety and fear of crime are a political and social concern that is distinguishable from actual crime or risk. Policies on local crime prevention and community safety not only address causes of crime but also address the feelings of anxiety and unsafety that surround crime (Gilling, 2001). However, it is difficult to define unsafety as well as deal with it. As a concept, it often becomes a measure of how safe one feels from specific types of crime and in specific situations. This study takes an alternative approach to feelings of unsafety, the symbolic paradigm. Feelings of unsafety are understood and measured as a perception of societal develop-ment and how safe the surrounding society is (see Elchardus *et al.*, 2008). The study looks in particular at the role place plays in this perception.

Two theoretical models on the role of place on feelings of unsafety were tested. The findings from Model 1 show that place has no unique effect on how unsafe one perceives the world to be. Theoretically, this finding indicates that place can be reduced to its structural variables. However, Model 2 shows that place has a moderating effect on feelings of unsafety. Hence, a primary conclusion is that more complex mechanisms than direct effects should be considered when determining the effect of place and when searching for mechanisms behind feelings of unsafety.

Living in Vivalla changes the influence of other factors on feelings of unsafety. In Örebro (and as reported in previous research) the variables with a unique effect on general unsafety are gender, age, and education, together with generalised trust. The fact that women, the elderly, and socioeconomically weaker groups experience greater feelings of unsafety is often ascribed to their greater vulnerability (Hale, 1996), and, for women in particular, it is connected to a socially constructed identity with an inferior power position (*e.g.* de Beauvoir 1986; Listerborn, 2001). In Vivalla, these factors with an established relationship to fear of crime do not influence feelings of unsafety. The factors that have a unique effect on feelings of unsafety are institutional trust, trust in the police, and generalised trust.

This is a limited and explorative study and we cannot draw general conclusions from the results presented. However, the findings challenge established explanations, and further research is needed to determine their scope. The results point in a partly new direction that assigns public institutions a central role in preventing feelings of unsafety in disadvantaged neighbourhoods. This result indicates that it is particularly in such areas that trustworthy institutions have the potential to generate feelings of safety and to neutralise the higher vulnerability and the greater risks these inhabitants face. These results are particularly important at a time when the welfare state is (or risks) being dismantled, when decommodification and redistribution are being rolled back, and when nations are considering reducing social services in deprived areas.

Concerning the understanding of place, this study suggests that we need to consider that place may not only have direct effects, but also may function as a moderator. Depending on the type of place where we live our lives, different aspects come to be more or less important, in this case, for example, regarding how (un)safe we perceive the world to be.

References

Austin, Mark D., Furr, Allan L., & Spine, Michael (2002). 'The effects of neighborhood conditions on perceptions of safety'. *Journal of Criminal Justice*, 30: 417–427.

Bauman, Zygmunt (2001). *Community: Seeking Safety in an Insecure World*. Cambridge, UK: Polity Press.

Beauvoir, Simone de (1986). *Det andra könet (Le Deuxième Sexe)*. 4th Ed. Stockholm: AWE/Geber.

Beck, Ulrich. (1992). *Risk Society: Towards a New Modernity*. London: Sage.

Björkemarken, Mariann (2009). *Medborgarskap otrygghet brottslighet*, Göteborg: Göteborgstryckeriet.

Borg, Elisabet, & Westerlund, Joakim (2006). *Statistik för beteendevetare*. 2nd Ed. Stockholm: Liber.

Brunton-Smith, Ian, & Jackson, Jonathan (working paper). 'Neighbourhoods Matter: Spatial Spill-over Effects in the Fear of Crime'. In; V. Ceccato (ed.), *Urban Fabric of Crime and Fear*. New York/Berlin: Springer)

Castells, Manuel (1997). *The Power of Identity*. Oxford: Blackwell.

Cops, Diederik (2010). 'Socializing into fear: The impact of socializing institutions on adolescents' fear of crime', *Young*, 18 (4): 385–402.

Crawford, Adam (2009). 'Situating crime prevention policies in comparative perspective: Policy travels, transfer and translation'. In: A.E. Crawford (ed.), *Crime Prevention Policies in Comparative Perspective* (pp. 1–37). Devon, UK: Willan Publishing.

De Donder, Liesbeth, De Witte, Nico, Buffel, Tine, Durey, Sarah, & Verté, Dominique (2012). 'Social capital and feelings of unsafety in later life: A study on the influence of social networks, place attachment, and civic participation on perceived safety in Belgium'. *Research on Aging*, 34(4): 425–448.

Ditton, Jason, & Farral, Stephen (2000). *Fear of Crime*. Aldershot: Ashgate.

Doran, Bruce J., & Lees Brian G. (2005). 'Investing the spatio-temporal links between disorder, Crime and fear of crime'. *The Professional Geographer*, 57(1): 1–12.

Elchardus, Mark, De Groof, Saskia, & Smits, Wendy (2008). 'Rational fear or represented malaise: A crucial test of two paradigms explaining fear of crime'. *Sociological Perspectives* 51 (3): 453–471.

Esping-Andersen, G (1990). *The Three Worlds of Welfare Capitalism*. Cambridge, UK: Polity Press.

Forrester, Ray, & Kearns, Ade (2001). 'Social cohesion, social capital and the neighbourhood'. *Urban Studies*, 38(12): 2125-2143.

Gabriel, Ute, & Greve, Werner (2003). 'The psychology of fear of crime: Conceptual and methodological perspectives'. *British Journal of Criminology* 43:600-614.

Garson, G. David (2011). 'Correlation', from *Statnotes: Topics in Multivariate Analysis*. Retrieved 04/11/2011 from http://faculty.chass.ncsu.edu/garson/pa765/statnote.htm.

Garson, G. David (2011). 'Univariate GLM, ANOVA, and ANCOVA', from *Statnotes: Topics in Multivariate Analysis*. Retrieved 05/02/2011 from http://faculty.chass.ncsu.edu/garson/pa765/statnote.htm.

Giddens, Anthony (1991). *Modernity and Self Identity*, Cambridge, UK: Polity Press.

Gilling Daniel (2001). 'Community safety and social policy', *European Journal on Criminal Policy and Research*, 9, 4: 381-400.

Goldsmith, Andrew (2005). 'Police reform and the problem of trust'. *Theoretical Criminology*, 9(4): 443-470)

Hale, Chris. (1996). 'Fear of crime: A review of the literature'. *International Review of Victimology*, 4: 79-150.

Hartmann, Frank. G.H., & Moers, Frank (1999). 'Testing contingency hypotheses in budgetary research: An evaluation of the use of moderated regression analysis'. *Accounting, Organizations and Society*, 24: 291-315.

Holloway, Wendy, & Jefferson, Tony (1997). 'The risk society in an age of anxiety: Situating fear of crime'. *The British Journal of Sociology*, 48(2): 255-266.

Hummelsheim, Dina, Hirtenlehner, Helmut, Jackson, Jonathan, & Oberwittler, Dietrich (2011). 'Social insecurities and fear of crime: A cross-national study on the impact of welfare state policies on crime-related anxieties'. *European Sociological Review*, 27(3): 327-345.

Jackson, Jonathan *(2006)*. 'Introducing fear of crime to risk research'. *Risk Analysis, 26(1):* 253-264.

Johansson, Marcus (2002). *Exkludering av invandrare i stadspolitiken – Makt och maktlöshet i Örebro 1980 – 2000*. PhD dissertation, Örebro University.

Langer, Gary (2003). 'About response rates – Some unsolved questions'. *Public Perspective*, May/June, 16-18.

Lee, Murray (2001). 'The genesis of "fear of crime"'. *Theoretical Criminology*, 5(4): 467-485.

Lee, Murray, & Farral, Stephen (eds) (2009). *Fear of Crime. Critical Voices in an Age of Anxiety*. London: Routledge.

Lidskog, Rolf, & Persson, Monika (2012). 'Community safety policies in Sweden. A policy change in crime control strategies?' *International Journal of Public Administration, 35(5)* 293-302.

Lilja, Elisabeth (2008). 'Den meningsfulla förorten – Statsrum och offentlig plats i en segregerad stad'. In: H. Forsell (ed.), *Den kalla och varma staden – Migration och stadsförändring i Stockholm efter 1970*, Stockholm: Stockholmia Förlag.

Listerborn, Carina (2001). 'Rädslans geografi – om "privata" kvinnor och "offentliga" män', *Kvinnovetenskaplig tidskrift*, 2: 83–98.

Örebro Municipality (2012). *The municipal statistical database*, http://www.orebro.se/3843.html.

Pain, Rachel (2000). 'Place, social relations and the fear of crime: A review'. *Progress in Human Geography*, 24(3): 365–387.

Persson Monika. (2013). 'The relative importance of institutional trust in countering feelings of unsafety in disadvantaged neighbourhoods', *European Spatial Research and Policy*. 20(1): 73–95.

— (2012). 'Local sensemaking of policy paradoxes – Implementing local crime prevention in Sweden'. *Public Organization Review*, 13(1): 1–20.

Police, Örebro, Criminal Intelligence Service (2009). *En liten bok om Vivalla – Problem- och resursinventering 2009*.

Putnam, Robert D. (2007). 'E Pluribus Unum: Diversity and community in the twenty-first century. The 2006 Johan Skytte Prize Lecture'. *Scandinavian Political Studies*, 30(2): 137–174.

Ross, Catherine E., & Joon, Jang Sung (2000). 'Neighborhood disorder, fear, and mistrust: The buffering role of social ties with neighbors'. *American Journal of Community Psychology*, 28(4): 401–420.

Rothstein, Bo, & Stolle, Dietlind (2008). 'The state and social capital: An institutional theory of generalized trust', *Comparative Politics*, 40: 441–467.

Sampson, J. Robert, Morenoff, D., Jeffery & Gannon-Rowley, Thomas (2002). 'Assessing "neighborhood effects": Social processes and new directions in research'. *Annual Review of Sociology*, 28: 443–478.

Sandstig, Gabriella (2010). *Otrygghetens landskap – En kartläggning av otryggheten i stadsrummet och en analys av bakomliggande orsaker, med fokus på medias roll*, PhD dissertation, Göteborg University.

Stolle, Dietlind (2007). 'Social Capital'. In: R.J. Dalton. & H-D. Klingemann (eds), *The Oxford Handbook of Political Behavior.* Oxford: Oxford University Press.

Stoutland, Sara E. (2001). 'The multiple dimensions of trust in resident/police relations in Boston'. *Journal of Research in Crime and Delinquency*, 38(3): 226–256.

Svensson, Ylva, Håkan Stattin, & Margaret Kerr (2012). 'School as a safe haven in disadvantaged neighborhoods'. In: Y. Svensson (ed.), *Embedded in a Context: The Adaptation of Immigrant Youth.* PhD dissertation, Örebro University.

Taylor, Ralph B., & Hale, Margaret (1986). 'Testing alternative models of fear of crime'. *The Journal of Criminal Law and Criminology,* 77(1): 151–189.

Tyler, Tom R. (2005). 'Policing in black and white: Ethnic group differences in trust and confiden-

ce in the police'. *Police Quarterly*,
8(3): 322–342.
Vanderveen, G. (2006). *Interpreting
fear, crime, risk, and unsafety:
Conceptualisation and measurement.* Den Haag: Boom
Juridische Uitgevers.

Walklate, Sandra (1998). 'Crime
and community: Fear or trust?'
The British Journal of Sociology,
49(4): 550–569.

Appendix 1: Questionnaire

General unsafety

The dependent variable was measured using a 6 item index (α =
.823),[9] with the respondents being asked to respond to the following statements: 'Compared to fifty years ago, the world has become
more unsafe'; 'Over the last ten years, the streets have become less
safe'; 'At night, you have to be particularly careful when out in
the streets'; 'A burglar alarm is essential nowadays'; 'It isn't safe
enough to let kids play out in the streets alone'; and 'The police are
no longer able to protect us from criminals'.

The respondents could choose responses coded on a 5-point
Likert scale (which was used throughout the entire questionnaire).
The responses, ranging from one two five, were 'strongly disagree',
'disagree', 'neither agree nor disagree', 'agree', and 'strongly agree'.
High responses indicate high levels of general unsafety.

Place

Place is measured as the geographical place of residence. Vivalla
(coded as 2) is contrasted with Örebro (coded as 1). Hence the aim
is to capture the particularities of a separate and segregated area,
with its particular characteristics, in relation to the general area
(*i.e.*, the average for Örebro as a whole).

---

9   The alphas of the indexes have additionally been calculated for both subgroups
    (Vivalla and Örebro). No significant differences were found. The indexes have
    strong reliability for both groups.

Gender

Men were coded as 1 and women as 2.

Age

The respondents were asked to state their year of birth. Hence, higher year numbers indicate younger age.

Descent

The respondents were asked to select the best response from the following choices: 'You and your parents were born in Sweden'; 'You were born in Sweden, but your parents were born in another country'; 'One of your parents was born in Sweden and the other was born in another country'; 'You were born in another European country'; and 'You were born in a non-European country'. In the regressions, a recoded variable was used: born in Sweden was coded as 0 and born abroad was coded as 1.

Education

The respondents were asked to describe their highest level of education. They were offered the following choices: 'I have no education (0)'; 'Elementary school or the equivalent (0)'; 'High school or the equivalent (1)'; and 'University level or the equivalent (2)'.

Employed/unemployed

The respondents were asked to describe their employment status. They were offered the following choices: 'Employed'; 'Retired'; 'Student'; 'Unemployed'; 'Job training or course through the Employment Office'; 'Other'. Employed, retired, and student were coded as 1. Unemployed and job training or course through the Employment Office were coded as 2.

Civic engagement

The respondents were asked how they would describe their civic engagement (for example, sports, church, choir, culture, or similar).

They responded on a 5-point Likert scale in which the responses ranged from 'very large' (coded as 5) to 'very little' (coded as 1).

Exposure to crime

The respondents were asked if they had been the victims of any of the following crimes in the past 12 months: vandalism, burglary, robbery, threat, or physical abuse). In the coding, 1 is 'not exposed', 2 is 'exposed to one crime', and 3 is 'exposed to two or more crimes'.

Generalised trust

The respondents were asked the standard question for measuring generalised trust (and sometimes social capital): 'Generally speaking, would you say that most people can be trusted or that you need to be very careful in dealing with people?' The respondents were offered the following alternatives: 'People in general can be trusted'; 'People in general can often be trusted', 'neither in general nor often'; 'People in general can seldom be trusted'; and 'People in general cannot be trusted'. High numbers indicate high levels of trust.

Institutional trust

A 6-item index was used to measure institutional trust ($\alpha = .851$). This measurement combined the respondents' level of trust in the Swedish Government, the Swedish Parliament, the courts, the police, the compulsory schools, and the social services. The choices ranged from 'very little trust' to 'very much trust', with high numbers indicating high levels of trust.

Trust in the police as an institution

A 4-item index was used to measure trust in the police as an institution, using the following statements ($\alpha = .836$): 'I am confident that the police can do their job well'; 'I trust the leaders of the police to make decisions that are good for everyone in Örebro'; 'People's basic rights are well protected by the police'; 'The police care about the well-being of everyone they deal with'. High numbers indicate high levels of trust.

Appendix 2: Correlation matrix

		1	2	3	4	5	6	7	8	9	10	11
1. Place	Pearson Corr	1	.119	.010	.070	.422	-.251	.243	-.258	-.088	.039	.157
	Sig. (2-tailed)		.021	.834	.161	.000	.000	.000	.000	.090	.442	.002
	N	401	376	401	401	399	395	379	397	373	383	371
2. General unsafety	Pearson Corr	.119	1	.099	-.123	.025	-.240	.058	-.336	-.322	-.196	.049
	Sig. (2-tailed)	.021		.054	.017	.634	.000	.276	.000	.000	.000	.359
	N	376	376	376	376	374	371	355	372	353	365	349
3. Gender	Pearson Corr	.010	-.099	1	.072	.059	.018	-.012	.003	-.011	.029	-.063
	Sig. (2-tailed)	.834	.054		.152	.244	.723	.816	.953	.838	.565	.223
	N	401	376	401	401	399	395	379	397	373	383	371
4. Age	Pearson Corr	.070	-.123	.072	1	.198	.214	.082	-.118	-.014	-.090	.123
	Sig. (2-tailed)	.161	.017	.152		.000	.000	.112	.019	.782	.077	.017
	N	401	376	401	401	399	395	379	397	373	383	371
5. Descent	Pearson Corr	.422	.025	.059	.198	1	-.109	.183	-.329	.040	.032	.035
	Sig. (2-tailed)	.000	.634	.244	.000		.031	.000	.000	.444	.527	.505
	N	399	374	399	399	399	394	378	397	373	382	369
6. Education	Pearson Corr	-.251	-.240	.018	.214	-.109	1	-.164	.178	.133	-.121	.026
	Sig. (2-tailed)	.000	.000	.723	.000	.031		.001	.000	.011	.019	.622
	N	395	371	395	395	394	395	374	392	370	378	365
7. Employment / unemployment	Pearson Corr	.243	.058	-.012	.082	.183	-.164	1	-.187	-.123	.012	.104
	Sig. (2-tailed)	.000	.276	.816	.112	.000	.001		.000	.020	.813	.050
	N	379	355	379	379	378	374	379	376	356	363	352
8. Generalised trust	Pearson Corr	-.258	-.336	.003	-.118	-.329	.178	-.187	1	.305	.174	-.158
	Sig. (2-tailed)	.000	.000	.953	.019	.000	.000	.000		.000	.001	.002
	N	397	372	397	397	397	392	376	397	371	380	367
9. Institutional trust	Pearson Corr	-.088	-.322	-.011	-.014	.040	.133	-.123	.305	1	.565	-.144
	Sig. (2-tailed)	.090	.000	.838	.782	.444	.011	.020	.000		.000	.007
	N	373	353	373	373	373	370	356	371	373	363	349
10. Inst. trust in police	Pearson Corr	.039	-.196	.029	-.090	.032	-.121	.012	.174	.565	1	-.130
	Sig. (2-tailed)	.442	.000	.565	.077	.527	.019	.813	.001	.000		.014
	N	383	365	383	383	382	378	363	380	363	383	358
11. Exposure to crime	Pearson Corr	.157	.049	-.063	.123	.035	.026	.104	-.158	-.144	-.130	1
	Sig. (2-tailed)	.002	.359	.223	.017	.505	.622	.050	.002	.007	.014	
	N	371	349	371	371	369	365	352	367	349	358	371

Appendix 3: Descriptive statistics

	N Statis-tic	Min. Statis-tic	Max. Statis-tic	Mean Statis-tic	Std. Dev. Statis-tic	Skewness		Kurtosis	
						Sta-tistic	Std Error	Sta-tistic	Std Error
General unsafety	376	1.00	5.00	2.36	.83	.67	.13	.37	.25
Gender	401	1	2	1.49	.50	.025	.12	-2.01	.24
Age	401	1935	1994	1964.2	16.56	.08	.12	-1.12	.24
Descent	399	.00	1.00	.27	.44	1.05	.12	-.90	.24
Education	395	.00	2.00	1.18	.75	-.311	.12	-1.16	.25
Employment	379	1.00	2.00	1.10	.29	2.77	.13	5.72	.25
Exposure to crime	371	1.00	3.00	1.35	.62	1.59	.13	1.31	.25
Generalised trust	397	1	5	3.47	1.09	-.68	.12	-.33	.24
Institutional trust	373	1.00	5.00	3.19	.78	-.37	.13	.27	.25
Trust in police	383	1.00	5.00	3.31	.87	-.42	.13	-.06	.25
Place	401	1	2	1.41	.49	.35	.12	-1.89	.24
Valid N (listwise)	306								

The Construction of People and Place in Swedish Residential Projects

Maja Lilja & Peter Sundström

Introduction: Actors in a deregulated housing market

Ideas about how cities should be designed are fundamental to city planning (Tunström, 2009:18). However, these ideas are not static, but tend to change over time. From the 1930s until the end of Sweden's 'Miljonprogram'[1] in the mid 1970s a central concept was to plan residential areas as strictly defined spatial units, often termed neighbourhoods. The overriding idea was to divide the city according to functions and means of communication (Franzén & Sandstedt, 1981). In opposition to this method of city planning, and paralleled by broader concerns about growing residential segregation, the idea of mixed housing[2] was brought up at the national level in the early 1970s.[3] It was decided that mixed housing should be the guiding principle in all municipalities (Holmkvist, 2009:21f.) or, put differently, all residential areas across the country were to be mixed with regard to housing structure (type of housing, form of tenure, and size), and population composition (in socioeconomic, demographic, and ethnic terms) (Holmkvist, 2009).

Though slightly modified, the goal of mixed housing still prevails in today's city planning. One current question is whether all resi-

---

1 The Swedish 'Miljonprogram' is the commonly used term for the political resolution whose aim was to build a million new residences across the country in the period between 1965 and 1974 to resolve the shortage of residences and to enhance the housing quality.
2 Mixed housing is synonymous with a social mixture, see Holmkvist, 2009.
3 Mixed housing became a national goal within Swedish housing policy in 1974, see Proposition 1974:150.

dential areas should be differentiated, or if this only should apply to disadvantaged neighbourhoods. Another is whether there must be a mixture of all kinds of housing types and/or if there only should be a mixture of ethnic groups. Studies of mixed housing often state that the goal of mixed housing may have prevailed but the means for accomplishing it has not (*ibid.*). Reasons often cited for the failure to effectively achieve the goal of mixed housing are related to recent developments on the housing market. At the time when the goal was formulated, the public housing policy was very progressive. Mixed housing was related to a number of different public interventions including housing and financial and tax-related issues. Together with a strong non-profit housing corporation and an ambitious land policy on municipality level the means for accomplishing mixed housing were well established. Over time, as a result of deregulation of the housing market, these public subsidies and grants have been removed, housing benefits to residents have replaced production subsidies, and the non-profit housing corporations have been criticised for inhibiting competition. Today the housing market is dominated by a large number of private developers. In today's housing market, new construction is therefore strongly demand-driven, or undertaken for the benefit of those who pay the most. In addition to using the tool of converting building types, public planners might try to encourage private actors to build in certain ways to achieve the goal of mixed housing (*Ibid.*: 257ff). In light of these developments, it is important to examine these private actors and their contribution to the reshaping of the city.

In this chapter we will study the private actors that comprise the supply side of today's housing market and the way they build. We will not focus on the physical end-result of these residential areas; rather we will analyse the manner in which these actors try to sell them. The aim, therefore, is to examine the branding of new residential development projects and scrutinise the target groups and values constructed in the process. The place branding of four different new residential developments in the cities of Stockholm, Örebro, and Gävle will be used as examples. The main question to be answered is as follows: How are people and their environment constructed in the branding of new residential developments in Swedish cities?

The expanding field of place branding

The post-industrial restructuring of city econòmics (Bell, 1999; Short, 2006) has gradually led to harsher competition between cities and regions for new in-migrants, global capital, businesses, and visitors (Heldt Cassel, 2008; Book, 2006). This has led to an expansion of the field of place branding, though it is by no means a new phenomenon. Place marketing practices began to develop during the era of European colonial expansion, and continued with regard to tourist destinations in the mid-nineteenth century (Jakobsson, 2009; Ward & Gold, 1994). Today almost every locality, city, region, or nation is involved with place marketing (Book, 2006). The practice of place marketing has over time taken on some new forms. In the past it mostly involved commercial advertisements and catchy slogans, but now it is often part of more comprehensive economic and social development strategies. In this context, which began to emerge in the 1990s, traditional marketing of places is integrated within broader branding processes that seek to construct (or reconstruct) and establish (or re-establish) the place as a brand that is associated with certain values and directed at a selected group of people or several distinct target groups. Within the public sphere, branding processes tend to involve many areas and different actors. These branding practices commonly develop through public-private partnerships (Jakobsson, 2009; cf. Cochrane, 2007).

One consequence of marketing activities is that the particular location tends to be streamlined or smoothed over. This streamlining of places is fundamentally linked to the involved actors' ambition to create embellished images. Place branding is a communicative practice that revolves around associating the place with certain attractive values that are appreciated by the intended target group. Unique features of specific locations which do not fit with these images, are therefore smoothed over or are overshadowed by the prioritised set of values. Sometimes the branding process is primarily about changing the image of a place, that is, replacing characteristics considered negative or less attractive with new, more appropriate ones. In these processes of place creation and re-creation, identities are formed and carved out, or even reshaped. Research has shown that these values often follow a 'global formula'. The global recipes are available in several versions depending on whether the target audience is composed of businesses, new residents, or tourists.

The place branding process is nourished by the construction of trademarks for products and companies. One problem that arises when places are treated as if they were products in a marketplace is that they hardly can become fully equivalent to a consumer product without damaging the diversity and variety of the actual place. Place identities always exist in several versions, and there are always several ways to describe them. These variations arise from diverse experience and perceptions of a place, while at the same time the place has a unique material embeddedness. Although similar, places are always unique. Once a location is reduced to a consumer product in a marketplace, stereotypes are automatically created. These stereotypes conceal diversity, differing and/or conflicting interests, and internal power relations pertaining to the particular place (Jakobsson, 2009; Heldt Cassel, 2008; Aronsson, 2007).

Method

The chapter is based on a study of four residential projects. The most important criterion when selecting the residential projects was that they should differ from each other. Therefore, the projects are geographically spread, being located in Stockholm, Örebro, and Gävle. Two are located in the urban periphery, and two in the central areas of the selected cities. Furthermore the projects have been developed by five different companies, Skanska, JM, HSB/Peab, and Besqab, and generally target three distinct groups: families with children, young couples, and older/middle-aged couples.

In this study we aim to analyse both texts and illustrations. Hence, we combined a content analysis of the written parts of the marketing with an analysis of the visual images. As John R. Gold (1994) has argued, studies about place marketing are often limited to analyses of written text, which implies that the equally important pictorial representations often are neglected. By studying both texts and illustrations, we believe we will get a more comprehensive understanding of the projects, since illustrations and text often complement each other.

Table 1. Description of the four projects examined.

Project	Location	Developer	City
Hertigen	Inner city	JM	Örebro
Längtan	Outskirt of town	Besqab	Stockholm
Nyhamn	Inner city	Skanska	Gävle
Åstaden	Outskirt of town	HSB/Peab	Örebro

This combined approach resulted in our being able to identify three pairs of different but interrelated themes: people and lifestyles, history and modernity, and nature and urbanity. These themes will be treated in the following three sections of the chapter.

People and Lifestyles

Above we have argued that in place marketing, developers often create their own version of the place. In the marketing of residential projects, developers construct the particular residential project as offering a dream-home that is free of any negative or deviant elements (Ward, 2004). The construction of home is often expressed with emotional language imbued with idealised versions of prevailing norms of family life or ways of living (*ibid.*). In the construction of the ideal home, not only is the place itself described, but the writing and images used to describe it also show what kinds of people and activities are imagined as living there. We will here investigate who the developers construct as living in these residential projects and how they are constructed as living their lives.

In the marketing, the four residential projects are often described in an idealised way, for instance as being 'idyllic', an 'oasis', or a 'dream home'. The projects also imagine a certain idealised life style of the presumed customer. The reader is presented with a number of activities, from sport to cultural offerings, which will be available if you move to the residential project. In the marketing of Hertigen these activities are constructed as something which can 'enrich' your life:

How about a visit to the local theatre followed by dinner at
one of the many restaurants in the city, or to the cinema or
a sport event at Behrn's Arena? With abundant cultural and
entertainment offering right around the corner, it is easy for
you to lead a full and rich life. (JM, 2010:2)

Though the marketing often describes the presumed customer as
living an active life, it is also emphasised that the residential project
can offer you calm and relaxation. In the same residential project
as above, Hertigen, this theme is exemplified when describing the
bathrooms in the apartments: 'Here you can slide into a nice bath,
light candles, and just be. Or enjoy a hot shower after running or
walking alongside the smooth surface of Svartå river' (JM, 2010:4).
Here the particular project is constructed as a place that can offer
a presumed customer relaxation and calm within the surrounding
busy and hectic life characteristic of contemporary society.

The active, relaxed, and happy life described in the text is also
present in the illustrations. A common motif is smiling people in
relaxed poses, which can be exemplified by the materials for the
residential project Längtan, the front page of which is covered by
a smiling child. The presence of smiling people in the illustrations
gives the impression of a home where people are joyful and happy.
Furthermore, the weather in the illustrations is always warm and
sunny, emphasising this ideal image of the neighbourhood. Only
Åstaden has a winter image, though it still shows an idealised
motif: a woman and two children playing together in the snow.

Furthermore the residential projects are constructed as places
where you live together with others. This is visualised in the
illustrations, where people often are socially involved with others,
both in the neighbourhood and their apartments. In many of
the illustrations, people are positioned in a way which gives the
impression of their being socially involved with each other. In the
marketing materials for the residential project Nyhamn, it is stated
that the neighbourhood facilitates social encounters:

The neighbourhood is calm and safe, without through-traffic,
and there are plenty of natural meeting places where you can
get to know your neighbours. An example is the benches along
the canal where you can relax on sunny days. (Skanska, 2010:4)

Figure 1. People dining in Nyhamn. Source: Skanska

In the branding of the residential project Hertigen, this is also a crucial theme: 'Hertigen is a way of living that creates emotions; it is open and welcoming for meeting others and experiencing a sense of community' (JM, 2010:2). The emphasis on living in a social atmosphere where you can get to know your neighbours goes hand in hand with post-war city ideals of building in a way that facilitates encounters between people (*cf.* Jacobs, 2004; see also Franzén & Sandstedt, 1981).

However, even though the marketing emphasises that you should live together with others, the residential project is often constructed as a unique place, implying that you are special if you have the chance to move to this particular residential project. For instance in the marketing of Åstaden it is stressed that those who move to these properties 'can enjoy having a place to live in one of the absolutely most beautiful environments' (HSB/Peab, 2011:5). This theme is even more salient in the marketing of Hertingen, in which it is claimed that if you move into this neighbourhood you are privileged: 'If you have the opportunity to move into a newly built apartment in this soulful neighbourhood you are indeed privileged' (JM, 2010:2). Emphasising that receiving an apartment in this neighbourhood is a privilege might be understood as a way to make a presumed customer feel special, but it also implies that this project is so exclusive that only a privileged group can afford to live here. This shows that not only does the marketing imagine the lifestyle of the presumed resident, but how the texts are written and how the bodies are positioned in the illustrations also constructs *who* is imagined to live here and *what* activities they are expected to be involved in. In the case above, there was imagery about the economic resources and perhaps even the social class of the presumed resident. In the marketing of Längtan as well, the developer is imagining an upper- or middle-class target group by referring to activities that often are associated with this group, such as golf and tennis.

Moreover, the marketing of the projects builds on norms of the heterosexual family, which becomes salient by the frequent images of heterosexual couples. The illustrations also show a strong gender division between men and women, as is particularly visible in the cases of Längtan and Åstaden, both of which are projects for families with children (*cf.* Ward, 2004). Except for one illustration where a man is carrying a child on his shoulders, it is usually women who are seen together with children. One of the illustrations in Längtan's brochure shows a woman sitting on (her) terrace near two children who are playing with a dog. Beside the house two men in suits are walking on the road, looking as if they are involved in a conversation with each other. Another illustration shows a woman who is occupied with something in a baby carriage while a child (hers) stands beside her (see figure 2). These illustrations reproduce traditional family values in which women take care of children. It is interesting that women and children often are placed physically close to the home. This may be interpreted as being because women often are seen as a symbol of home (Mallet, 2004).

If we look more closely at how children are constructed in the marketing of the residential projects we can see that there are many children in the illustrations for the suburban projects, Längtan and Åstaden. However in the case of the two urban projects, Nyhamn and Hertingen, children are almost entirely absent. In Längtan, children are shown playing on the grass with a dog, and in another image with a ball. In one illustration, a smiling man is carrying a laughing boy on his shoulders. These images, with children smiling and playing, construct Längtan and Åstaden as good neighbourhoods for families with children. This is also emphasised in the text: 'In Längtan, children will grow up in a wonderful park-like environment with birdsong right by the house and school and

Figure 2. Women and children in Längtan. Source: Besqab. Illustration 3D House

preschool in the immediate vicinity' (Besqab, 2010:8). This statement appeals to the romantic idea of letting children grow up in the countryside, something that goes hand in hand with the construction of the ideal home. It must be stressed, however, that it is only small children who are mentioned in the marketing; teenagers are almost entirely absent, being neither mentioned in the text nor shown in the illustrations.

Not only constructions of social class, gender, sexuality, and age can be observed in the marketing of the projects, but also of race and ethnicity. All the people in the illustrations have what is commonly seen as a white appearance, *i.e.* fair skin and blond hair (*cf.* Dyer, 1997). Though Sweden today often is described as a multicultural society, it has been argued that whiteness is one of the crucial dimensions of who is constructed as 'a Swede' in contemporary Sweden (Mattsson, 2005). By placing particular bodies, with fair skin and blond hair, in visualised images, and excluding other bodies, the residential developers produce and reproduce whiteness as a dominant norm. Also, placing only white people in the images can be seen as standing in contrast to the idea of mixed housing described above, given that one of the latter's aims is to mix people with different cultural and social backgrounds.

To sum up, in this section we have seen how the marketing of the residential projects constructs a very limited version of the residential projects, in that they are described by choosing whose bodies are included in the illustrations and whose are not, and what activities the presumed customer is imagined to engage in. Here we can see how dominating norms about gender, sexuality, class, and race together produce the imagined customer as a white, middle-class, heterosexual family or couple, and in so doing exclude other kinds of bodies and ways to live your life.

Nature and Urbanity

A common theme in the marketing of the residential projects is nature, with both texts and illustrations emphasising the presence of green areas, water, and other things usually associated with nature. Nature often plays an important role in place marketing (Gold, 1994). This is thought to be because nature has a special value in Western countries, and perhaps especially in Sweden where nature is considered by many to be a crucial part of the construction of Swedishness (Ehn *et al.*, 2005; Crouch *et al.*, 2008; Arnstberg, 2005). Moreover, nature is often used in place marketing to transmit abstract ideas (Gold, 1994). For instance it has been argued that 'urban nature' is used as a way to express emotions, such as calmness or harmony (Dixon, 2002) and is often constructed as something which may contribute positively to people's lives (Uggla, 2011). In the materials we have analysed, nature is often constructed in a way that captures feelings of pleasure; for instance in Längtan 'the ready-planted garden makes it possible for you to enjoy walking barefoot on the grass right away' (Besqab, 2010:8). This theme is also salient in Nyhamn:

> Walk around the neighbourhoods among sun-warmed piers
> and promenades, enjoy the sea smell, and watch the seabirds
> bob up and down on the waves. (Skanska, 2010:2)

In these projects, nature offers many various ways to experience life, since the natural environment of the neighbourhood is constructed as making the presumed customer use diverse human senses, such as touch, smell, and sight. The notion of nature, and particularly of nature as something that enriches people's lives, can also be seen in several of the images, for instance when people are shown having coffee on their lawn, walking in the park, or taking a boat tour on the canal.

When describing the natural environment of residential projects, it is common to refer to their close proximity to water. In particular, the marketing materials use the imagery of a marina when describing the projects.

> The neighbourhood has a strong connection with water and nature. Svartån river flows past right beside the houses, a few hundred metres away you find Örebro's small-boat harbour, and within walking distance you can find both city and lake-influenced natural areas along the west shore of lake Hjälmaren. When we were working with the sketches of the house prototypes, we looked for marine themes to be able to design something that would give the area a unique character. (HSB/Peab, 2011:5)

As we can see in the excerpt above, water and imagery of the marina play a special role in the marketing of this residential project. The reference to the marina can be viewed against the background of the contemporary planning efforts to expand the city by redeveloping old harbours or industrial areas close to the water, as can be seen in a number of international cities such as Baltimore (Inner Harbor), San Francisco (Fisherman's Wharf), and London (Docklands) (Brownill, 1994), but also in recent years in Swedish cities (Ramberg, 2006). This development is a consequence of these areas having been abandoned following the industrial crises from the 1970s onward (Book, 2006).

Nature is also expressed in the marketing of the residential projects through the presence of both wild animals and pets, which are explicitly mentioned in the written text as well as shown in the pictures. Dogs occur most frequently, but birds and seals are also mentioned. Wild animals can naturally be understood as

Figure 3. Child and dog walking by the artificial lake in Åstaden. Source: HSB/Peab.

underlining the residential project's close proximity to the natural environment. However dogs are used in a somewhat different way. In Längtan, which is a suburban project, a dog is seen playing with two children on the grass. This scene could be seen as emphasising the natural environment, since dogs and children may be interpreted as part of nature, but dogs are also often seen as important family members (Belk, 1996), and can here be interpreted as highlighting a happy family life.

Not only do the marketing materials refer to the residential projects' close proximity to nature, the closeness of the city is also often stressed. In particular they create the image of an active urban life associated with culture, nightlife, and shopping. Even though the respective emphasis on city and nature varies between the projects, they all stress the importance of living close to both. Everything should be within walking distance (*cf.* Gold, 1994). In the marketing of Åstaden, it is said that this is the perfect place for someone who wants to live close to nature but with convenient access to the city, as exemplified by its title: 'A dream home – Close to nature for city lovers' (HSB/Peab, 2011:1). This theme can also be found in the marketing of the urban project Hertigen. Here, however, the particular project is constructed as a calm oasis in the middle of the city: 'The garden is a harmonious oasis in the middle of the pulsating city life with comfortable seats, grill, playground, boule pitch, and newly planted plants' (JM, 2010:3). Paradoxically, this residential project is located in the middle of the city but at the same time to some extent is constructed as a calm oasis outside the city. It must, however, be pointed out that it is not wilderness that is emphasised here, but rather a very specific, controlled version of nature (*cf.* Uggla, 2011).

Nyhamn and Hertigen, both of which are located in the city with everything it has to offer in the way of culture and entertainment, have marketing materials that stress the residential projects' closeness to nature, while the opposite can be seen for the projects Längtan and Åstaden, where it is stated that what the city can offer can be found at a convenient distance. In Längtan this is also illustrated by an image of central Stockholm. In these projects, the city should be nearby, but at a distance appropriate for families with small children. This shows that nature and urbanity are important components of the marketing of both the suburban projects for families and the urban projects for young or elderly couples. Nature and urbanity have commonly been seen as standing in opposition to each other, which is connected to the nature/culture dichotomy. For instance, urban nature (for example green areas and parks) has been seen both as a vital part of the city but also sometimes as an obstacle to the growth of cities (Uggla, 2011). In the marketing of the residential projects we have analysed, nature and urbanity are never placed in contrast or opposition to each other. Rather it seems crucial to construct the project as closely connected to both nature and the city, regardless of whether the project is located in the city or in its outskirts.

History and modernity

History is generally very important for place marketers (Graham *et al.*, 2000; Jakobsson, 2009) as it can be used to anchor the place of today in a particular favourable past. In the place branding of residential projects, it is important as well, even though the projects often have not yet been built, and consequently lack a material basis to which past events can be connected. When new residential settings are described, they are often put in a historical context that borrows historical elements from the nearby surroundings, sometimes combined with more or less fictional elements (Graham *et al.*, 2000). There is an abundance of historical events and time-lines that can be brought up and used in marketing a place. For a place marketer, these historical elements must be carefully selected to suit the branding strategy of the new project. The mediation of a suitable history is therefore a very important place-marketing practice. In the same way, it is also very important to neglect certain historical elements that can potentially harm the impression of the place and the attractiveness of the new residential project. Consequently, history functions as a two-way framing tool, as it both opens a door to the past and at the same time closes doors to other disturbing histories.

In Åstaden, a residential project in the outskirts of Örebro whose marketing focuses on the proximity of water, a particular history is described and ascribed to the place:

> There was a time when Örebro was a busy shipping town. A hundred years ago the ships headed up the river Svartån and made land in the eastern harbour in Skebäck. Örebro was the innermost creek of the seven seas, and big passenger ships and cargo liners moored along its quays.
>
> Once again the banks of Svartån are beginning to seethe with life. And it is here, by the historical waters, that Åstaden is being built. (HSB/Peab, 2011:2)

The project developer of Åstaden opens the door wide open to shipping and Örebro's past as a seaport, even though shipping never came to play a central part in the history of Örebro or for that part, in that of Skebäck[4]. But closeness to water is an important quality in today's construction of the ideal city (*cf*.Tunström, 2009).

The marketing of the inner-city project Hertigen (the Duke) begins by stating that the new development is a 'First class pearl in historical Vasastan' (JM, 2010: 1). On the following page the historical anchoring continues:

4   In the times when much of the transports were taken on by shipping, Skebäck and other areas along the river Svartån for obvious reasons was used to ship various goods to Stockholm and elsewhere.

Figure 4. The 'fin-de-siècle' style of Hertigen. Source: JM

A modern classic in an urban environment with fine old tra-
ditions. JM is building a beautiful five-storey fin-de-siècle
building close to the river Svartån in central Örebro. This is a
residence in the traditional style, located in one of the greenest areas of Örebro, with historical echoes from the days of
Gustav Vasa and Duke Karl. The apartments are characterised
by a classic rustic style and are framed by beautiful elms. (JM,
2010:2)

Two stories from history are told in this passage. First the place in
which the new residential project will be developed is anchored in
the age of great kings and rulers, signalling a long and prosperous
past, though far away from the castle in the city centre. Secondly,
there is a reference to early twentieth-century architecture, with
the reader being informed that the new buildings will adopt the
classic fin-de-siècle style that has been praised since the modern-
ist era of housing construction began to be heavily criticised (see
Tunström, 2009). These are the two doors to history that are
opened for us in Hertigen.

Sometimes there seems to be a strategic need to reconstruct
the place and its history. In Längtan, located in the outskirts of
Stockholm, new housing is to be built on the site of the now closed
but still well-known mental hospital of Beckomberga. The strategy
in the place marketing of this project seems to be to highlight the

area's history before it became associated with mental illness. As with Hertigen, the history of Längtan goes way back in time:

> Looking back in time, we find that Beckomberga has been inhabited since at least the Bronze Age. Burial grounds, tools, jars, and gold objects tell how people lived hundreds of years ago. In the 1300s there was a village here with three farmhouses: Södergården, Mellangården, and Norrgården. The name Beckomberga is mentioned in writings from as early as 1347 and has been interpreted as meaning 'the people who live on the hill by the stream'. For the subsequent five-hundred years, Beckomberga was ruled by several warlords and noble families, including the Stierncrona family, who also owned the nearby castle of Åkeshov. (Besqab, 2010:2)

This is the historical context with which the place marketer wants to associate the new residential housing, conjuring up a place with idyllic Swedish farm names (Södergården, Mellangården, and Norrgården), beautiful nature (streams and hilly landscapes), and wealthy noble families (the Stierncronas). The mental hospital period, which lasted from 1932 to 1995, is mentioned in the same passage but in a different manner, focusing on the natural sceneries created during the period:

> Beckomberga was purchased by the municipality of Stockholm, and in 1932 Beckomberga Hospital [not the mental hospital, our note] stood ready. Around the hospital buildings a beautiful park was built with broad, open lawns, large planted borders, and tree-lined paths.
>
> Today a new garden city is under construction around the old hospital park: Beckomberga – the idyllic heart of Bromma [the district of Stockholm where Beckomberga is located]. (Besqab, 2010:2)

When it comes to the last residential project examined in this study, history does not have a big role to play. The history of the place must be mentioned according to the branding strategy, but it really does not matter because the new development belongs primarily to the future. It is simply a reconfiguration of the old place without any clear or obvious tensions involved with reference to historical events. There is no competition with history in this kind of redevelopment; instead it bring back some life to a place that, according to the new branding, has long been almost deserted:

> This is an area with an illustrious past in which the nearby sea has played a significant role. In the nineteenth century about 40 shipping companies and 350 trading firms were located here. And it was in places like this that many people boarded the ships to America. After a less fortunate twentieth century, when shipping was losing importance, Gävle Strand has now become one of the most interesting parts of the city. (Skanska, 2010:2)

To summarise, history is used in at least three different ways when it comes to the marketing of a new residential project. Firstly, as shown in the cases of Åstaden and Hertigen, historical elements serve as a straightforward anchor for the new place, although deliberately selected and packaged so that the right version of the past is brought to the fore. Secondly, history may be used to reconstruct the place. Beckomberga is well known for its large mental hospital, and the residential developer tries to sidestep that by introducing a history of farming lands, famous warlords, and noble families. In the last example, Gävle Strand (Nyhamn), history is used in a slightly different way. Here, history functions as an incentive for the developer to undertake the new residential construction project. The intention is to enrich the city of Gävle with new kinds of living possibilities. There almost appears to be a historical need for that.

But history does not work alone. Together with modernity, it forms a vital place-making tool for constructing the identity of place. Metaphorically speaking, history seems to enclose modernity. The interiors of the apartments or houses are exclusively connected with modernity. History serves as the wider, outdoor context for the modern interior of cooking islands, open plan arrangements, and bathrooms clad with tile and clinker:

> The first thing you might notice upon entering the apartments is how bright they are. Thanks to the open spaces and

the generous ceiling height of 2.6 m, sunlight penetrates freely. (Skanska, 2010:3)

The bathroom is modern and stylish, as is the interior of the rest of the apartment [...] The washstand is dark stained oak, and the tiles and clinkers have sober, light colours, making it easy to transform the room with textiles. (JM, 2010:4)

Most apartments have a cooking island and carefully planned details giving them an exclusive touch. (JM, 2010:5)

Figure 5. Light colours, cooking islands and open spaces in Hertigen. Source: JM

The convenience of modern life, with simple, comfortable, and stylistically pure solutions for the modern person – in a word, modernity – is always present, and is constantly combined with a consciously crafted history of the place. Just as history points to a favourable and attractive past, modernity is the guide to the future, making the historically unique neighbourhood a place to dwell in for a long time.

Conclusions: Uniform 'exclusification'

Some preliminary conclusions can be made concerning the nature of the place-branding processes studied in this chapter as they relate to the field of branding as a whole. In contrast to the most common marketer in Swedish urban contexts, the municipality, actors on the supply side of the deregulated housing market are profit-maximising entities operating within an often global market. The local contexts in which they work are consequently reduced to an opportunity of exploitation. This becomes most obvious in the small print next to the images in the branding materials, where it says that 'The house in the picture is for illustrative purposes only. There is no correspondence with reality, either internally or externally' (HSB/Peab, 2011:2). Consequently, these actors both cut themselves off from and shield themselves from the actual local context, from the place they are about to develop and exploit. At the same time they are constructing it in a certain way, forming the local social geography. You will never see such a comment in the branding processes coordinated by a truly local actor who first and foremost is promoting the actual place. This screening off of the local context tends to result in uniform constructions of both places and the people inhabiting them.

To summarise and conclude, the people constructed in the present study are all variations on a prosperous middle class that is localised in settings that are attractive combinations of nature and urbanity as well as modernity and history. However this apparently straightforward construction of Swedish middle-class well-being contains an inherent paradox. This crack can be summarised as a form of 'exclusification' of place. Although uniform in comparison with each other, every single place investigated here seem to be thoroughly perfect. In this uniform world the particular place is superior to others. At same time, this middle-class heaven on earth, this stereotypical and uniform construction of people and place, can be seen as a blatant example of why the goal of mixed housing is not being achieved in today's urban development.

References

Aronsson, Lars (2007) 'Bilder av platser', in Aronsson, Lars, Bjälesjö, Jonas & Johansson, Susanne (eds.) *Kulturell ekonomi. Skapandet av värden, platser och identiteter i upplevelsesamhället.* Lund: Studentlitteratur.

Arnstberg, Karl Olov (2005) *Sprawl.* Höör: Symposion.

Belk, Russel W. (1996). 'Metaphoric Relationships with Pets', *Society & Animals: Social Scientific Studies of the Human Experience of Other Animals,* 4 (2), 121–145.

Bell, Daniel (1999) *The Coming of Post-Industrial Society.* New York: Basic Books.

Besqab Projekt och fastigheter AB (2009) Längtan, Bromma. Täby: Besqab.

Book, Karin (2006) Vardagsliv kontra imagebyggande. Planering och utveckling i den postindustriella staden. www.idrottsforum.se (ISSN 1652-7224)

Brownill, Sue (1994) 'Selling the inner city': Regeneration and place marketing in London Docklands', in Gold, John R. & Ward, Stephen V. (eds.) *Place promotion. The Use of Publicity and Marketing to Sell Towns and Regions.* Chichester: John Wiley & Sons.

Cochrane, Allan (2007) *Understanding urban policy. A critical approach.* Malden, Mass.: Blackwell.

Couch, Chris, Leontidou, Lila & Petschel-Held, Gerhard (eds.) (2007) *Urban Sprawl in Europe: Landscapes, Land-use Change & Policy.* Oxford: Blackwell.

Dyer, Richard (1997) *White: Essays on Race and Culture,* London: Routledge.

Dixon, Terell F. (2002) *City wilds: Essays and stories about urban nature.* Athens :University of Georgia Press.

Ehn, Billy, Frykman, Jonas & Löfgren, Orvar (1993) *Försvenskningen av Sverige: det nationellas förvandlingar.* Stockholm: Natur & Kultur.

Franzén, Mats & Sandstedt, Eva (1981) *Grannskap och Stadsplanering. Om stat och byggande i efterkrigstidens Sverige* (Neighbourhood and City Planning. State and Housing Construction in Post-War Sweden). Uppsala, Sweden: Acta Universitatis Upsaliensis.

Gold, John R. (1994) 'Locating the message: place promotion as image communication', in Gold, John R. & Ward, Stephen V. (eds.) *Place promotion. The Use of Publicity and Marketing to Sell Towns and Regions.* Chichester: John Wiley & Sons.

Graham, Brian, Ashworth, G. J. & Tunbridge, J. E. (2000). *A Geography of Heritage. Power, Culture and Economy.* London: Arnold.

Heldt Cassel, Susanna (2008) 'Platsmarknadsföring, regional image och jakten på attraktivitet' in Andersson, Frida, Ek, Richard & Molina, Irene (eds.) *Regionalpolitikens geografi. Regional tillväxt i teori och praktik.* Lund: Studentlitteratur.

Holmqvist, Emma (2009) *Politik och planering för ett blandat boende och minskad boendesegregation – Ett mål utan medel?* (Policy and planning for mixed housing and reduced housing segregation – A goal without means?) Geografiska regionstudier 79, Uppsala universitet.

HSB Mälardalen (2011) Åstaden. Drömboendet – Naturnära för stadskära. Västerås: HSB

Jacobs, Jane (2004) *Den amerikanska storstadens liv och förfall.* Göteborg: Daidalos

Jakobsson, Max (2009) *Från industrier till upplevelser. En studie av symbolisk och materiell omvandling i Bergslagen.* Örebro: Örebro Studies in Human Geography.

JM AB (2010) Brf Hertigen. Förstklassig pärla i historiska Vasastan. Örebro: JM

Mallet, Shelley (2004) 'Understanding home: a critical review of the literature'. *The Sociological Review* 52, 62–89.

Mattsson, Katarina (2005) 'Diskrimineringens andra ansikte – svenskhet och det vita västerländska', in de los Reyes, P. & Kamali, M, (eds.) *Bortom vi och dom. Teoretiska reflektioner om makt, integration och strukturell diskriminering. SOU 2005:41.* Stockholm: Fritzes.

Proposition 1974:150 *Angående riktlinjer för bostadspolitiken m.m.*

Ramberg, Klas (2005) 'Stadsplanering och stadsliv', in Forsberg, Gunnel (ed.) *Planeringens utmaningar och tillämpningar.* Uppsala: Uppsala Publishing House.

Short, John Rennie (2006) Urban theory. A critical assessment. Handmills Basingstoke: Palgrave MacMillan.

Skanska Sverige (2010) Nyhamn, Gävle. Låt havet bli en del av din vardag. Gävle: Skanska.

Tunström, Moa (2009) *På spaning efter den goda staden.* Örebro: Örebro Studies in Human Geography.

Uggla, Ylva (2012) 'Construction of 'Nature' in Urban Planning: A Case Study of Stockholm', *Town Planning Review*, 83(1): 69–85.

Ward, Stephen V. (1998) Selling places. The marketing and promotion of towns and cities 1850–2000. London: Spon Press.

Ward, Stephen V. & Gold, John R. (1994) 'Introduction', in Gold, John R. & Ward, Stephen V. (eds.) *Place promotion. The Use of Publicity and Marketing to Sell Towns and Regions.* Chichester: John Wiley & Sons.

Contributors

MARCO EIMERMANN is a human geographer and member of the Centre for Urban and Regional Studies (CURES) at Örebro University, Sweden. His PhD thesis *There and back again? Dutch lifestyle migrants moving to rural Sweden in the early 21st century* (2013) combines insights from population geography and rural studies. Marco is interested in rural areas attracting new residents and everyday practices in post-migration lives. In spring 2014, he started working in a post-doctoral project at Umeå University (Sweden), focusing on Swedish rural hotspots and local socioeconomic impacts of incoming entrepreneurs.

INGEMAR ELANDER is senior professor at Örebro University, Sweden. His research interests cover urban governance in a broad sense as exemplified in publications on cities and climate change, environment and democracy, faith-based organisation and exclusion in European cities, urban partnerships and public health. He is currently doing research on sustainable development and urban renewal in Swedish neighbourhoods and cities. He is co-editor of *Urban Governance in Europe* (Eckardt & Elander 2009), and twin author of Faith-based organisations and social exclusion in Sweden (Elander & Fridolfsson 2011).

HÅKAN FORSELL is associate professor in history at the University of Stockholm. His main fields of interest are comparative studies and urban sociology in a historical perspective. From 2004, he has worked periodically at the Center for Metropolitan Studies at

Technische Universität Berlin, Germany. He has also been affili-
ated with the Centre for Urban and Regional Studies at Örebro
University, Sweden. One of his recent (2013) publications is
Bebodda platser – studier av vår urbana samtidshistoria, a compilation
of essays and articles.

CHARLOTTE FRIDOLFSSON is a member of staff, lecturer and
researcher in political science at the Department of Management
and Engineering, Linköping University. Her PhD thesis *Deconstructing Political Protest* (2006) investigates the ideological organisation
of political protests and what makes some subjects or political
gestures tolerable and legitimate and others less so. Since then she
has been doing research in the area of faith-based organisations'
work against poverty in European cities. Another research project
concerns education among Swedish elite politicians.

EVA GUSTAVSSON is a PhD in human geography and teaches at
Örebro University, Sweden. Her research covers climate change
mitigation at local level and sustainable development. She is
currently doing research on sustainable development and urban
renewal in Swedish neighbourhoods and cities.

CHRISTINA HJORTH ARONSSON is a member of the Centre
for Urban and Regional Studies (CURES) at Örebro University,
Sweden. In her PhD thesis *Structure, Action and Spatial Morphology*
(1999) she describes the renewal process of a social housing area
from the Swedish 1960s and the planning and building process of
a new urban area in the beginning of the 1990s. The focus in the
thesis is on planning and decision-making processes due to public
and private ownership. After the dissertation she has been teaching
as a senior lecturer in social work with older people (gerontological
social work) at Örebro University with a main interest in the importance of the housing environment. She is also Vice Head of the
School of Psychology, Law and Social Work at the University.

MAJA LILJA is a PhD-student in sociology at Örebro University,
Sweden. Lilja is interested in housing segregation and especially
how majority Swedes contribute to segregation patterns. In her
PhD-thesis *The best for my child; Mothers with small children in the*

divided city, she analyses how mothers construct ethnicity, race and class in relation to their children and how these constructions are related to the ethnic and social polarisation of the city.

SUSANNA NORDSTRÖM is a PhD in sociology and lecturer of social psychology at Skövde University, Sweden. Her previous research concerns young adult identity construction in relation to subculture. She is currently doing research on subcultures as forums for identity creation and risk-taking in a changing late modern world.

MONIKA PERSSON is a political scientist and a member of the Centre for Urban and Regional Studies (CURES) at Örebro University, Sweden. In her PhD thesis *The dynamics of policy formation – making sense of public unsafety* (2014) she explores mechanisms that shape and constrain the way a policy problem is understood and addressed. In particular, she emphasises the interrelationship between policy and research and between definitions of problems and institutional settings.

PETER SUNDSTRÖM is a human geographer and associate member of the Centre for Urban and Regional Studies (CURES) at Örebro University, Sweden. In his PhD thesis *Localities in the vicinity of cities* (2013) he describes and analyses socioeconomic and demographic changes in localities in the vicinity of the biggest cities in Sweden for the past 40 years, partly within the context of the two processes of reurbanisation and counterurbanisation, partly in relation to the ongoing segregation of cities. Since 2012, he is working as an urban planner at Örebro municipality planning department.

ANDREAS K. G. THÖRN is a PhD student in history and associated member of the Centre for Urban and Regional Studies (CURES) at Örebro University, Sweden. In his PhD thesis *A successful stranger – The Philadelphia Church in Stockholm's group identity, as expressed in historical narration and work 1910–1980* (2014) he studies an organisation's strategies for unity in a changing society.

ANDERS TRUMBERG is a human geographer and member of the Centre for Urban and Regional Studies (CURES) at Örebro

University, Sweden. In his PhD thesis *Divided schools – Processes of segregation in the Swedish school system* (2011) he describes the change in the Swedish compulsory school system and how it has influenced the school as a meeting place for pupils with different socioeconomic and/or ethnic backgrounds. In autumn 2014 he is working at the Centre for Urban and Regional Studies at Uppsala University (Sweden), studying whether the pupil's choices of schools have any impact on their future life.

www.ingramcontent.com/pod-product-compliance
Lightning Source LLC
Chambersburg PA
CBHW030648270326
41929CB00007B/267